OVER MY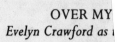
*Evelyn Crawford as*

Chris Walsh, B.A.(Melb), B.Ed. (Monash), M.Ed.(Tas), was born in Melbourne in 1925 and is a member of the world-wide Presentation Sisters Congregation. She learnt to write with a slate and squeaky slate pencil and now writes with a personal computer. A teacher since 1942, she has worked in government and independent schools and universities in Australia, the UK, USA and New Zealand and with students of all ages from preparatory to post-graduate levels.

Chris counts her friendship with Evelyn and her family, and the trust they have given her, as one of the most enriching experiences of a full and rewarding life.

# OVER MY TRACKS

*Evelyn Crawford*

*as told to*

*Chris Walsh*

**Penguin Books**

Penguin Books Australia Ltd
487 Maroondah Highway, PO Box 257
Ringwood, Victoria 3134, Australia
Penguin Books Ltd
Harmondsworth, Middlesex, England
Viking Penguin, A Division of Penguin Books USA Inc.
375 Hudson Street, New York, New York, 10014, USA
Penguin Books Canada Limited
10 Alcorn Avenue, Toronto, Ontario, Canada M4V 3B2
Penguin Books (N.Z.) Ltd
182–190 Wairau Road, Auckland 10, New Zealand

First published by Penguin Books Australia, 1993

1 3 5 7 9 10 8 6 4 2

Typeset in 12/12½ Perpetua by Post Typesetters
Made and printed in Australia by Australian Print Group, Maryborough, Victoria

National Library of Australia
Cataloguing-in-Publication data:

Crawford, Evelyn, 1928–   .
Over my tracks.

ISBN 0 14 023093 9.

1. Crawford, Evelyn, 1928–   . [2]. Aboriginal Australian teachers –
New South Wales – Biography. 3. Women teachers – New South
Wales – Biography. 4. Teachers – New South Wales – Biography. I.
Walsh, Chris, 1925–   . II. Title.

371.10092

Publication of this title was assisted by the Australia Council,
the Federal Government's arts funding and advisory body.

*To Gong
and our family*

*in the hope
that all Australians will learn to share
a better understanding*

# CONTENTS

# PREFACE

In 1987 I had one of the most significant experiences of my life. Aboriginal friends in Sydney recommended that I meet a lady named Evelyn Crawford. So I made a detour from Southport to Melbourne via Broken Hill! And it was certainly more than worth it. I entered a new world and made a great friend, great in every sense of the word.

We have sat together, two grannies, *Wimpaatja* and *Wudjiin*, and yarned by the hour on the banks of the Darling-Barwon above the thousand-year-old Aboriginal Fisheries, and by the waterhole on the Red Hill, at Brewarrina.

I have learned what it feels like to be accepted in spite of my white skin. I have shared my city childhood, and been taken through the shimmering heat of the Australian outback into the childhood of my friend. I have shared my experiences of the privations of the Great Depression, and seen them mirrored and magnified in the life of my friend.

I have laughed until I cried, and cried until it hurt.

Chris Walsh
Melbourne

# INTRODUCTION

Here I am goin' over my tracks, takin' people with me.
I hope they see them tracks the way I seen 'em, and live
the days along with me.

All the things in my life are part of me now, and that's
like the core of the person I am. When I think of all these
things, not so very far back, people today wouldn't think
they existed. The fastness of the changing – it's incredible,
isn't it? I tell my kids, "I remember this happenin'," and
then I see it in books, and I look at the date and think,
"Gord, I can't be that old!"

Tellin' all this to Chris to make the book, it's been like
sittin' down with a friend, yarnin' about old times. There's
not many people left you can yarn with. I hope the people
who read it will feel like that too. My Dad used to say,
"Your friends are where you find them." Or where they
find me, I suppose.

I read all the time. It's one of my greatest pleasures.
My kids know I love to read, and somehow they seem to
buy the book they **know** I'd like to read. Some of my
treasured possessions are my books. So for me to be able
to read a book that tells the story that is **me**, yeah, I'm
pretty excited about going back over my tracks.

You know, I never knew how old I was. I never knew the
date, or even the year. From what Mum told me, I was
born in their tent and she was helped by the old grannies –
the Aboriginal midwives. It was the darndest thing how I
found out.

I was working in Broken Hill as Regional Aboriginal Co-ordinator for Western New South Wales – that's the whole of the State west of Dubbo. Administration was always on my back, "Your age, we need your age..." The people in our office kept passing on the message. I suppose they had to keep their pieces of paper up to date.

"Don't know what year I was born."

"Oh, come on, Ev, that's incredible." I suppose they thought I was one of those coy white ladies that try to hide their age!

"It's not incredible. You better believe it. I don't know what year I was born. All I know is Mum said it was gettin' on for winter."

One day in 1985, I was going back to Broken Hill from Brewarrina where I'd been working with teachers and I passed Rossmore Station, not far out of Bourke. I drove in and asked some station hands, "Who's the boss here now?" They called the young feller who owned the property then and I asked him, "Who was the boss here about 1930?"

"My grandfather – they lived in that old house over there. Why?"

"I was born here, in a tent under those trees near that tank over there, me and my sister."

"Is that so? Come on over to Grandma's old house, see if we can find anything. There's still the old station books there."

We went over to the old place and in the room that had been the station office we found this little old book. And written on one page it had:

Born, to station, calves – 9
       lambs – 28
       foals – 2

Born, to Hannah Black and Jack Mallyer, one girl baby.

We was on the Station ledger, like we was their stock! My date of birth was registered there, and not any place else, 'cos I was a station kid. Back in those days Aboriginal babies didn't have to be registered. We weren't citizens so we was nobody. But if the parents worked on a station the baby could be entered on the station books. That made us what was called 'station kids'. At least it gave us some bit of protection from the Aboriginal **Protection** Board who couldn't move us without the station owner's permission. On the other hand, the owner could call in the Board to get rid of us if he wanted to.

Them bullocks and sheep were written in on the same day I was born, the 18th of May, 1928. Maybe that was just the day the bookkeeper brought his records up to date – and I found out in 1985. Anyway, that's the date I keep as my birthday, 'cos it's the only one I've got. Even today people find it hard to believe I didn't have a birthday till I was fifty-eight.

The young feller was shocked. "Fair dinkum! I can't believe it," he said. "Would you like to have this book, Mrs Crawford? It's no good to us, and it's important to you." I was just standin' there, couldn't believe it myself. We went through the book, and there was my cousins and uncles and aunties, all in that stock book.

I took the little book and when I got back to Broken Hill I took it to the TAFE Administration and said, "There you are! That's the year I was born. Happy now?"

Those men in the office went quiet, and one of them said, "Ev, you keep it. And if anyone asks you again, just say you don't know when you were born."

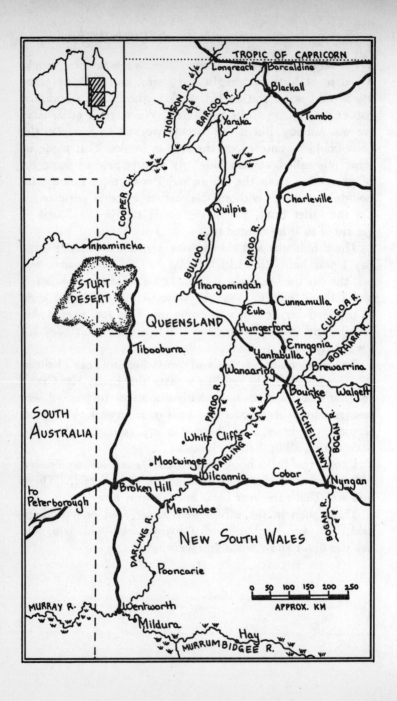

# YANTABULLA

*'We was all happy then*

*... a family together'*

I don't remember much about when I was very small, just the usual things of a little kid runnin' round and playin' about with the rest of the kids. I only vaguely remember when my sister Gladys was born but I do remember her as a baby sittin' up, that I was allowed to pick up and carry around. From then on, I always had her on my hip. Then she was nice to play with, and she became part of my life.

Mums wouldn't let you pick babies up till they could sit up straight, 'cos they always feared you'd hurt their backs. Older children always had their baby brothers and sisters with them. You threw 'em on your hip, and they clung with their arms around your neck and legs wrapped round your waist so you could hold their two feet with one hand and git on with playin'. You ran after balls, played chasin', and the kid was still there! They were like little native bears! We were still growin' ourselves, and a lot of us grew up a bit crooked.

My father, Jack Mallyer, was born on Cooper Creek below Hammond Downs Station, and so was his sister Kate. I just assumed that his parents, both full-bloods, came from up that way too, because they spoke *Wankamurrah*, the language of that area. They only spoke English to white people. I used to wonder how my Mum could talk to Granny Mallyer when Mum didn't know *Wankamurrah*, only *Baarkanji*. But Granny knew *Baarkanji*. You'd get to know your in-laws' language so you could talk back and forth, and Granny always seemed to have a lot to talk to Mum about, even if it was only about straightening us up. Granny Mallyer's totem was teal duck. I didn't know much about the rest of Dad's people.

Aboriginal people belong to their mother's tribal group. Mum's people were *Baarkanji*, so I'm *Baarkanji* too. My mum was born Hannah (Annie) Knight, and her totem was eagle hawk, so we're all bird people. Her mother, Granny Knight, and her aunty, Granny Moysey, were born at Louth near Bourke. Granny Moysey lived at Wilcannia where most of the people are *Baarkanji*. She was a remarkable person, a very strong woman in her own views, and very, very important with the *Baarkanji* tribal people. A lot of us were afraid of Granny Moysey, the things she stood for. She was the same lightish colour as myself but a very strong, very tribal woman. What she told you, and the way she told you, made big impressions, like putting a dent in a new piece of tin. It was there forever, no matter what you did! You had it for the rest of your life. She was the keeper of the knowledge and the enforcer of the law in Wilcannia as long as I can remember. She must have been about ninety-three when she died.

Gladys was toddlin' when Dad got a message from his parents who were living at Yantabulla. That's near the Queensland border, not far from Hungerford. They were both gettin' old and Dad had been on Rossmore for a long time, so he decided to pack up and go. None of mum's people were near Rossmore, so she didn't mind leavin', I suppose.

There were big preparations for this **long** trip. It took ages because Dad still had his work on the station. While he was away Mum greased the axles on the buggy; I kept Mum's bantams together and checked on the buckets and tins. All the time, I was draggin' Gladys around by the hand and she was carryin' bits of wire for me to make handles.

When Dad was home he fixed all the harness and tested all the parts of the buggy. He was worried about the horses. We had five and they were too fat. I remember him sayin' to Mum, "Annie, these horses won't go in the daytime, it'll be too hot for them. We'll have to travel at night."

Mum made heaps of bread and brownies so she wouldn't have to be doin' a lot of cookin' on the road, and they loaded up the buggy, leavin' a great hole in the middle for us two to sit in. But no, not me! I wanted to ride one of the horses.

"If I don't ride Ginger, he won't follow the buggy, Dad. That lazy old feller'll just stay behind."

Mum must've thought, "Let her go. She'll soon get sick of it." I soon did, and tied him to the side of the buggy and crawled in with Gladys. We never had many arguments about what Mum and Dad wanted me to do. If I thought I had a better idea, I'd voice my opinion even when I was pretty small. So they might say, "Yeah, alright, Ev," and let me go. Lots of times I was the loser even though I thought I'd got my own way. I wouldn't listen, even at that age!

It took us two days to go from Rossmore to Bourke. We camped at the billabong just out of Bourke and Dad rode in for Vicks and Aspros and things like that. He was a great believer in Condy's Crystals and Eucalyptus. Years later we went through his box after he died and we found twenty-one bottles of Parrot Eucalyptus! He used to say, "If you see a thing you know you'll need some day, buy it if you've got the money, because you can be sure you won't be near it when you do need it." When I got a family of my own I found I was doin' the same thing!

When it was just gettin' on to red sundown, we moved out, on the edge of the big Wagdon Plain. Dad said it would take us all night to cross that plain, and it did. I just remember being pulled out of the buggy and wrapped in a blanket on the ground and it wasn't real daylight. When I woke up properly it was day and we were at a bore. We camped all that day because the old ginger horse was looking knocked up.

My cry every start-off was, " 'e's jist lazy, Dad. I'll git 'im goin'", as if I was the only one who could do it.

I can't remember how many days it took to get from Bourke to Yantabulla, but Dad was getting excited as we got closer. He wasn't a man that talked a lot, but he seemed to be talkin' all the time and laughin'. Then he started pointin' out things he'd seen when he was a kid.

It was the first time Mum had been away from the Darling and she kept sayin', "There's no rivers out here, Mullya, all there is is bores." She always called him Mullya – it means Big Man. If we did come across a creek or a small lagoon we'd camp and swim, give the dogs a bogey (bath), and Mum'd do a bit of washing. It was like a sort of holiday, just takin' your time and enjoyin' the goin' along.

We were travellin' at night and it was real quiet. No bitumen out there in them days, so the horses were just walkin' along quiet in the soft sand, just the noise of the chains rattlin'. Then we could hear dogs barkin'. Dad said, "We're either at a station or we're gittin' close to Yantabulla. D'ya want to ride the horse, Ev?"

The summer moon was really bright and I could see along the side of the road behind a broken-down fence – a ceme-tery! Well, who wanted to git out in the dark and sit on a horse? Not this girl! "Nah, nah, Dad, I'm alright in 'ere. I'm tired." Pretty soon we got to the town, which consisted of nine houses, a pub, and a store that leaned on an old mulga telegraph pole that was leanin' too. Talk about the Leaning Tower of Pisa – it had nothing on that little store! We pulled up and Dad waited till someone came out of the pub and he asked them where old Jack Mallyer lived. I heard the white feller say, "Up in the scrub on the sandhills."

When we got there, old Grandfather was sittin' out by the fire rubbin' down boomerangs. They used them to kill meat 'cos they weren't allowed to have guns. We pulled up in the buggy in the dark and Grandfather sang out, "Who's that?"

"It's me, Jack Mallyer."

Then Grandfather's callin' out, "Katie, Katie, git up quick. This boy's 'ere."

I was gigglin' at anyone callin' Dad a boy, and I giggled more when Grandfather said, "You got your kids with you, Jackie?" because everyone we knew called Dad Mullya. Granny came out and was pullin' us out of the buggy and huggin' us. It was the first time we'd seen her and the first time for Mum too. Granny Mallyer was a full-blood, a big tall, very dark, big-hearted person, and, as I soon found out, a real smart old lady. A big welcome we had then, the fire built up, billy on to boil and a big feed. I don't know what time they finished talkin', I was asleep.

I was up early next morning, lookin at this new place. You could hear kids talkin', dogs barkin', and now and then you could hear a bit of music – Harry Lauder on the old wind-up gramaphone – but you couldn't see anybody. Then the others woke up and when we were havin' breakfast Granny said to Mum, "Annie, when I come home from work, we'll go up on the hill and you can meet all them people." Granny was the housemaid and cook, and Grandfather milked the cows and worked as a handyman, at the Yantabulla pub. He had an old horse he used to drive in their spring cart down to the pub early in the morning.

When we went to visit the camps in the afternoon, there were a real lot of kids and we were all nearly the same height. They seemed nice friendly kids and I wondered how long we'd be stayin' because some I'd like to have for friends and some I'd like to play with. I didn't realise we'd be there for years. We didn't get back till after dark because Granny took us to about eighteen families, each camped a fair way from the others. She was very proud of the long hair me and Gladys had, because she had long wavy hair herself, as white as anything. She wrapped it round her head in a knob.

I liked Yantabulla. It was a nice place. Everything was so good.

We set up camp just over from Granny's. At first we had a canvas tent high enough to stand up in, just big enough to sleep in and keep our clothes in. Over the top was a fly made of woolbales. Mum split them open and sewed them together. When it rained, the hessian would get real tight and the canvas didn't get wet and drip inside, so we had a dry camp.

Dad built a bough shade out the front – four forky poles, about eight foot high, with bushes to make the roof. If a bit of wind come up and it was cold, then Dad cut more bushes and stood them round like a wall. Under the bough shade we had the table. That board top we carried everywhere we went, so all Dad had to do was cut four forky sticks, put 'em in the ground and tie the table on 'em through the holes he'd bored in the corners. It was swingy but we were used to it. If you leaned on it, it would move, so you made sure you didn't, 'cos if Mum was mixin' somethin', you'd get a hit on the head with the spoon. We learnt to remember the hard way!

It was a pretty comfortable camp. Dad stretched long pieces of wire high up across the shed, where we hung our pints (enamel mugs) on wire hooks. Our plates were enamel or tin, put upside down on a box or they'd collect dust. Mum had a lot of tin plates, 'cos she liked makin' jam tarts. Apricot jam tart and custard was her favourite pudding.

A bit away from the bough shade was the fire, with a frame built over it where the billy cans hung. If there was any sheets of tin about, the fire had a windbreak too. If there were stones we put iron bars across the fireplace to sit the cooking pots on, and the boilers Mum used for washing.

We had a hurricane lamp, and we used carbide lamps too. Carbide looks just like lumps of stone. You put three or four pieces in a bowl, poured a bit of water on, and poked a sort of tube down into it. At the top end was a smaller tube with a hole in it. When the carbide got wet it went 'shh-hh-hh' and a gas came out the little hole. You lit it and there was your lamp. When you wanted to put your light out you pulled out the tube and tipped the little rocks out on the ground and in the morning they'd be dry ready to use again the next night. They made a nice bright light, but the carbide itself had a terrible smell, worse than rotten eggs.

Dad was doin' odd jobs, helpin' Grandfather with fences, so he decided to make us a *gurrli* – a more permanent place. So Mum packed a tucker box and we all went with Grandfather up to the pine trees on the sandhills to cut poles. She cut with the men, and us kids made tea and got the food ready. A couple of young fellers come along on horses and jumped off and done some cutting. When it was time to take all the rails back, there was buggies and spring carts – I don't know where they came from! But they were all there, with young fellers and old fellers puttin' posts in and tyin' them on, and that big job was done in no time. Some of the people who helped us get set up, we didn't even know their names. It was their way of being friendly, welcoming new people to the sandhill community. It didn't matter what anyone started to do, always someone turned up to help. A woman would be doin' her washin', liftin' the clothes out of the boiler with the big stick and another would come over and help wring 'em out and someone else'd be hangin' 'em out with the old dolly pegs. That's what it was like in those little communities back then, all helpin' together.

7

That *gurrli* was like a big log cabin, with an earth floor, and the big bough shed out the front, and a little bough shed over a deep hole out the back, so we were set. Our beds were made with four forky sticks and a wool bale. Down the sides of the wool bale went two long poles that were propped on the forks. It was a bit hollow, and you just put your blankets on top. If it was a good season we'd get some *nardoo* grass and make it into a kind of mattress, but you didn't carry a stuffed mattress when you were travellin', 'cos the grass would all break up and the sharp bits would stick into you. In the bed you'd be about knee-high off the ground, so I'd think to meself, especially when we'd seen a snake track on the ground we'd swept, "It's high enough. A snake won't git me here." When you moved on, you left the forky sticks in the ground, and the poles with them. When someone else came along, they wouldn't build their camp in the exact same place, but they'd take the sticks to use themselves. On Willara Station someone reckoned one lot of bed sticks had been used seventeen times!

In that sandhill country they made everything out of mulga. Dad brought the mulga branches in to make all sorts of things and mum used the small sticks he trimmed off. She cut all the straight pieces, the ones about two inches thick, and fitted them tight together side by side in the red dirt in the part of the room where Gladys and me slept. That made a bit of a board floor. Mum knew what she was doin'! Like all kids we used to drop our clothes on the floor when we took 'em off, and it was terrible hard to get the sand out when you washed them, and the red stain was worse. So we were the only ones that had a little stick floor.

We had plain tucker, but enough to eat. Dad went huntin', 'cos all our meat was wild meat. You'd buy flour in 25-pound white rag bags, tea and salt and sugar, onions and potatoes and a bit of rice. There was always someone in the camp growin' vegies so we could cadge a few carrots or turnips, sometimes green peas, till we grew our own. Granny Mallyer would bring us leftovers – cold meat and things – from the pub kitchen, or cakes and brownies and yeast bread that she'd made. Sometimes she'd be cooking all day, poor old thing! just to give everyone a loaf of yeast bread, which was luxury. She taught some of the younger women to make bread too, but it was a lot of trouble.

We used to watch Granny makin' bread at her camp. She'd boil up the yeast, bottle it with a couple of bits of potato, some sugar and salt, then tie the cork down. You'd look at it the next day, and you'd see it all workin'. There'd be a hell of a scatter when Granny decided to take the cork out! It never did explode – she'd been makin' it for too long to let that happen. I think we almost hoped it **would**. She'd stir the yeast up with the flour and water, work it into a dough, and put it in the square bucket.

The 'square bucket' was a petrol tin. Cut out the top and you had a deep bucket. Cut a few inches above the bottom and it was a cake tin. Cut it from top to bottom down the middle and you had baking dishes or mixing bowls or wash tubs or boilers for the washing. I've even seen little kids sittin' in 'em bein' bathed. The men took care makin' them – no sharp edges. They folded the sides over and hammered them, or rolled down the ends to make handles so you could lift a wash tub. When it was wash day, they'd put the tins on the back of the buggy, fill 'em at the bore and bring 'em back to the camp. You could put the clothes straight in and put the whole thing on the fire.

Petrol tins played a very important role in Aboriginal people's lives, and the lives of lots of white people in those little way-out towns. People made tin meat safes – cut a big square hole in each side, then covered the holes with hessian or gauze. Old white fellers even made boats. They nailed the sheets of tin onto a light wood frame, filled all the holes with putty, and painted it over.

They'd throw a petrol tin on a **very** hot fire, and the

ends would come undone and fall out, 'cos it was all leaded up. They'd have sheets of tin, which they nailed onto frames and made a tin house. You'd see these kerosene tin or petrol tin houses everywhere. There's still a few out back, all rusty now of course. The lead was used for solderin' because there was always something that needed repair.

The best forks and poles were made of yapunya, a tree that grows very straight with red bark, very tough, almost like ironbark. When our buggy pole broke, Dad would look for a yapunya, cut a new pole, trim it down and bore holes for a new shaft. That tree was used a lot for parts of spring carts and buggies, 'cos it's very tough wood.

The most interesting tree anyone could ever sit under is the belar. It's got long droopy needles like a she-oak. Belar trees grow very big and in the hottest day, when it's so still and so hot, you sit under a belar tree and you listen. You've got to sit right underneath, and lean back on the butt if you can. There's no wind at all, the leaves aren't moving, but you can hear this breeze blowin' through it, and that alone makes you feel cool. If there's a belar in a paddock, that's the one you'll see the stock under. Their imagination has got 'em, and they're thinkin' they're cool, just like people do.

Gidgee's the heaviest wood there is. The only thing they used it for was cooking. It's good firewood, but you've gotta know how to use it.

Mum taught me to cook and she learnt from her mother, and way back. If you had a gidgee fire, when the coals came you just moved the logs away and used the hot ground. You dug a hole and put your dough in the bottom part of the Bedourie oven, and buried it in the hole with hot sand heaped on top. We cooked everything in the hot sand underneath the fire. You loosened it up a bit and put a damper straight in, or spread out a goanna, and sprinkled the hot sand on the top. Then we'd pile cold sand, better still, wet sand, on top to keep the heat in. In the meantime there'd be a big fire burnin' in another spot hottin' up another bit of ground. You move your fire in little circles all the time, so you're better off than a white woman with only one oven. And you don't have to pay your gas bill, or your power bill! All we needed was to pick up a few brambles and sticks.

Gladys and me, our job was to sweep all round our camp, everywhere, with the little bush broom we used to make. It was called Brunda Bush – the white feller calls it Butter Bush. It has beautiful flowers, mauve flowers, pink flowers. We tied three or four limbs together and made it like a straw broom. We did the sweeping in the late afternoon, just before sundown. First thing in the morning we'd git up to see what tracks were there. That was our job, and to keep wood by the fire, and to keep the buckets filled with water, no matter where we were. If we didn't, we'd get a hiding, or have to do someone else's work as well. Eight or ten of us camp kids'd get up early in the morning and go across to where we got our water at the station. We liked the company and a mob of us would be safe if anything went wrong or we got into mischief. We had to go across a big patch of hop bushes, then through a fence.

Two white ladies lived there, old spinsters called Miss Moran, and they had five brolgas (native companions) as pets.

Every morning these birds would fly down to the tap where the bore water came up. As soon as we'd turn the tap on, one would want to put his beak under and drink, so we'd have to wait until he'd finished, and then the other one, and then the next one – and all this time our mother was back on the other side of the hop bushes singing out, "Hurry up, you kids, with the water. You'll be late for school." If you dared to push a bird's head away they'd all start singing out, and they could make a terrible noise. One of the old women would run out of the back door with a broom yelling, "What're you kids doing to my birds? Leave my pets alone, or I won't let you get any water here."

She couldn't stop us, 'cos it was a government bore, a watering place for everyone. This used to go on every morning and Mum would get mad, and it often did make us late for school. We didn't mind in the afternoons, 'cos we'd stoke those birds up a bit, and stone 'em a bit, while one of us filled the billycans. Then we'd all run with the birds flying over our heads and we'd get back to our camp with only half a billycan of water each. So Grandfather Mallyer made billycans with lids on so we could run and not spill any water. Those brolgas would pick holes in the waterbags too if they were hanging on the fence. Gee, they were bad bloody birds. But even that was fun for us kids. We could knock fun out of anything.

None of the children in that tiny township of Yantabulla had ever been to school. The children of the station owners had governesses, and when we were near the homestead we would sit at the edge of the verandah and listen. No one hunted us away, but we didn't share the lessons. So the dads in the place must have decided to ask the government to send a teacher and they all got together and built a bush school, and a bush school it sure was! It was just a big shed, with beefwood uprights at the corners, and long beefwood beams to support the roof. The walls were filled in with wired bundles of canegrass, solid up to about six feet, then there was a gap about three feet high all round to let in the light, and then the roof – more bundles of canegrass. We couldn't see out unless we got up on the desks, or put our toes in the wire and climbed up the side like spiders. The floor was just red sand. Later on they built a proper schoolroom with a wooden floor and a tin roof, but we still used the canegrass shed when it was really hot.

The long desks – long enough for five or six kids – were split beefwood logs with split pine planks for seats. You know how splintery pine is, so you could say there was one schoolful of kids who didn't wriggle in their seats. We learnt the hard way – a splinter in your *thithee* (bum) hurts more coming out than going in! The teacher's desk and even her chair was split timber, but I don't know if it was as splintery as our seats. Anyway, she had long petticoats and skirts, and she didn't wriggle.

The men cut the tops out of square five-gallon petrol tins, painted them inside and out, and the teacher had them piled two by two, four high, on their sides with the mouths open. That was her 'filing cabinet' where she had all her stuff.

The blackboard was on a three-legged easel made from bush timber, with holes bored through to take the pegs the board rested on. There was another homemade table where she kept things like book pencils, slate pencils, rubbers and chalk, and where we stacked our slates. We used slates and squeaky slate pencils most of the time, and cleaned our slates with tiny pieces of rag tied on bits of string nailed to the desk all along, swingin' there all the time.

We had one special book with our name on it and we used to do sums in that book, or a bit of dictation, or our best writing. It was a very special day when we worked in our book. We used little bits of pencil stuck in a tin holder. The teacher cut pencils in four to make them' go round. They were red pencils, but they wrote black. She sharpened them with a pocket knife Granny Mallyer cadged from Grandfather. He used to keep it sharp for her.

There were forty-two kids in that little school, but I don't ever remember seeing forty-two there all in one day. There'd always be ten or twelve missing. Aboriginal kids didn't have to attend school in those days. If they came along the teacher taught 'em, if they didn't, well, that was it. It must have been real hard on the teacher. If their mums and dads understood what school was they'd send the kids most days. My mother and father could read and write pretty good for blackfellers at that time so me and Gladys went to school most days. It wasn't only that kids stayed home to play.

Whenever dads got work on stations any big distance away, they took their whole family with them. No one would ever say to a kid's Granny or Aunty, "We'll leave so-and-so with you so he can go to school." Being with your family was the most important thing.

In our little school there were Aboriginal kids and white kids from the town and the nearby stations. There wasn't any calling names like 'black kids' or 'white kids'. If you were born on a station or lived there you were 'station kids' and if you lived in town you were 'town kids', black and white alike. All of us had to call all grownups Mister, Missus, Uncle, Aunty, Granny, Grandfather, whatever was respectful, even if they weren't our real Uncle or Granny. We had real good times together and got into mischief together – just kids.

That first day in the little Yantabulla school was real strange. Not one of us, even the white kids, had ever been to school, and we were all ages. The young white lady teacher hardly spoke to us. She was whingeing and sniffling, then she was really crying. Every time we looked at her she was wiping her face with her hanky. She put something on the board but we didn't know what to do with it, and she just sat at her table with her back almost turned to us. We just sat there too and looked at her and looked at each other. We didn't know whether to speak to her or touch her like we did if someone in our family was sad. Nobody dared to ask her what was wrong. We'd never been in that close contact with a grown-up white person before. We didn't know if she'd rouse on us if we touched her, but we certainly felt very very sorry for her, even the big boys.

As soon as we were let out to play we all huddled together and tried to work it out.

"What the matter with that new *wudjiin*?"

"Dunno. Never seen one like that before."

"Reckon she don't like it here?"

"Where she come from?"

"Dunno. Maybe a long way 'way."

"I know. She comes from Bourke, and my mum says it's big, real big. Maybe she don't like this place – too little."

So we went back into the classroom knowing no more than when we came out and she cried all the afternoon too!

First thing when I got home to our camp I said to Mum, "Mumma, that white lady teacher **cried** all day!"

"What's wrong with her?"

"None of us kids know. She just kept cryin', and her hanky was a real wet ball, all spoilt. I saw when she took it out this morning. It was lovely then – a white hanky with a purple flower in the corner and lots and lots of pretty lace."

"Something must be making her cry. Those big kids been actin' up, or you little 'uns? Come on, tell me."

"No one been actin' up, Mum. True. She just cries."

"What's wrong with her, then?"

"We don't know – none of us knows."

Mum went across to Granny Mallyer. She'd know the answer to everything. Granny came back to our camp where all us kids were sittin' playin' in the sand. She stood over us, and the red thick stockings she always wore were real close to me. She looked right down at me, Granny with her big voice just like I've got now. Everyone listened when she talked.

"What you bloody kids doin' to that little *wudjiin* down there, makin' her cry?"

"No, Granny. We not doin' nothing', but we sorry for her."

"Well, just don't make her cry any more."

The next morning when we went to school, Miss Cook was cryin' again. We looked at each other. We'd never said nothin', we'd never done anythin' to make her cry. So we started pattin' her on the hand and sayin', "You sick, Miss?

We'll run across to the pub and tell Granny." The pub was just across the road from the school.

We hadn't been inside very long when Granny, all dressed up in her long white starched apron, came over to the school. She marched in, came up to the teacher and said, "Hello, girl. What's your name? I'm Granny Mallyer."

The teacher said, "I'm Leanne Cook."

"I heard you was cryin' all day yesterday." And that started her off again! All us kids were staring with big eyes and stretching our ears! Granny put her hand on the teacher's shoulder and said, "What's wrong with you, girl? What these bloody kids been doin' to you? These kids been gettin' cheeky? They been playin' up, not doin' the right thing? You tell me, girl, I'll soon fix it for you."

Miss Cook just stood there crying and shaking her head. I heard her say, "I miss my mum and dad, and I miss Bourke."

"You poor little thing!"

Granny told us all to go and play but not to go far away. As we went out I saw her give Miss Cook the end of her nice white apron to wipe her eyes on, and she said, "Sit down, girl, and listen to me." They both sat outside the school door on an old log, talking, but we didn't dare stay close enough to listen – we all knew Granny Mallyer!

When Granny came over to talk to mum that night we found out that Miss Cook was lonely. Even if the teacher had told us that on that first day, we wouldn't have known what '**lonely**' was. We were always together with our family. We would have had to take that word back home for Mum to explain it to us. It was the first time Miss Cook had ever left her home and family. She was only young, a very thin girl, but very tall.

Granny Mallyer said to her, "You want feedin' up, girl. You want a lot of good tucker. You'll be right when you get a good feed – you won't get upset and lonely. You're just not strong enough." But what she had to be strong for, just reading and writing, buggered if we knew, and we didn't dare ask Granny!

Every morning after that, Granny used to come over at half-past-nine with a tray of fresh cakes and a big white enamel jug of milk fresh from the cow. She'd come into the schoolroom and say, "Pull up now, girl. No more teachin'. Sit down there and eat these cakes now and drink this milk. Come on, you kids." She'd have cakes and milk for us too. But the teacher, she said, "Now, Katie, we can't have recess at half-past-nine. We have to have it at eleven o'clock. That's why they call it eleven o'clock break."

"Girl, I got no time to be messin' about at eleven o'clock. I gotta be cookin' pub dinner at eleven o'clock. I'll bring this milk and cakes over to you every day and you'll eat them."

So Granny Mallyer invented our nine-thirty recess. She came every day, rain, hail or sunshine, so we got used to half an hour in school and then a break. Most days Granny would just leave the tray with milk fresh out of the cow, and cakes just out of the oven and go back to work. Then one or more of us would run back with the tray and jug and plates.

One day Miss Cook asked, "What do you think Granny Mallyer puts in her cakes?"

"Flour, Miss . . . eggs, Miss . . . sugar . . . fat, Miss," 'cos we'd never heard of such a thing as butter. I think most of the time Granny did cook 'em with fat like Mum did at home.

One day Granny outdid herself. She brought cakes with icing sugar and tiny little lollies all over the top. We were bumpin' each other all in a little heap, you know, when she put them down.

"Oh-h-h-h! I like that pink one . . . I like that white one . . ."

Course we didn't grab 'em. We waited like always, the way Miss Cook had taught us, till they were handed round

17

on another little plate and you had to take one and pass the plate on. That day it seemed to take ages for her to pass them round with us waitin' to see what it tasted like with the pretty stuff on top. So that was the big story for the day when we went home.

Next day the teacher explained they were Hundreds and Thousands. One kid asked, "Why they call 'em that, Miss?"

"Well, you remember what they looked like. There were hundreds and thousands of them, weren't there?"

We couldn't imagine what a hundred or a thousand of anything would look like. Numbers like that didn't mean nothing to us. We learnt to count and do sums with sticks Grandfather Mallyer made for Miss Cook. I bet Granny got him to do it! They were about six inches long and as thick as Grandfather's thumb. He used to sit around the camp and cut them. We used them as counters, and for add-ups and take-aways. We only had sixty sticks so if we went past that, like up to eighties, we had to use stones as well. I tell you it was hard work! We used Grandfather's sticks as clap-sticks too when we sang songs.

Some mornings, if Granny stayed talking to Miss Cook when she brung the milk and cakes, we'd sneak off for a swim. At the back of the pub was this big lagoon that ran right up past the school and past the police station. There were lots of ducks, wild ones as well as tame ones, with swans and pelicans, and we swam too. In the summertime, when the teacher blew her whistle after recess and after lunchtime, we'd come in all wet and muddy. But there was nothing to worry about – we only had wooden seats and a sand floor so there was nothing to spoil. But the teacher wasn't used to that sort of thing.

At first I think she worried about it. She'd say to us, "You kids'll get a cold", and things like that, and go crook at us sitting around in wet clothes, because we'd go in swimmin', clothes and all. Girls wore only knickers and a dress and the boys shorts with a singlet or shirt. Most of us had pretty scaly feet from running in the mud and not wiping them. She got us to bring a piece of towel so we could dry our heads. She had combs hanging on strings around the shed. She'd plait the hair of those who had long hair, and tie the plaits with bits of pretty rag. Gladys and me had lovely long plaits, so long we could sit on them! We got to like Miss Cook very much, and, I suppose, respect her. We didn't swear in front of her, or fight.

We asked a lot of questions and she always seemed to have time to answer. Any sort of question she'd answer. Like, she had a pair of red boots, the most beautiful pair of boots I've ever seen in my life. I'd never owned shoes. There were times when I'd be there wrigglin' me toes, tryin' to imagine what it felt like to have me foot in shoes. I'd lean on the desk and just look at those red boots with their black buttons up the side.

I said to her one day, "Miss, where'd you git them red boots from?"

"My mum and dad bought me them for my graduation, and they're just new." Course I didn't know what that big word meant. I used to think to myself, "By gee, if I had a chance, I'd shake them boots." It's funny, the only thing that was important to me was them red boots! She had a wide red leather belt too that was just like the boots. She was a very snazzy dresser. She had fair hair done in a big bun in the back, and always wore blouses buttoned right up to the neck, pinned with a cameo brooch. She wore a long black skirt and a white petticoat with lace around the hem. Sometimes we'd be pickin' burrs out of the bottom of the petticoat instead of doin' our schoolwork. She'd start to do it and we'd offer to help, and she seemed to have lots and lots of petticoat underneath. The frills at the bottom of her dress in winter time were velvet and woolly. I didn't know how she could carry it about for someone so bony!

It was very hard for Miss Cook to understand lots of things we said when she first came. In those days lots of the kids could only speak the lingo. Nearly all of us used mostly our Aboriginal language, *Burunji*, even in the school. Most of the white kids could speak *Burunji* too, 'cos we all grew up together. We didn't know she couldn't understand our language until Granny Mallyer got at us and said, "Now listen, you kids. That little *wudjiin* don't understand our lingo. When the kids say words she don't know, you tell her what the word is in English. She's good to you. You all help her."

So white kids and black would translate for her. One of the boys might say, "*Tharnee nginga*, Miss", so we had to tell her that he said, "I'm goin' over there", and she tried to teach us 'going' and 'gone' and she couldn't understand that '*tharnee*' meant either 'going' or 'gone', depending on how you said it, and what other words went with it. We had to chop up our Aboriginal sentences into a lot of little pieces so she would understand what we was talkin' about. She got one of the dads to make more holes in the legs of the easel so she could put the board lower. Then the little kids could draw on it to tell her what they meant when they couldn't say it in English.

One day there was a bit of an argument in the school between my cousin Elsie and Ray Eulo, a very dark full-blood boy from up around Cunnamulla. He was cryin', and when Miss Cook said, "What's the matter with you, Ray?" he said, "Elsie poked me in the *munga* with a pencil." The pencil didn't go right into his ear but the point of it went in somewhere and his ear was bleeding.

Miss Cook said, "If Elsie doesn't watch what she'd doing, I'll poke her in the *munga* with the cane !"

We all cocked our ears and said to each other, "Ah, she can say an Aboriginal word." So, without discussing it with each other, I think we decided that we'd teach her our *Burunji* language. We'd say more words, sometimes ten or fifteen words a day. She'd ask what they meant, and then we'd say, "Go on, Miss, you say it."

I'd go home and say, "Mum, Miss Cook knows '*mookoo*', ... '*munda*'." Then she got to know our Aboriginal names, and by the end of the year that was all she used. She'd shout them when we were doin' something wrong. A lot of the time she'd use *Burunji* for her ordinary teaching, because she knew we'd listen and she didn't have to keep repeating things like she had to in English, because we didn't hear much English at home. Sometimes I'd go home that tired tryin' to teach her. I never thought, "What's **she** got to teach us?" Oh, it was a mixed up way, and of course us Aboriginal kids were tryin' to learn in a foreign language. I never thought about it that way then, but I was only just a kid. But I thought about it in 1974 when I got into the Kinder classroom in Brewarrina. "Here I am, doin' the very same thing with this teacher as I was doin' for Miss Cook in Yantabulla when I was a little girl!"

When we got to school in the morning, Miss Cook would be there waiting, and she'd ask us if any more were comin'. We didn't have a school bell – she blew a whistle when she wanted us to come inside after recess and lunchtime. Besides reading and writing and sums, we did lots of drawings with coloured chalks. We drew houses and coloured 'em in – no aeroplanes 'cos we'd never seen any, but we did draw camels 'n waggonettes and buggies and sulkies, and trucks and tractors. We'd seen them.

I can remember the first racin' car I saw. It was a Friday.

We had this funny feller in the class called Alec Edwards, he sat on the side of the room near the road. He called out, "What's that noise comin'?" and put his toes in the wire and climbed up the wall.

"Quick, look at this, look at this thing. It's a motorcar."

That was the first time we seen a T-model. It was a red one with a black top and yellow wheels, and two fellers sittin' up in the front. So we all raced over to the side and climbed up to watch it go past. All the dust settled, and there was another one came along, a green one – square with a black top, and bigger, a four-seater. So we raced over again, and this went on all morning.

We found out later there were car races up at Hungerford, and the cars were all coming through.

The day they was comin' back, it was a Sunday, all the Aboriginal people were down on the main road all day, watchin' all these cars go past on their way back home.

We didn't know what sort of cars they were, or what made 'em go, we just knew they went. Tractors we knew about, and the big old trucks they used on the stations to cart wood and things like that, but we'd never seen anything like those T-model Fords. After that, the biggest competition we had in school was who could draw the best car.

Miss Cook taught us all to knit, too, the boys as well. She gave us little balls of wool, and our knitting needles were two 4-inch nails, brand-new ones. She said we had to knit little squares. We'd sit in the shade at the side of the cane-grass shed, and we'd all be knitting with our 4-inch nails. I think she kept those squares as a keepsake when we all left, all the Aboriginal children, and there were only white kids there.

We learnt to sing songs, and do the Irish Jig and the Irish Reel. Uncle Archie Knight, my mother's brother, played the accordion and he'd come down to the school and play these quick-steps. The dust would be flyin' in the canegrass shed, with little black and white Aussies doin' the Irish Reel. We didn't do our Aboriginal dances there, though, only in the camps.

When the school was started, all the kids were taught the same things, because no one had been to school before . . . but some kids learnt faster than others, and soon they were very flash, 'cos they could spell 'treacle' and 'golden syrup' and 'flour'. Talk about learnin' to read off the jam tin! Most of us did just that, and very proud of it too we were. There'd be a big scurry to the white man's tip to take the labels off every tin or bottle we could find, and bring them back to our camps. Those labels were our treasures, and to find a new one was like findin' gold! 'Uncle Toby's Oats' was one that was hard for a lot of us. 'Onion' had us a bit tangled up too. 'Pumpkin' was even harder, because we said it like 'punkin'. I had a hell of a time tryin' to spell 'Marmalade Jam'! 'Jam' I could spell, but all them extra letters! 'Holbrook Sauce' was another big word I couldn't wrestle with. So was 'Vinegar'. 'Bushells Tea' I had trouble spellin'. I recognised it because it was a blue packet with an orange line around it. I could say it, but I still **needed** to be able to spell it. No one made me, just me myself. We could spell '*Yantabulla*' because it's an Aboriginal word and we wanted to know it. It's the word for 'plenty to eat' in the *Burunji* language.

The kids that learnt quicker than most of us – I wasn't one of the quick learners – sort of helped us at home. There'd be heaps of us kids together sittin' on the ground under a little tree, or a bough shade, learnin' each other, teachin' each other. It was more than just kids playin' school. You'd say the letters over and over, then close your eyes and you'd remember that sauce bottle or packet, and you'd spell that word. You'd read the letters off from inside your head. It was like homework we set ourselves.

One little boy used to say, " 'urry up, 'urry up so I can still 'member it," 'cos if you waited a few minutes longer he'd forget what was the next letter! He'd be real disappointed and he'd say, "You spoilt it for me, you spoilt it!"

Because Miss Cook was our friend we wanted to prove to her that we could learn words in her language. The look on her face was our reward for all the work we'd done to learn that English word. She would have liked us to tell her how to spell words in our language but there was no way in the world we could do that. I still can't. The best we could do was to say the word real slow for her, and she'd write it down her own way.

Yantabulla is almost on the Queensland border. The heat was bad enough in the mornings, but in the afternoons the sand was red-hot. None of us had shoes. All you could do was run as fast as you could from one tree to another, and where there wasn't any trees you'd run from one bush to another where you could put your bare feet on the little patch of cooler sand in the shade. When we could cadge a ride home from school with Grandfather in the spring cart we'd all crowd on. Grandfather would rouse because we were making it too heavy for George, his lazy old horse.

Sometimes, someone else's dad would hitch up a buggy and be waitin' for us when school finished. We thought that was great, but it only happened when it was real hot. Just the opposite for white kids in towns. Their parents give them a ride when it's raining. When it was cold or wet, our mums and dads just told us to run fast and we'd be warm by the time we got to school. Then we'd be sittin' in the canegrass shed gettin' cold again.

There was no heatin' in the school, but we had a big fire-bucket outside. We had big rocks right round it, where we could sit. Everybody rolled his own stone down from the hill. "This is my stone – this is mine." Because you'd gone and rolled it yourself, no one else had the right to sit on it. Grandfather Mallyer provided the wood for the fire bucket, and, I can tell you, some mornings, sittin' there round that fire bucket, and Granny with her nice warm milk and her fresh hot cakes, it was pretty good. Yeah, it was pretty good.

Winter and summer, we went barefoot. I remember the first time I wore shoes – I could never forget it!

A white lady had given Mum a bag of clothes and three pairs of shoes. They all fitted Gladys's feet and none fitted mine, but I was determined I was going to wear the black leather pair so I forced 'em on. I got a blister, and Mum used to say, "Ev, they're too small for you, you know," but I wouldn't listen. I wanted to wear them shoes, even though I was old enough to know I shouldn't wear 'em with a blister. My feet used to ache and throb in the night, and I'd cry. Mum would soak my feet in *gweeyuhmuddah* water. The *gweeyuhmuddah bush* (dogwood) grows on the sandhills. We boil the leaves, the water goes à greenish-brown and we drink it for upset stomachs. It's rather bitter so you put some sugar in it for kids. *Gweeyuhmuddah* is great for cuts, best cure in the world for sore eyes, for almost anything.

The next morning my feet would feel better and I'd force them shoes on again. One mornin' I couldn't find the shoes. When we were puttin' the fire out, I found the buckles! Dad had thrown my shoes in the fire and left just the one pair that were on Gladys's feet so I couldn't get at 'em. There I was, walking around with bandaged feet. I got blood poisonin' and Mum was dosin' me with bush medicine so I lost a lot of weight, because when you're using bush medicine for a severe sickness it takes a lot of strength out of you as well as takin' out the poison. I was pretty sickly after that for quite a few months, 'cos we didn't have anything fancy to live on, like milk. I know I must've been bad because Mum and Dad didn't get me doin' so many jobs. They knew I wasn't a lazy kid, so if I was layin' down, they'd leave me and do the job themselves.

I really wrecked my feet, you know. Even now, after all those years, they're very tender. It sort of took the hard skin away from both my heels. Yeah, I went mad for shoes.

The first pair of shoes I had that really fitted me was sandshoes. I felt pretty proud of them, wouldn't call the King me uncle, struttin' round in the burrs with my new sandshoes on, and black socks, up to the knees they went, yeah, right up to the knee. Granny Mallyer bought the shoes and socks off the old Afghan hawker, Ahjune, that used to come through. That's what he had with him that trip, so every kid in Yantabulla had white sandshoes and long black socks. Imagine what they looked like on the real black kids, all with skinny legs! So proud of 'em we were that we kept 'em white with *kohpie* – a glassy kind of rock. You put it in the hot fire, and the inside goes real white. Then you scrape off the outside black, wrap it in a rag, hammer it and mix the white powder to a paste with water.

One night we were all sittin' outside round the fire and the dog barked. We all looked to where the dog was lookin' and Uncle Arch said, "Don't like this too much – all I c'n see is a pair o' white shoes comin'!" When they got in the firelight Ray Eulo was in 'em! His Granny had sent him over to borrow some black tobacco from Granny Knight. She was stayin' with us at the time and all those old grannies smoked pipes.

In his van Ahjune had hooks with coathangers for the clothes he sold, and heaps and heaps of beautiful silk material. I've never seen anything like it since in my life. He had hats and shoes, and things for sewin'. The white hawkers used to sell books and comics as well as clothes and hair ribbons and clips and scents. Scenty soap was the main thing that we liked, you know, those egg-shaped cakes of scenty soap.

The white man's school was only a part of our life, and not the most important part. We had the white feller school all day, then in the afternoon we'd have to learn all our Aboriginal training. Our teachers were our grandparents and our oldest aunty – in our customs she's our second mother. If anything went wrong with our own mother, this aunty would take us on. But the most special teachers were uncles – our Mum's brothers, not Dad's.

Mum had two brothers, one just a bit older than me, and an older one, Archie, and he was the one doing the teaching. There were eleven of us in our mob, mainly *Baarkanji* kids, all related. There were other classes too, different tribes – *Muruwadi*, *Wankamurrah*, *Burunji* and *Ngemba*. Their languages are different, but closely related. All tribal kids could speak *Burunji* because the words were easy to pick up and put together. But when you got older, say thirteen, fifteen, you had to talk the language of your tribe. Ours is *Baarkanji*, and the words are much different from *Burunji*. I think that made a little gap among us kids when we got a bit older, and had to speak the language of our tribe. The friendliness didn't seem to be there as much. We didn't drop back into *Burunji* even when there were no grown-ups around. We only spoke it if we were talkin' to smaller kids. I guess we were proud of belonging to our tribal group. It put us closer to the grown-ups.

A kid started in the class as soon as he could talk. Even small kids had to learn to walk long distances without shoes because that was part of the traditional way of life. On hot days we carried the little ones over the scorching sand and stony ridges – our Aboriginal classroom.

Uncle Arch would say, "We're trackin' birds today. Creep real quiet."

When we cut a fresh bird track we'd listen, all quiet, to see if we could hear that little bird close by. Sometimes we'd catch the bird and actually make the track with his foot so we could identify it always. Like policemen, fingerprintin', I suppose. A big bird would sink into the sand and the pattern of his track would disappear, just a little hollow left, but the tracks of little birds would still be distinct on the surface. Magpies and bower birds have almost the same track, except the bower bird's big toe is crooked so he c'n rake up shiny things out of the ground. The crow's track is wider, very much a "I'm here, I'm crow, this is my track!" sort of thing.

When we found a feather, Uncle would ask us, "Who do ya think lost this feather?" The little kids'd be so happy if they found a black feather and be able to say "crow" and be right. We'd carry home all the things we found, and keep them in a special place. We'd look at 'em, and talk about 'em, so nobody could forget 'em.

Another big lesson was which bird owns which egg. The crow has the same egg as the blue crane, the brolga, believe it or not, just the same size, a greeny sort of blue, a very pale pastel colour, but the crane's has the tiniest, tiniest orange spots on it, just a few, but they're there. Snake's eggs are on a string, like a row of elongated beads. The outside is soft and flexible, not hard like a bird's egg. Carpet snake eggs are the size of the big joint of a man's finger, the brown snake a bit shorter. The mulga snake has a short round egg like a marble. They are different colours and shades of colour, and some are pure white. *Thurooh*, the snake, nests in hollow logs, especially logs that have sand in them. We'd hit a log and all the sand would fall out and there would be the eggs. We'd 'kill' them all so there'd be less snakes in our world. Some people eat 'em, run the string of 'em through the fire just as they are. They're like tiny boiled eggs, white and yellow.

We'd find a goanna's track. Uncle Archie would ask us, "What track's that?" He'd be testin' us.

"Goanna track."

"You sure it's goanna, and not blue-tongue lizard?"

"No, he's goanna alright. Lizard walks different, his feet turn a little bit backwards, like echidna."

A goanna track was always exciting because you knew that at the end of that track was something good to eat.

Goanna eggs are much the same as snake's, but a bit bigger. *Kulyah*, the black goanna, has real white eggs. He's not real black, just black markings on him. He's the one that chases you and can run faster than any racehorse. He bites. If you grab him, he'll grab you back, and he's got real big teeth, just looking at him you can see he's vicious. He's a smart feller, never lays with his belly on the sand. If anyone comes by he stands up on his four legs all the time, with his tail up at the back, ready for anything.

Not like *Thirridya*, the little sand goanna. He's got yellow legs. That feller can't even climb a tree, just runs into a hole or a hollow log. He fattens himself up all the summer, then digs a hole in roots and rabbit burrows where he spends all the winter. He's good eatin' if you dig him out early in the winter while he's still fat.

*Burrnyah* looks like a sand goanna, but he's got brown legs and back, a yellow belly and a really long tongue. He'll climb a tree and get out on a limb, then he'll let go and drop on your head! He thinks, "I'll give 'em a fright, and they'll run away, and leave me to get away and live another day." He won't bite you or scratch you, unless he gets in your shirt. Then he'll scratch you, tryin' to get out, but he won't bite.

When I was in my twenties, one day I was throwin' sticks at *Burrnyah* to get him for tucker and he fell down on this white feller who didn't know enough to stand away from the tree! It was a big joke, but not to the feller under the goanna. *Goolgah* is even bigger. That feller lives in the big gum trees, 'n he's yellow with a grey stripe. He'll grow to 14 or 20 inches wide across the belly. We learnt to track *Kultha*, the blue-tongue lizard with his rough black scales and *Thulyee*, the shingleback lizard.

Uncle Arch taught us what eggs we could eat. None of us would eat snake eggs, because I suppose we had imaginations of a snake comin' alive in your tummy, although the egg would be cooked. Goanna eggs we ate, cooked in the hot sand. They've a different taste from birds' eggs, different altogether, a weedy flavour. You could taste 'em in anything, just like garlic is distinct in anything you eat. Fish eggs are different again. We didn't eat any of the small birds' eggs. We'd take an egg home and learn it. We'd keep the egg in the shade in the cool so it didn't go off and the birds that laid it would still hatch it. Then, no matter if it was six weeks after, we'd take it back to the nest. Once birds lose eggs and don't see the shells round anywhere, they know they haven't been eaten by snakes or lizards, so they hang around, and they keep the nest for the next nesting time anyway. So we had no worry about robbin' nests and them not gettin' baby birds.

We became that expert we didn't have to take eggs home. We'd go back every day to the same nest and I guess the birds got a bit worried about kids being there.

But only one kid was allowed to go right to a nest. The rest of us stayed a long way away, and that kid went with a bunch of leaves or a bit of rag, 'cos you didn't touch the shell with your fingers at all, so there'd be no smell of you on the egg. That way the bird would accept it back. Another reason you sent only one kid was so he could climb up the tree without breakin' anything off it. That way you did no damage to the tree.

We all had a turn at doin' this sort of thing. If you did touch the egg you had to admit it, then you'd have to go back and learn to do it without touchin'.

Uncle Archie explained it like, "What if someone come with paint on their hands and they grabbed you, and your mother, she'd rouse and say, 'I don't want you any more. You're painted a different colour.' What about that?" I used to think, "Gee, surely Mum would want me even with a bit of green paint on me." Uncle had funny ways of explainin' things, but he made us understand and remember.

Other times we'd have an afternoon on the river. When Uncle Archie took us to the Cutterburra Creek, first thing he'd say, "Yous c'n go and have a dive," and a dive it would be. You'd go in and dive under and wet yourself all over and come out, and that was it. You were ready to work again. We'd learn to track the birds that lived along the water then.

We found duck tracks up on the sandhills. Some of them nested in the old stumps and hollow trees away from the river. We'd wonder how they got their baby ducks to the river half a mile away without a fox or a hawk gettin' them, but they managed somehow. We could tell what kinds of duck had made the track. The teal is the smallest, the brown duck a bit bigger, and the biggest was the black duck. His track said he was the same show-off as the crow. "I'm the big duck of the river!" sort of thing. He has very long toenails, so when he goes to fly he c'n dig them in deep to give himself a push-off. We even had to identify different duck poo so we'd know which duck was campin' in that spot. If grown-ups said, "We'll go and get a few ducks," we'd be real proud to say, "We know where the ducks are campin'." Ducks lay in the hollow stumps, so we'd look for even a piece of feather caught on a splinter. We'd get a stick, put it in the hollow stump and move it around. If it had duck feathers stuck on the end you knew there was a nest. But you never put your hand in because snakes love eggs as much as people do, and they love sleepin' in ducks' nests too. So you'd swirl the stick round inside to stir the snake up and get a long way back thinkin' he'd come out. Sometimes, he did!

If there was no snake, you'd get only what eggs you wanted, leave the rest, and put all the down back in.

We were taught never to take **all** of what we found. Uncle said, "You take all you find, that old mother duck won't 'ave no more sons and daughters. Then no more eggs and no more ducks. No more food, no more blackfeller." You didn't kill anything that was young, because he'd grow up into something big that would make a real meal. You never deprived yourself by killing the smallest of anything.

We got crayfish – *boogoli* – out of the holes in the hard mud along the creek bank. You'd put your hand or foot in one hole and sort of pump it, like when you unblock a sink. You'd see where the water came up in other places, so that's where the crayfish would come out. They always come out backwards, so someone would stand over that hole while you pumped at the first hole. In the waterholes we'd catch crays and shrimps with a lump of meat on a string, and we'd scoop 'em out with a wire net. Our liveliest time was when we were findin' mussels – *thilli*. We'd go into the shallow water, walk around on the mud and we'd feel the mussels, hard and lumpy. They travel in a line, five or six one behind the other. We'd dive down, pull 'em out and chuck 'em on the bank. The smallest kids heaped them up ready to take home.

In our class we had two boys, cousins to each other and cousins to us – Fred Leppert and Hope Knight. Freddie was a bit older than me, and Hope younger. It didn't matter what we were doin' or learnin', they would muck up, always make a big game of it. When we were on the sandhills trackin', they'd be wrestlin' or rollin' down. We'd go to the river and they'd stay swimmin' and divin'. Uncle Archie didn't spend much time checking them, 'cos he had other kids to teach. He told them, and the rest was up to them. Aboriginal teachers were very different from white teachers. We'd be told a second time, but never threatened. Never once was a stick raised, or a voice raised.

The end of the year come, and we had to do our test. We had to go with Granny Mallyer, or whoever important was there, and a real old Uncle that was no relation to us at all. They come with us and Uncle Arch, and we'd tell them all the things we'd learnt. They'd take a kid in turn, just like the white teachers'll say, "Will you get up and read something for me?" Of course, Fred and Hope were sort of lost doin' some of the things because they hadn't been paying attention. Then the grown-ups said, "Right, you two. You'll have to do another year with Uncle Archie." They cried and they cried but it didn't do any good. They had to pass their lessons, and that was it. The rest of us got patted on the head, even though we made some stumbles.

We were taught how to collect the *nardoo* seeds. *Nardoo* grass grows about knee-high, waist-high in a good season. We'd break it off just where the seed is, 'cos the horses had to feed on the grass stems. We'd shake it into the *coolamons*, even though we knew we were robbing the little

birds, but we needed tucker too. They weren't real carved
wooden *coolamons*, just big pieces of bark. The old people
used to gather dead wool, or wool caught on thorns and
fences and roll it on their thighs to make yarn out of it.
We'd tie the bark into a dish shape with that.

We'd grind the *nardoo* seeds on the table, or better still
on a *nardoo* stone – a big flat hard stone – with a special
smaller stone, till the husks came off. You blew them away,
then you kept on and on crushin' till it become flour. **Very**
tedious work! It would take all day to get enough for a
damper. There was no time to play when there was *nardoo*
to be ground, everybody helped. It was like the nice brown
flour you get now in the Health Shop, and the taste was
sweeter because it was so fresh.

In the swamps yams grew. When there were flowers you
knew the yam down in the mud was ready to be picked.
It's a black hairy thing and when you cook it in the ashes
or hot sand, inside is the creamy-coloured 'potato'. If you
boil it without the skin on, the water gets inside and spoils
the taste. Yams soon dry up and shrivel and they'll keep
like that for ages. You soak 'em and they expand again and
you can cook 'em. If you try to eat them withered up,
they're just like a bundle of sweet hair!

Mum would put wild spinach in stews and soups, or boil
bundles of it with corned meat. A little bulb – *kaalaakah* –
grows only in the sand, but very small. You'd dig all day
before you'd get a pintful of them but they were lovely,
very sweet. Wild bananas – *gaakaalah*, and the wild orange –
*mookraali*, are not like bananas or oranges in any way. I don't
know why the white man called them that. Quandongs make
very nice jam and pies. Wild lemons – *tooli* – are a little
round fruit, very tart. Split Jacks – *naypaans* – are a long
yellow fruit with seeds like a passion fruit, but the substance
inside is white, not orange, very sweet. When they're ripe,
if you see a pad of little black ants, get down low and
see which way they're goin' with a load, and which way

they're comin' back without a load. If you follow the empty fellers, you'll find your *naypaans*. There are two kinds of lilies, and if you pick the wrong one it could give you terrible bellyache. Both lilies have a purple flower, one a big flower, one tiny. One has a white centre, one has a yellow centre, and that's the one you eat, a big bulb like an onion.

Lots of these plants you can use for bush medicine. The best of all is the *gweeyuhmuddah*. There's also a leopardwood tree – *girrinyuh* – that we use for medicine, mostly the roots but the bark too. You take the bark off, smash it up and boil it. It makes a thick red substance and you put it in the hole of a tooth that's aching badly. It's like quinine, but very raw. If it got on your tongue you'd think your tongue was goin' to curl up, like old boot leather! Then, three weeks later, your tooth would start to fall away and come out from your gums. But what would you do in the bush with an aching tooth anyway? On that same tree there's gum that you boil up with sugar to make a syrup. It puts a coating on the stomach and stops dysentry, bad diarrhoea, any kind of bellyache. The gum, especially when it's just oozing out of the tree, is beautiful to chew. There's good chewing gum on other trees too, like the river wattles – *willyuhdoo*. Uncle Arch taught us all this too. I don't think there was anything about the bush he didn't know.

But all the grown-ups were concerned about our learning. Some grown-up, even from the next camp, would sing out, "What bird is that, Ev?" and you had to tell 'em, 'cos if you didn't know, that would be a little black mark across your lesson, and that was something you really had to concentrate on to learn. I guess everybody was our teacher.

Every night Uncle Archie would sit and talk to old Grandfather and Granny Mallyer and Granny Knight.

Granny Knight smoked a pipe, and she used the stem to point at you, especially when she was telling you off! She was only at Yantabulla for a little while, but she liked it better than being in Bourke.

The old people didn't seem to like being in towns at all. They wanted to be out in the bush where they could walk. They'd say to you, "Ev, come on for a walk," and, mate, you'd be walkin' for miles! That's all they wanted to do in the bush – walk for miles, and you'd come home dogtired and go off to sleep sittin' down eatin'. If they walked in town, they'd see a white person in a car or a buggy or on a horse, and they hated runnin' into white people. They'd rather be out in places like Yantabulla where they could walk and walk and not see anybody. If we went for a walk with anyone they'd expect us to tell them what was there, how to go about catchin' it. They wouldn't ask us or tell us, because they weren't our teachers, but we were suposed to take every chance to show what we knew. If we didn't, they'd go back and report to our teacher that we knew nothing, and we'd have to concentrate better. Even little kids knew why. For us it was survival, and no one could learn it for us.

The elders believed that to be really skilled at anything you had to devote all your time and interest to it. We all learnt the basics in all parts of Aboriginal learning, so that we knew enough to make a sensible choice. Then we 'specialized' in the thing we were best at, or were really interested in. I've always liked drawing. Our drawing board was the sandhill itself. You just spread the sand smooth and then you could draw anything you liked. Another Uncle was our painting teacher, and he wasn't the greatest painter in the world! But he used to say to us, "Just because I can't paint real good doesn't mean that you kids can't be good painters when you grow up. I'll start yous off and show yous how to do it, then maybe you'll be real good at it."

When we were introduced to bark painting, I really liked the idea that you could draw on bark with mud. But there aren't any ochres on the Cutterburra River because it is a flat sandy creek, not many rocks at all. Mostly we used the stones from the old fires Aborigines made years ago.

We crushed them up and made yellow and black paints, but it still wasn't smooth like real ochre.

Gladys decided to do the medicines, so she spent most of her time in a class with other kids learning from an old lady, Ruby Eulo, from Enngonia. Gladys knew all there was to know about it by the time she grew up. People would go to her when they needed medicines. Even now with the Flying Doctor Service and doctors all around, she's got stuff bottled and bagged so if she needs anything in a hurry all she has to do is mix it or boil it.

There was kids who wanted to learn all about languages so they learnt more of our language and the languages of other tribes. Teachers came from other places to teach them. If a boy wanted to be a singer of songs for corroborees, he was taught by the old singers, fellers who had **ver-ry big voices**. They trained him and his voice became stronger and stronger. Kids who chose to concentrate on the dances for corroborees had different teachers.

All kids learnt some corroboree dancing and it was great. Leaves were tied around your ankles and every time you stamped your foot they rattled. You made a big noise and shook all over. We learnt that there was more to dancing than just jumpin' around. I wish I could do it now. Boys learnt spear throwing too – part of learning to survive. Hope Knight, much fairer-skinned than me, could throw a spear better than anybody. If he was alive today we could put him in the javelin mob for Australia. If he told you he'd put a spear in a certain tree, he'd put it in right there.

We had to go out with Uncle Arch in the rain too. When the ground's wet, grubs and beetles come out and birds run around in the rain pickin' up a little meal. We learnt which way the wind had been blowin' by which side of the tree was wet or dry, or how the rainwater had washed off the gum.

Cloudy days were frustrating when we were learning directions – you couldn't tell where the sun was. So we learnt that where the bark on the tree was really light, with the colour all gone, that was on the west, because the hottest sun comes from that way. You'd do it that way on a cloudy night too, when there was no Southern Cross to guide you. We used the Cross because a lot of Aboriginal and drovers' travellin' was by night. We'd tell the time at night by the Cross too. In the cattle camp you'd say to your relief, "Wake me up when the Cross turns over... Wake me when the tail's this way... or that way... or when the bright star's over 'ere..." and you'd draw it on the ground. You could tell every two hours by it.

We learnt to identify all the stars by their Aboriginal names. They had meaning for us, and there were stories about them all. I learnt the white man's names later.

In the Milky Way, as we get closer towards the winter, there's a black smudge shaped like an emu. Now when that emu is very distinct, the emus are laying eggs so that's the time you go huntin' for them.

We learnt to read the weather signs from the moon. A big ring around the moon meant a big rain, a little line was just a small bit. I think up until they got computers the white weather man went by that too! Sometimes the moon isn't right in the middle of the ring, but to one side or the other. That means there's wind coming. It takes a lot of explaining to understand it right. You gotta live a lot of years in the bush for that, but I've used it all my life.

Other things we learned were pottery, emu egg carving, wood carving, weaving with grass – mats, baskets, dilly bags, even the big mats you could sit on. The good grass for weaving grows where the bores run over into salty lagoons. So before we could make baskets we had to know where the reeds grew, gather them, bring them back and dry them. As kids we all made them the natural colour but a kid who specialized in that would have to learn the whole thing – which roots to dig up and boil for dyes to colour the grasses.

We wove dilly bags from ordinary grasses or vines or thin strips of kangaroo hide or the longest emu feathers. In fact you'd see little babies sittin' on the mother's back, in a fancy grey carrybag – *mulka* – made of emu feathers. It was easy weaving with feathers, long ones like emu or crane, because you sharpened the end and used the point as a needle. To decorate an ordinary grass basket, we'd weave in long coloured feathers.

We made use of small coloured feathers too. We plaited them into strands of human hair and put that in with the grasses. We weren't allowed to kill a tiny bird for his feathers, but we'd watch out for where they'd preened themselves. There were always lots of galah feathers because we lived on them as meat.

We didn't eat cranes because they tasted too much like fish, so does a pelican. Yet it's a strange thing, the duck who lives in the water and eats the same things as the pelican and the crane, his meat tastes like meat, not fish. Crane meat is very black. We'd feed it to the dogs.

The only wild meat dogs don't eat is porcupine – *thiggibilla*. I've never tasted it either. In our Baakanji tradition it was taboo for me because I'm the oldest in my family. But it smells good! A lot of times I'd like to 've tried it when the others were havin' it.

Boys spent time with their father learnin' how to be good dads, and we spent time with Mum, who taught us how to look after babies and sick kids. They didn't teach us how the babies were born until we were older, about twelve. When there was a baby to be born they'd build a special tent a long way from the camp and take the woman over there. They'd say to us kids, "Get more wood for that fire . . . you make sure that bucket's filled up . . . we gotta have plenty of hot water." We got to the stage of asking, "Why do they want all this hot water for just one tiny little baby?" Course, Hope and Freddie said, "They're gonna cook it!"

We'd all have to stay a long way back. First it was out

of sound, then we were allowed to come a bit closer. As we got older we had to stand at the tent door, always one girl and one boy, never two girls or two boys together. I'll admit it made my hair stand up the first time I seen it. We'd seen pups born, and calves, foals, cats, but to think this happened to people!

The midwife was Aboriginal, an old Granny or Aunty, never a white person. That baby became a special part of the midwife's family. If anything happened to the parents, she would own that kid. In a way it was like the godmother at a Christening, but stronger. If the midwife couldn't take the kid, the next person in line was the mother's sister. In kinship, she was your second mum, and your father's brother was your second dad.

So our Aboriginal schooling about every part of life went on and on and on, but in the white man's school it was straight stuff.

You learnt c-a-t, b-a-t, but if we didn't know them, we weren't made to go back and concentrate on them like we did with our own learning. So I guess we took the white man's learning – reading and writing – just as something to do. But I didn't see what we could use it for. If you'd walked up to a white man and spelt c-a-t, would he give you a cat. Who wanted a cat? What if you spelt h-o-u-s-e or t-o-w-n? Nothin' happened!

I saw Miss Cook reading a story out of a book, but I never thought **I** could ever do that. I always thought I'd have to be white to read good, to look good – to do all the things **they** did.

I didn't think about any kind of life ahead except the way we lived at Yantabulla. What I had, and what knowledge I had, I was satisfied with.

I suppose you could say we went to the white man's school because it was somewhere to go every day, and we liked this *wudjiin* who got lonely and cried and didn't care if we seen her cry. We liked it when she'd teach us songs, like 'Yankee Doodle Dandy' and Christmas songs that we'd never heard before.

When Miss Cook got married to a drover, Tom Rushton, Granny crocheted a lovely pillow sham for **her** *wudjiin*.

One night not long after that we were all asleep and dogs barking and people singin' out woke us up. Gladys said, "Get up quick, Sister. Something wrong." We started calling out for Mum and Dad but they were already gone. We could see big flames through the cracks – Granny and Grandfather's camp was burnin'. Gladys started cryin' and so did I. We were very fond of our grandparents. We could hear everyone singin' out, and we wanted to go over but we knew we shouldn't, and anyway we were frightened. When someone shouted, "Drag 'er out, get her out!" Gladys said, "Must be Granny's old dog". I think we both had an idea it was Granny but we didn't want to say it to each other so we went into our hut and sat down and waited.

We were there all that night by ourselves and when daylight came we wanted to look out but were still too frightened. We stayed huddled up under our blankets. Then Mum sung out, "Come on, you girls, get up and have some breakfast." She had made tea and fried scones. So we were sittin' at the fire dippin' them in golden syrup in the one plate and Gladys said, "Mum, where's Dad?"

"Oh-h-h, he took Granny to Bourke. She got burnt in the fire last night."

In them days they had no ambulance out that way, and it was too far away for the Flying Doctor in the tiny planes they had in the 1930s.

We just kept on eatin'. I used to always enjoy hot pufftaloons and golden syrup, but it didn't taste right. Mum could see that there were a lot of questions we wanted to ask but didn't know how. She said, "It was Grandfather's pipe started the fire. We think it set the pillow alight."

We were sittin' there when Uncle Archie come along on

his horse and got down real slow, like he didn't want to come over. Mum said, "What's wrong now, Brother?" My Uncles and Aunties called each other Sister and Brother, and so that's the way we grew up. My kids do it sometimes too.

"The old woman died, Annie ... just down the road. She was burnt too bad. They're bringin' her back up to the Police Station." They had a sort of a shed there they used as a morgue, with a bit of a timber yard at the back where they put coffins together.

Mum said, "You kids stay here and don't go away. Just wait here till me and your father come back."

We watched and saw all the grown-ups goin' from their camps, and kids were left in their own camps. All day we were there – all day. Kids older than us went and got the *gweeyuhmuddah* bush to make a smoke. They made big fires, they smoked the camp and they smoked everybody. Each of us in turn had to stand in the smoke so the spirits wouldn't bother us. No one had to tell 'em to do it. It was a ritual thing grown-ups did as soon as anybody died.

When it came towards sundown we got frightened. We called the dogs and tied them in front of the hut and at the back. We were sittin' there till late, then the oldest kids said, "You littl'uns go to bed." They fixed up for one big kid, a twelve or thirteen year old, to stay in each camp with the smaller kids. I was the biggest in our family but I had to have a big kid lookin' after me. We made a fire and put the billys right around. When there's trouble you have a fire goin' all the time and you have water boilin' in case somebody comes along for a drink of tea. Then we went off to sleep.

In the morning we got up real early, just daylight. Still no Mum and Dad home, nobody's mums and dads. The big kids took us all away from the camps to the big claypan on the edge of the cane grass, and told us to stay there while they went and got tucker for breakfast. They made a fire and fed us, and we stayed there in that open place on the edge of the claypan until just on sun-down.

We seen all the mums and dads comin' along then. We could hear them cryin' comin' along the creek. We didn't go back home straight away – I suppose we were scared with all the cryin'. We were usin' the moon for a light and it was nearly down when we went back. Probably only went then before it got really dark, 'cos everything that moved, we thought it was Granny – terrified of ghosts we were. Nobody tells you there's a *gurrnki* – it's just built in you. Although we knew Granny wouldn't harm us, we were still afraid of seein' her because we knew she was dead.

Mum gave us a feed and we went to bed. When we woke up in the morning Dad was gone. He was workin' fixin' windmills on Arara Station. When he was away we could talk loud and play, but when he come home it had to be all quiet. Kids could play but you weren't allowed to raise your voices for about a month after a death. That wasn't just for our camp – all the camps kept everything quiet. That was the law and culture we grew up with.

When Monday morning came and it was time for school we were all happy about it, 'cos we got away from the camps where this sadness was hangin' all the time. It was a heavy thing on all of us. When we got to school the feeling was **worse**. Miss Cook, the sadness from her sort of rubbed off onto us, because of Granny being so good to her. There was times when we didn't have any lessons at all. We'd just sit round and talk. All over again it was like when she first come, us tryin' to bring her out of the depression she was in, so she could teach us. Her husband was away droving most of the time. When he'd come home she'd be happy so we'd be happy at school too. If Miss Cook came to school sad we'd have a sad day, and we'd be glad to get away from her and go home. But then it was sad at home. So the only happy place for us at that time was between school and home but we had to be home before sundown. None of us could explain to the grown-ups why we didn't want to come back to the camps. We couldn't explain – we didn't really understand it ourselves, but we felt it.

We were real good friends with our Dad, me and Gladys. He was more than our Dad, he was our mate. If anything went wrong he'd patch it up. Arms fell off dolls and he'd put 'em back on for us. So we'd talk to him all the time, whereas we shouldn't have been talking to him at all. Kids were not supposed to talk to anyone who was a close relative of someone who died, for the whole time of sadness, unless the grown-up spoke to them first. Gladys's like me, a chatterbox, and we'd both talk to Dad. Granny was dead and she was buried, and to us that meant he needed someone extra to talk to, because Granny wasn't there for him any more. We didn't say it to each other, Gladys and me, but I think we decided in our own minds, wherever Dad was, that's where we'd be

Granny Knight used to say to Mum, "Annie, them girls! They'll be sendin' Mullya up the wall, they're talkin' too much to that old feller."

"He'll tell 'em if they talk too much."

Grandfather Mallyer, he just closed up. He wouldn't talk to no grown-ups, just us kids. Later on he used to say, "I wish you little fellers would've come over and talked to me when Granny died. I 'ad no one to talk to, only me dogs."

We didn't know if we should have spoke to him or not. Our Aboriginal law was strict.

Dad and the others built him another camp three or four hundred yards from where Granny got burnt, because blackfellers don't stay in the same place where someone died. He lived in that camp for about eight months when they woke us up again shouting that a camp was on fire and it was Grandfather's. He was dead when they found him. It was daylight by then so we could see them wrap him up in blankets. The police rode down, then the men put his body on his old spring cart and took him to the Aboriginal burying ground.

After Grandfather Mallyer died, it was all sad again at the

school, because both those old people had spent a lot of time at the school, helpin' Miss Cook. They were the first two people who befriended 'er. She'd sit down and ask them questions and listen to them for hours before she got married, and after, when Tom was away drovin'. Dad was very sad after Grandfather's death, coming so soon after Granny's. He was not eating and was losing weight. We didn't really notice that, 'cos he was tall and skinny anyway, but Mum kept sayin' it. Gladys said to him, "Dad, you ought to go and smoke yourself."

"We already been smoked, girl, all of us."

"You ought go down the *gulpa* (deep gully) and sit there and smoke yourself, stay there all day."

"Yes, baby, I'll do that."

He did do it, too. We never seen Dad for a couple of days, and some of the other men went with him. He seemed to pick himself up after that. He came back, rolled his swag and got a job over a bit further, mendin' fences. Things were gettin' bad then, not much work around, what they called the Depression. We never seen Dad for about nine days. Then when he came back, he rode up singin' out, "Hello! . . . g'day, Ev! . . . how're you goin', Glad?" and there was our father again! . . . the father that we'd lost all those months while all these bad things were happenin' to him. His voice was Dad's again. He had emu eggs and berries and quondongs. It was great, just like someone went shoppin' and came home with all these goodies. That night out came Dad's old accordion and he sat at the fire and played.

We was all happy then, we was a family together.

Mum's brother, Uncle Harry Knight, lived on Waverley Downs Station, a long way from Yantabulla, over the Paroo out towards the Four Corners. He had a fencing crew of his own and knew that Dad didn't have a job so he sent for him.

Things were tough. If it hadn't been for emu and kangaroo we'd never have had meat at all. Mum could put it in the pot with wild spinach and carrots and we'd have a good meal. If there was nothing else, we'd have soup. We didn't have bread if we run out of flour, because there wasn't always *nardoo* that you could grind up to make one or two seed johnny cakes, 'cos it only grows in the sandhill country.

It took us weeks to get to Waverley Downs.

If we were travellin', our job, us kids, was to see that all the leather things, all the harness, was intact. If anything was broke, we gave it to Dad to mend. We checked the chicken coop under the buggy to see there was no holes so the fowls couldn't fall out, that the water bags, billy cans and buckets had no leaks. We checked the dogs, and the cats Gladys had as pets. We cleaned out the tucker box – a home-made one Dad had put together out of deal boards.

Dad's job was to repair the harness, check the wheels and shafts of the old buggy, see if the horses' hooves needed trimmin'. They weren't shod – we couldn't afford to buy horse shoes. Dad had a few rusty bent horseshoe nails but we were never able to pick up enough shoes to shoe even one horse.

Mum's job was to cook, to have everything ready for us in the tucker box, and of course to keep us clean. The travelling food was mostly cold meat and damper. We sat in the buggy and rode for miles eatin' raw cauliflower, carrots, turnips, or munching on a raw cabbage leaf! Strange, isn't it? The meat wouldn't keep unless you cooked it, and the vegetables wouldn't keep if you did!

Mum would make jam tarts, put two together, tin plate on top and tin plate on the bottom, and then wrap 'em in a piece of clean cloth, and we'd munch on those while we travelled. Whatever tea we had left over from breakfast camp would hang on the side of the buggy in the billy can, so if you wanted a drink, all you had to do was lean over with your pint, dip some out and sweeten it up.

On Waverley Downs they were doin' a fence on a stony hill, and if you ever sat under a tree watchin' four men tryin' to dig post holes on a stony hill, you'd hear a thing or two! Us kids made the fire and put the billy on and took tea to the men along the fence. We'd help run a bit of wire, thread it through the spreaders for the men to take up at the strainer posts. It was a hard job. It wasn't so bad draggin' the wire. The really bad bit was dodgin' the *bindi* burrs, 'cos nobody had shoes. A good feller owned that place. When he'd come out to look at the fence he'd bring heaps of fruit and eggs for all the kids. There were other camps too, not just ours, but they were seven or eight miles apart. While we were there, that was the whole world for us, nobody else, just us four.

Every time we'd move camp to another part of the fence, Dad'd say, "Come on, you kids, we'll make your cubby house," and he'd put four forky sticks in the ground and build a bough shade for us. It got that way that people would say, "Mullya must have been workin' this bit of fence. There's his kids' cubby house."

We'd gather rocks and sticks, like bower birds, and play House. Sometimes Gladys'd whinge and Mum'd sing out, "What're you doin' to her, Ev?"

"Nothin'."

I did a lot of 'nothing'. She'd do something and I'd tell her not to and she'd cry, or I'd tip over her mud pies and she'd cry, or I wouldn't join in the little tea party she wanted to have and she'd cry. So I got a lot of hits for a lot of nothing. It was always, "Ev, don't do that . . . What're you doin' to Gladys, Ev? . . ."

"Nothing!"

Sometimes I'd get sent to bed without any tucker for 'nothing'. I'd lay there and sulk a while and say to myself, "I don't want any supper anyway." I'd be hungry, but that tired from playin' and helpin' and runnin' all day sleep would overtake me. But I found out a bit later that all I had to do was wait till they went to sleep themselves and creep out to the tucker box and get myself a feed. I'd be first up next morning, fire goin' and the billy on. Mum or Dad would say, "Ah, gee, Ev must be hungry, went to bed with no supper last night." I wouldn't answer them because they really knew I'd been in the tucker box during the night. We were all good mates.

Mum used to drive the truck to drop the posts off for Dad, and our job was to mark where the posts were to go. We had a special chain with a spike at each end. Gladys would stop at the end to be sure the spike didn't pull out, and I'd stretch the chain and mark where the next post was to go. We'd do that all day, chaining, just the two of us, until maybe we'd think we heard a strange noise in the bush and we'd get frightened and run back to the camp. Terrified of everything we were, but safe with Mum and Dad.

I never thought that one day we'd be all split up. I thought there'd always be us four. We couldn't imagine not bein' with Mum and Dad. And the mates that me and Gladys were, we couldn't have imagined being without each other.

When we got back to Yantabulla after that job there was nothing, just nothing. We found that most of the Aboriginal people had moved away. Only the Zooches and three other families were still there.

"Where's everybody, Charlie?" Dad asked Charles Zooch.

"Some've gone to the Government Mission at Brewarrina. They reckon you get food for your kids, and a house to live in."

"Who said you can?"

"Some government fellers came while you were away, told us all about it. They made it sound really good."

We felt isolated way up on the sandhills, with all the empty camps around. The feelin' where there'd been deaths wasn't good either. So we all moved down near the lagoon behind the pub. The publican said, "Mullya, you can't drink that water. The ducks and geese and swans and pelicans swim and shit in it. You'll all get sick. We'll run a pipe

47

across from the pub tank and put a tap on it and you c'n all use it.'' He was a good feller.

Dad thought about the Mission and talked a lot to Mum about it. He'd almost made up his mind to go. Mum was friends with Charles Zooch's wife, Nellie. Nellie grew up on the Cherberg Mission and spoke very little English – always called her husband Wookermun. She told mum, ''Wookermun 'n all us goin' too. We gonna travel with you fellers.'' Then he came over himself and said, ''Mullya, if you're going to Brewarrina to the Mission so that things will be better for your children, then I'll come too.''

Now this Charles Zooch was one of the kids that Syd Kidman (the Cattle King, they called him) took from Naryilco Station, one of his huge properties, and sent to a College in Adelaide where the squatters' sons went. He gave him the name Charles Zooch. Charles was a full blood, but he was better educated and spoke better than most white men. When Kidman's 'boys' left school they worked on his stations until they married but they were always free to do what they wanted. Kidman never made them feel that he owned them because he'd educated them. I don't know how many he did that for, but it was a big number, boys and girls.

When they'd hear that Kidman was comin' to the town or station, little kids would throw out their chests and put on their best smiles thinkin', ''We goin' with Kidman.'' The parents trusted him because he was a good man, a man of his word, and really looked out for the kids. In their minds he wasn't anything like the Aboriginal Protection Board.

One day Dad said, ''Annie, I think we'll go to this Mission in Brewarrina. We might get a bit more food there for the kids, be able to live.''

''Alright, Jack, whatever you think best.'' (When Mum called Dad 'Jack' we knew it was a real serious thing.)

''Now listen, you kids, we'll start gettin' ready to pack up tomorrow because we're goin' a long way from here.''

''To Bourke, Dad?''

"Yeah, then we're goin' to Brewarrina."

"What's Brewarrina? Where is it?"

"It's a town and there's a Mission there. All the black people got houses and they get rations every week, kids go to a big school with a lot of other kids."

I thought, "That'll be alright. I can write my name, and I can spell things and I can read." I wasn't worried about whether I would fit into that school or not.

We told Miss Cook we were goin' away and she said, "Oh, Evelyn and Gladys, I'm sad to lose you."

"Not only us, Miss, the Zooches're goin' too.

"But I won't have any Aboriginal children at school, hardly any children at all, only the few white children."

It was especially in the last couple of weeks we was with her that I felt she was **my** friend. I said, "Miss, I'll be right in that Mission school 'cos I can read and I can write."

She said, "Yes, you can do this ... you can do that ..." and she give me all this confidence in myself. I'm pretty sure she made each one of us feel special.

We asked our parents if we could buy her something so we could say "Thank You". But no one had any money. Old Grandfather Jack Ellis said, "I'll make some boomerangs and carve 'em for you, and you kids can give her them." So him and the boys made the boomerangs and we all gave them to her. She cuddled us and kissed us all on the forehead, and gave us hair clips and combs and ribbons, and the boys a pocket knife, little different things, one thing each. She said, "Just so you won't forget me."

Those gifts were very valuable to us, because they were given to us by someone who liked us, somebody we liked.

Then we had to stay for another couple of days because Charles Zooch had a horse he was just breakin' in to a cart and needed to settle it down. So there was time for us to have a little party at school – cakes and home-made ginger beer.

Then it really was time to move on.

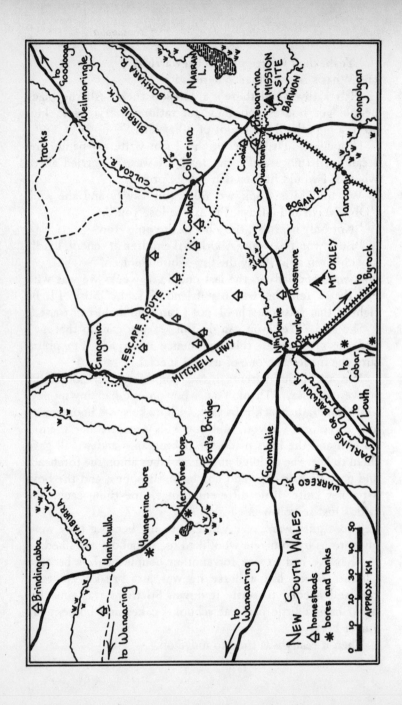

# THE MISSION

*'There was nothin' to look forward to'*

I must've been eight or nine, I dunno. I know I could hook an arm over the horse's neck to buckle the collar.

When we got goin', the excited talk seemed to drop out of all of us. Zooches were in the front buggy, our parents behind, with Gladys and me riding our loose horses. Every now and then someone would look back. The stone police station with its white roof was the last part we saw of Yantabulla, then we turned the corner where the big box trees are. After that, nobody spoke for a long while.

When we camped for dinner they started talkin'. Charles said, "Wonder what this place is like? We could even be sorry and regret that we've left Yantabulla."

Dad said, "I don't think so. Anyway, we can always come back."

"We could do that too, Mullya."

When us kids had finished eating, Dad said, "You c'n all walk on ahead. You'll come to a bore. We'll camp there tonight, so you have some wood gathered."

We got to the bore and Gladys and me picked our spot and the Zooch kids settled on theirs. When Mum and Dad got to us we had the place all swept clear, and the fire lit. Soon as we had a feed everyone settled down. I think we were all tired from the gettin' ready, but much, much more from the goin' away. Next thing I woke up in the dark, bullocks roarin', dad shoutin', "Why 'aven't you bloody kids got more sense? – pitchin' a camp right on the track where the bullocks come to water!"

We hadn't really looked, just said to each other, "This'll do." We didn't get back to sleep real soon, tryin' not to let Mum and Dad hear us gigglin'.

When we got to Ford's Bridge, about half-way between Yantabulla and Bourke, Charles Zooch took a station job with Taylors, because the dads had decided to work their way along, takin' jobs wherever they could. They planned to meet up in Brewarrina before they went to the Mission. We kept on to Bourke. It was gettin' into November so we travelled at night. Big thunderstorms were about but no rain so the dust from the travellin' was terrible. We swam in the overflow from every bore we came to. When we got to Bourke Dad said, "We'll stop off here for a while with your people, Annie – give the horses a good rest. There's still over sixty miles to go." But it turned out to be more than a while. That was the first time I met all my cousins, the Knights. Grandfather Hero Black, Granny Knight and all the Knight family lived in Bourke.

While we were there Mum was very sick in the hospital, and as we were held up Dad got work at the Fort Bourke Station. When mum came home from hospital she camped out there with him and Gladys, and I stayed in Bourke with Aunty Grace, mum's sister, so I could go to school. A couple of weeks later Gladys came in to go to school too, but she lived with Granny Knight.

Most Aboriginal children went to the Convent school. Their parents liked it because their children were treated the same as everyone else.

The first morning, my cousin Edie took me and five other kids from the river camp. I tell you what, the first time we saw the nuns with their habits, we thought they were *gurrnkis* (ghosts). The priest in his long black gown was a *gurrnki* too, until we got to know him. We hadn't seen missionaries much in Yantabulla. Sometimes they went through, but the police wouldn't let them stop there. Once a missionary had tried to dominate the people, so the next policeman stationed there wouldn't let them anywhere near the Aboriginal people. He told Granny Mallyer he'd said, "You're only frustrating them. They're perfectly happy living the way they are. Go on about your business."

Edie took us to the great big Convent door and told us, "We gotta go in here."

I panicked! "No, Edie, look at all those *gurrnkis*! We not stoppin' here!"

There were some up on the balcony, and some walkin' about, and we knew they were behind us 'cos we could hear somethin' rattlin'. Then a *gurrnki* came out the door and was right there! She was a **big** woman, this Mother, with big eyes, grey, like big saucers, and her voice was very rich. When she spoke, the voice seemed like it went all round you.

"Can you read and write?" she wanted to know.

"Little bit – not much."

"That'll be alright," and she smiled at me. I began to feel just a little bit not scared, but I still wasn't too sure.

We had a little feller with us and he was standin' there makin' marks in the dirt with his big toe, no shoes on, and he was lookin' down at the ground, shakin' his head, noddin' his head. She didn't say once to him, "Look up when I'm speaking to you," or "Let me have a look at your face." She bent down, right down real low, veil hangin' down at the side – and she was **tall** – till she could look up into his face! He was there with one hand in his pocket and the other behind him. She caught his eye and said, "Oh-h, you're there. I didn't think you were, because I couldn't hear anything." Then he gave a little bit of a giggle, and of course she was his friend, and he was her favourite from then on. She was Mother Ala ... Alaphonsus, I think. Some funny name she had like that.

The priest was called Father Tracey. He was a big man too. He used to laugh so loud at all the silly things the kids'd do, but if a kid fell over and was cryin', he'd pick 'im up and cuddle him better. We all loved Father Tracey, claimed him as a 'grandfather'. He always had time to listen to us, he was always there for us, and so were the nuns.

In Yantabulla we'd played mainly Aboriginal games, and as for football, we hardly knew what it was. The football the Sisters taught us in Bourke wasn't Rugby football. It was a round leather ball, soccer. There'd be two sides made up of all of us. The little kids'd be standin' there all shy but the captains'd pick them too so they'd feel good. Some of the younger nuns'd join in, and they'd fold that long black gown up round their waist, tuck it in at the back and they were off! They were very fleet of foot, those nuns! I knew when they were near me 'cos I'd hear the beads rattlin' and I'd put on a burst of speed but no use. They'd run, and cheek us ... I dunno, it was good.

Father Tracey would sit in his yard on a big high chair and watch over his fence. He'd bent the tin over at the top so he could lean his elbow on it. When the nuns won he'd clap like anything, and we'd be kickin' stones goin' back to the classroom, pretendin' to sulk. When we'd win, we'd wait for that clap too, and he'd make us wait for it. We'd think, "He's not gonna clap us," then he would clap and we'd all go away feelin' real good. When we played rounders the Sisters would really throw the ball to put you out and sometimes you'd go home with the red mark on your legs.

We'd played marbles at Yantabulla all the time. You could say we were professionals almost. We'd start off with glassies – those big green glass stoppers out of the lemonade bottles – and use them to win the pretty taws and milkies and aggies the white kids'd buy in the shops. The Sisters'd get down and play with us too. They'd cheat if they could but we never let them get away with it. We'd watch 'em like hawks and someone'd yell out, "Hey, knuckle down, Sister, no fudgin'!" That's when you poke your hand over the line scratched on the ground around all the marbles when you're playin' Big Ring. She'd just laugh and say, "I'm trying not to!" and I'd think to meself, "Yeah, you're tryin' not to git caught!" And we'd be playin' for Keeps too. But we all loved it when they played with us. They were real strict but we knew they were our friends.

There was a row one day. One girl whose father had the paper shop always had pockets of marbles, and I'd won 'em all off her, so she went to Sister. Sister Clare got me and said, "Evelyn, did you cheat playing marbles?"

"No, Sister. I don't cheat!"

"Dulcie said you cheated and that's how you won all her marbles. Come on now, tell me the truth."

"I didn't! She can't win marbles, 'er dad gives 'em to her. I won all them marbles **fair and square!**" I was real serious about it. That sort of stuck with Sister Clare, 'cos after that, every time there was some work I was supposed to have done, and I'd be just sittin' there, she'd say to me, "Evelyn, I'll give you five minutes to get that done, or you'll get no playtime – and that's fair and square!"

In school work we found the Bourke kids were ahead of us, but Sister Clare was very good helpin' us. She'd say, "Have a little bit of recess, have your bread and honey, then come back to me." Then she'd sit with us in a corner of the playground and give us little extra lessons. She'd say, all enthusiastic-like, "So's you can catch up with the rest." It wasn't no embarrassment to us that we were behind in our education. If a kid stood up to read and stumbled along, we couldn't see no reason why we should laugh at 'im, 'cos we were all learnin', we were stumblin' along too. But I've been in schoolrooms today when if a kid stumbles, the whole class laughs. All the teacher says is, "Settle down," instead of making them understand how cruel that is. No wonder kids drop out of school. Who wants to be laughed at!

If a kid didn't know a word, Sister would put it on the board and I'd think to meself, "Right, next time when I'm readin' that story I'll know that word." Probably other kids in the class didn't know the word either, or couldn't spell it, or didn't know what it meant, but wouldn't say so. That way we all learnt. We got so we could read Ginger Meggs comics, and Bib and Bub, and Popeye, but we left Bourke before we got up to the School Magazine. I could read a little bit in the prayer books and the catechism that we had to learn, because God was givin' orders to the Sisters that we had to. I learnt to do running writing real neat, too. I was very proud of my writing.

You had to do something pretty bad to get the cane. Stood in the corner, yes. Made to write words lots of times, yes. But canin' was the last straw, and I tell you, when you got it, you knew it. I've had the cane from teachers but they didn't seem to hit as hard as the nuns. They seemed to come down **in** the cane!

I'd talk out of turn sometimes in the classroom, me and me *wrutoo yalka* (big mouth). Sometimes I'd go home and they'd say, "Milk the goat, Ev."

"'ow c'n you milk a goat with four sore fingers?"

"Oh-h, got the cane again to-day, did you, Ev?"

But it didn't happen all that often because we wanted to please them. We knew somehow they cared about us.

We used a lot of our own language in that school and Sister Clare never said, "Don't talk like that. Speak English." She'd catch one of us by ourselves and she'd say, "That word you were saying to so-and-so, what does it mean? Say it for me." She knew if there was a mob of us we'd all try to help her at once and she couldn't understand how to say it.

I got into trouble when I hit a white boy and knocked him down and his glasses fell off. He'd called me a bony-legged skinny little black gin, and I hit him!

Sister Clare said, "I'll have to give you the cane, Evelyn."

I said, "Yeah, alright. I s'ppose so." Then I looked at him and said, "I'll punch ya again too."

Sister said, "You can't do things like that! What about if you'd broken his glasses?"

Afterwards she said, "I know you don't like being called a black gin."

"A bony-legged skinny little black gin, 'e said, Sister. I can't help it if my skin's this colour."

"I know, but all through your life, Evelyn, you'll meet people who'll say things like that to you. Are you going to punch every one, and hit them and knock their glasses off?"

"How many do ya reckon'll say it, Sister?"

"That depends on how old you get to be. If you live to be an old woman a lot of people will say it, and all you'll be doing is punching people and knocking their glasses off."

She told me to think about it, and I did. Next day I told her, "Sister, how about (I was pointin' to my ears) if I let it go in 'ere and out there? 'ow will that work?"

She gave a bit of a smile and said, "You just try it, Evelyn." And I did, and it worked.

There was another dear old nun – she must've been old 'cos she was bent over – used to give us home-made bread and honey, bush honey. They made jam too, and one time we were given a little jar to take home with us. One day we were all invited to have a look in the kitchen, and they were a busy lot of people in there. They had big aprons on, the old stove was goin'. They had boarders then, heaps of kids from out on the properties. Till then I didn't know they all worked real hard at other things than just teachin' us kids in school.

We took our lunch to school, mostly damper and syrup. We'd get sick of that, so we'd put it down where all the bags and lunches were, and nick some white kid's lunch, nicely wrapped up, thinkin' he'd have something nicer. Couple of times we struck cold meat sandwiches with yeast bread, a real feast to us, but most of the time we struck damper too! The white kids never complained about it, but the Sisters knew us all better than we knew ourselves. I think they'd make these damper lunches, in a nice-lookin' parcel, to trick us. We'd wonder then what white kid in that class was bringin' damper sandwiches for his lunch. It soon fixed us for swoppin' and nickin' dinners!

About three months we had in Bourke, three good months they were. We were Confirmed while we were there. We went to Church every Sunday morning, went across in the boat, carrying our shoes and socks till we got to the other side 'cos the old boat was leakin'. There was a lot of Aboriginal people at Father Tracey's Mass, 'cos he was a welcoming man. Whenever I was in Bourke when I was growin' up, I always went to visit the nuns. I even took my husband in to show him, and when we wanted the kids baptised we went back to that church. Just like we'd thought all teachers were like Miss Cook, I thought all nuns were like our Sisters at Bourke when I was a kid, but I found out later on that wasn't true either.

When we got to Brewarrina at last, we found that the Zooches had got there about a week ahead of us. Our parents decided we should go to school again, so Mum and Nellie Zooch

took us along to the Public School, me and Gladys, and
Harry and Neeta. The school was only one big room. We
were all on the verandah and our mums were talkin' to
the teacher and we heard the teacher sayin', "No, we can't
take them. Aboriginals can't go to this school, they have
to go to the Mission."

While we were there, all the kids came out to play and
hung around the verandah, and there was this little white
girl about my age, kept pokin' her tongue out at us when
the teacher wasn't lookin'. We didn't know why. We hadn't
done anything to her. We knew nothing about this 'You're
black and I'm white' thing. The four of us looked at each
other, and I decided in my mind she was just a cheeky
little girl.

Mum took us home to the camp and said to Dad, "We
can't send the kids to school in this town, they won't 'ave
'em. We've got to take 'em out to the Mission." Dad couldn't
get over it. He thought any kid could go to any school.
In them days it wasn't compulsory for Aboriginal kids to
go to school at all, but my parents wanted the best for
us. That was another good reason, they thought, for us to
go to the Mission, so us kids could get educated properly.
But in the end we didn't learn much more there than Miss
Cook and Sister Clare had already taught us.

"Alright," he said, "that settles it. We'll have to move."

Even then they waited on a bit because Dad and Charles
Zooch thought they might have been able to get some work
on the steamers. To them any work was preferable to just
linin' up for handouts, and in them days the steamers were
still working the Darling and Barwon all the way up to
Walgett. The Barwon is really the upper part of the Darling,
but it's not called the Darling until just upstream of Bourke.
In the end there was no choice. The bit of money they
had was whittlin' away and tucker was gettin' short, so we
packed up again, us and the Zooches, to make the last bit
of our trip to this wonderful Mission, more or less so we

could be sure of a feed. We were sort of lookin' forward to it, after all that time, and to us kids at least it was a big adventure.

When we got to the Mission in the afternoon – it was hot, middle of February – there were two other buggies ahead of us, the MacKellars, and people we'd picked up at Bourke, the Andersons. The only way in was through a big gate next to the Mission office. The Mission Manager came out, a big tall man. We were in the back of the buggy, sittin' waitin' . . . and listenin'. When it was our turn, Dad got down and Charles Zooch – he was travellin' right behind us – came and joined him.

The Manager talked quite reasonably to our dad, but when he came to Charles Zooch his manner was very different. I didn't know the word 'abrupt' then, but now I'd say he was very abrupt, because of the way Charles spoke. His English and grammar was much better than the Manager's, and you couldn't have an educated Aboriginal person on a Mission. You either starved him out, or boned him or shot him, but some way you got rid of him. It would never do for a white man to feel belittled by a full-blood Aboriginal, and Charles and Nellie were full-bloods. His features were like the drawings you see of Bennelong, and he was smartly dressed. I noticed all this at the time but I only understood it later on.

The Manager asked our dad, "What's your name?"

"Jack Mallyer."

"Where'd you come from?"

"Yantabulla, up on the Cutterburra Creek, Hungerford way."

That white feller'd have had no idea where that was, and he didn't care. We were just more Aboriginal people on his Mission.

"How many kids've you got?"

"Two girls . . . one wife . . . four horses . . . three dogs."

"Three dogs? Sure that's all? If you've got any more I'll send the boys around with the gun to shoot 'em."

The men's hackles went up at that. They'd had their dogs for years, and Charles was a stockman and used his dogs for his work.

"What'd you come here for?"

"There's no work about."

"Been in trouble with the police?"

"**Never!**" I can still hear Dad snappin' it. Gladys and I looked at each other real strange. None of us had ever been in trouble, not like that feller meant.

"Right. You'll have to sign a paper to say that you'll stay here."

"What d'you mean, 'stay here'?"

"That you stay here and don't leave. You stay here till you die."

"I'll see 'ow we like it first, see if we want to stay. If we don't like it we'll move on."

"Well, you can and your wife, but the kids'll have to stay."

Then Dad said, "I'll come back later and sign that paper. We're too tired now. Gotta get these kids settled."

While they were talkin', I was listenin' and thinkin', "Gee, what a bad lookin' feller that man is." He was an old bony feller and he sounded mean, specially when he was talkin' to Charles Zooch, like he didn't want to have anything to do with him. Charles signed the paper, because in that school he'd been to he'd grown up with white man's rules that were fair.

Then the Manager was askin' Dad, "D'you know anyone here?"

"Yeah, George Wilson and Violet Wilson."

George (everyone called him Muddy) and Violet were part of our family. So they showed Dad where we could camp, down the back of the Mission near Aunty Violet. Dad set up our tent and made our camp like he always did. The

Manager would come again and again lookin' for Dad to
sign that paper. The minute the Manager left his place on
a horse the word went all round that he was on the move,
and the furthest house knew right away. I don't know how,
but it must have been some sort of signal. Sometimes Dad'd
crawl under Aunty Vi's house to dodge him. An old dog
of Dad's used to follow him about, and he'd be sniffin'
under the house and poor Dad was layin' in the dust tryin'
to shut the dog up. We were scared the Manager would
notice and wonder what the dog was up to. We'd tell the
man that Dad was off fishin' or gettin' wood or fixin' the
horses down the bend of the river or somewhere. He'd say
to Mum, "You tell him to come over and sign this paper.
It's getting late now. He's been here months."

Dad was pretty cunnin' too. He'd know when the Manager
had gone into Brewarrina town nine miles away, then he'd
go over to the Office and ask to see the Manager. The
Missus'd say, "He's not here. He's in town." Dad would
act surprised. "Tell him I come to sign that paper, Missus."
There was method in his madness.

So he never signed that paper which he knew committed
him to stay on the Mission. If he did he would have felt
obligated to stay. There's no way in the world he would
have snuck off after he signed it. He was that sort of a
bloke. Mum and Dad would have died there, sad old people.
Charles Zooch was only there on the Mission a few days
when he was sorry he'd signed. If he'd been a rogue blackfeller,
he would've gone, but signin' was like givin' his handshake,
and he knew he was done. There was no possible chance
of goin' away, there was nothin' to look forward to.

We soon got settled in. Aunty Vi said to Mum, "There's
real big rules 'ere, you know. You've got to get up early
every morning, get the kids off to school, have the washin'
hangin' on the line and the camp cleaned up by eleven o'clock,
'cos the Mission Manager's wife and the Clinic Sister come

round to see if it's all done. They come inside your camp and poke into everything. And if they say anythin's not right, you're in big trouble."

Mum knew nothing about Mission life, 'cos we'd always lived on stations, where life was free, no rules we had to abide by. Dad was the only feller who lived by rules but they were good rules to get the work on the station done fair and safe, rules of the job. The only rules us kids knew were the ones laid down for us by our parents and grandparents and teachers. They were very strict but fair – good rules for livin'. Mum didn't want no trouble, so when the first Monday morning came she said, "Right, you girls, you gotta go to the school." We were pretty brave, 'cos we thought we knew what schoolteachers were all about, so we went happily off.

We went to school, and we come home from school in the afternoon, and I was sick in the belly. I'd been sick all day, couldn't eat the tucker Mum had given us to take for our lunch – I was really sick. I didn't know what she'd say or what she would do. Mum was at the fire thickenin' a stew when she saw us.

She yelled out, "Jack, look at these kids !"

Dad was trimmin' the horse's hooves and sung out, "What's wrong with 'em?"

We were just standin' there. I was cryin', Gladys was cryin', and we couldn't say anything.

"What you got them rag 'ats on for?" Mum almost yelled at us and snatched them off our heads. Then, all quiet-like, and in a funny sort of voice, "Where's y'hair?"

"Here, Mum." We had our plaits in our hands, still tied with the ribbons Mum had put on in the morning. Gladys had two blue bows and mine were yellow. They'd chopped off our hair, almost bald, about half an inch long all over. Dad heard all the commotion and ran over with the cutters in his hand, "What's the matter?" Then he saw. And it was Dad who'd never let Mum cut our hair.

"What'd they do that to you for, Gladys? Why'd you let 'em, Ev?"

"I couldn't stop 'em, Dad." He could hardly hear me, 'cos I'd started cryin' again. "They said all the kids on the Mission have to have their hair like this. They reckon we're lousy."

Mum's standin' there, Gladys's plaits in one hand and mine in the other, cryin' and sayin' to Dad, "Jack, what did we come to this rotten bloody place for?"

"Yeah, I know, Annie. I thought it'd be better than this too. We'll take the kids away from here the first chance we get."

It was Dad fed us that night. He dished out the tucker, Mum was too upset. Layin' on the old wire bed, she was, with her back turned to everybody. Aunty Violet said, "Yeah, that's what they do to all the kids here, Annie. They think they got lice, no matter how good the parents are, and how clean we keep the kids. There's no kids here with lice, but they still do it. None of the people got lice because we gotta wash in sheep dip." We found out that was true, we all had to, and we only got a small lump of rock-hard soap about once a month. We had to use that disinfectant that makes the water go pink. Everything smelt like sheep dip, everybody smelt like sheep dip.

Every morning before school we had to go to the Clinic and get pink eyedrops put in our eyes, and it used to burn us. While we'd be cryin', they'd give us the biggest spoonful of codliver oil.

In the summer time we'd bath in the river, but when it was colder we bathed in tin tubs. The tub was set in a little place with a sort of shelter round it where you could take all your clothes off. To heat the water you had a big drum you could light a fire under. Some lazy kids used to put a little bit of fire under the drum, wait till the water got warm then jump in. That way they didn't have to cart the water from the drum over to the tub. They'd splash around in the drum, and if it got too hot, they'd hop out and pull a bit of fire from under it. Their Mum would be singin' out, "You kids not s'pposed to be bogeyin' in that big drum. The *wudjiin'll* come along and she'll be rousin'. Get in the tub."

We bogeyed in our drum too. The drums were out in the open in the back yards, and sometimes you'd see kids in the drums in their yards, all in a line! In the drum you couldn't go naked, you had to keep your drawers on. When Mum caught us, she roused, and I got the blame for teachin' Gladys to do it. I was supposed to be the instigator, so I got a few slaps for that. You know, I never noticed any sores or scabies or itches or anything like that on the Mission. I never even seen fleas, nobody had lice. The only sickness people had was colds, especially the old people. Everyone shared the wild meat with them so that stopped them from gettin' too sick.

Our first day at the school was bad and it didn't get much better. We never had proper teachers there. The Mission Manager was the teacher, so was the Mission bookkeeper, the Clinic Sister – anyone was good enough to teach ignorant black kids. I found out years later that Mission schools only had to teach us to the standard of white kids' Grade Three. That was supposed to be enough for us. It was worse for us kids from Yantabulla after our Miss Cook, and 'specially for me and Gladys after the Sisters in Bourke. It changed my opinion of teachers.

I didn't like the Manager when I first seen him and it was worse when he was the teacher.

I'd always liked showing that I could write nicely and read, but in his school you never seemed to get the opportunity to do it well. You were never **asked** to read. It was "**Get out here to me and read.**" It took the enjoyment out of the story, and you were so nervous from that abrupt voice, and bein' near him, that you'd stumble all the way

along. He'd growl, "Sit down and learn to read it properly",
but we could read it properly when we weren't shakin'!
We'd read all the Red and Green and Brown Readers to
Mum and Dad at home. The school work we were doin'
was only a little bit further on than what we'd done already.
History, yes, we learnt History, all about Captain Cook.
Who the hell wanted to learn about James Cook? He was
just another white man. I thought, "If this James Cook's
like the Manager, I don't want to know 'im anyway!"

That Manager seemed to shout at us most of the time,
and if you done anything wrong you got whipped across
the bum with a piece of rope. He had pieces of rope –
the heavy kind of rope we tied horses up with – coiled up
and hangin' one next to the door at the end of the schoolroom,
and one each end of the front verandah, one on the back
verandah, handy for him to grab if he wanted to hit one
of the kids. The rope near the doors was ready if one of
the boys tried to run out of the room. He'd grab the boy
with one hand and the rope with the other. He'd bend you
across the desk, lift your dress up if you were a girl and
whack you. The rope never hurt me as much as the embarrassment in front of all the boys and girls in the classroom.
That did hurt, deep down. And he wouldn't have cared that
we hated him, because we were nothin' to him, less than
nothin'. His dogs were treated much better than we were.
That manager wasn't there very long while we were there.
His wife was rather a nice old lady, and because of that
she wasn't allowed to come anywhere near the school. He
wanted to be the big tough feller, you know. We were
always wishin' he'd go and were excited when we heard
a new Manager was coming. He was much, much worse!

His wife was a tall old thin woman. Reminded me and
Gladys of them old brolgas that used to peck us at Yantabulla.
We felt if you touched her she'd peck you, vicious old thing.
She had glasses and wore a straw hat. Big lace-up boots
with green-top socks she had. And a big voice. Always yellin',

**"What're you kids doing over there?"** If she'd come along some mornin' and seen us kids sittin' in the drums of warm water with the little tiny fire underneath, I'm sure she would've had a fit. But they never seemed to be able to catch anyone doin' the wrong thing – there was too many eyes everywhere, ready to give each other warning.

The Manager had a great big old labrador dog. Well, this dog was so old and so fat he couldn't walk. The Manager would walk across from his house to the school – about a hundred and fifty yards, and this old dog would howl from the front verandah. His wife complained about the dog howlin', so every morning he'd allocate four kids to go and carry that big fat labrador on a big board over to the school. They'd wet a bag and put it on the school verandah for the dog to lie on. Those same four kids would carry him back at play time when the Manager went home for his cup of tea, hang around till he came back to school, carry the dog back. Then do it all over again at lunch time, and again at home time. But we loved that old dog. None of us minded pickin' him up, 'cos he'd wag his tail and we knew he couldn't walk. We'd pat him and talk to him while we were carryin' him. Some of the little kids'd give him a cuddle – when the man wasn't watchin', of course, or he'd growl, "Leave the dog alone."

That Manager smoked a pipe, even in the classroom. He'd take the pipe out of his mouth and point the stem at you, and we knew which one was in trouble. Gee, he was a big man, with short-cut hair, like the bristles of a pig, and a loud voice. You'd be forty or fifty yards away and he'd sing out in this big deep voice, "**EVELYN!**" and you'd stop dead in your tracks and start shiverin', thinkin' "What've I done now?" You'd turn around real quick and start walkin' back to him, walkin' as slow as you dared. He always carried a ridin' crop, never without it.

One day after school he called me back to him. He'd been interested in a telephone thing the boys had made.

They had two meat tins with a long piece of string they stretched out tight between the tins and they could talk to each other, just like a real telephone.

"What did you do with that telephone, Evelyn?" He sounded like he was roarin' at me. I don't know how I had any voice to answer him, but he used to say we were bein' cheeky if we didn't answer him as soon as he said anything to us.

"Didn't do anything with it – didn't even 'ave it in me 'and. It's the boys' toy, and they don't let girls touch it."

A couple of the other girls tried to make him understand, but he wouldn't listen to us. He just said, "We'll see about it in the morning." I worried sick all night.

The next morning we went to school and we got his crop across our bum – for making up stories, he said. One of the boys tried to explain that the girls didn't ever have it. "Aboriginal girls not allowed to play with Aboriginal boys' toys."

"Rubbish! Toys are toys. Everyone can play with them."

No one from the Aboriginal Protection Board didn't give one damn for our culture or laws or anything we valued.

When we went home and told, Dad got the elders on the Mission to go across to the Manager and explain what was happening. One of them was King Clyde, and the APB themselves recognised him as the chief elder. That brute of a feller hit the old man on the knee with the riding crop, and after that King Clyde always limped. Us kids felt really bad about gettin' the old feller into trouble, though we hadn't done anything. But once you got that whitefeller mad, what happened was when you lined up for meat and rations you got less and less. He'd say that us kids were playin' up in school. So we had to watch our P's and Q's, else we'd have starved to death, because families only got rations for school-age kids who went regularly and behaved themselves. We were worse off than if we'd stayed at Yantabulla, 'cos there we could go out and shoot a kangaroo or emu for meat.

Every Tuesday and Friday morning we'd line up at the butcher's shop in the front part of the Mission to get our supply of meat. I'd go because I was the biggest, with me little tin plate. The white overseer was there, and Aboriginal fellers would be cuttin' up the meat and servin' it to people.

"How many in your family?"

"Four," and I'd get four chops, a lump of fat or a kidney with the fat on it, a piece of liver and half a neck.

On Friday we'd get two shanks and a kidney, and that was it, all the meat for four people for a week.

On ration day, once a fortnight, we'd get eight potatoes, four onions, four pints (a pint is an enamel mug) of sugar, two pints of tea leaves, four pints of rice, eight pints of flour, bit of salt, bit of pepper, some syrup, half a bar of soap. Sometimes Mum would come and help us carry it but we could carry it on our own, me and Gladys, it was so little.

If anyone on the Mission played up – started to make trouble, didn't work, didn't clean up the house, didn't send the kids to school, cheeked the Manager, anything – **everyone** in the family got chopped down on their rations. Then everyone depended even more on their gardens and on what fish they could catch. Every part of the river bank that was allocated to the Mission was taken up with bums, 'cos everyone was fishin', especially the old people. Everyone had their own possie that was worn right down. The job for us kids was to get mussels and bait for the old people. That way we knew we'd get a fish now and then to take home to Mum. There wasn't one fat kid on that Mission, but no terrible bony ones either. The parents gave the kids all the food they could get, but they must have been hungry themselves sometimes, even though the Mission had its own bullocks and sheep to kill. Everyone was stringy, from the hard food and the hard work.

Water was pumped up from the river, and Jimmy Barker looked after the pump and the Mission machinery.

Nearly everyone on the Mission wore the same clothes. There was a Government issue for summer and one for winter. The men and young fellers got two summer shirts and two flannel shirts, one jacket and two pairs of trousers. Boys got two jackets and two pairs of short pants, two summer shirts and one flannel one. Women and girls got one flannel dress and two cotton ones, one summer and one winter petticoat, two pairs of unbleached calico drawers and two calico vests. They called them 'chemises'.

All the clothes were grey with a red line through the material and everything was stamped 'Brewarrina Aboriginal Mission'. They stamped them anywhere on the outside when they gave them to you – on the hem of a dress, on the sleeve, anywhere. We **hated** it. People used to try to unpick the red line so that everyone wasn't exactly the same, and so you didn't look too different from people off the Mission. 'Gubby clothes' we used to call 'em. '*Gubba*' is an Aboriginal word for 'white people', because most of the white fellers they came in contact with in the early days had something to do with the Government. Everyone was scared of the 'gubmen'. Blankets had 'AUSTRALIAN ABORIGINALS' printed in great big letters right down the middle. I suppose so you'd know what you were when you woke up!

When Aboriginal girls on the Mission were thirteen or fourteen they would be taken away from their families, no matter what their parents said, and made to live in a dormitory – for their 'protection' the APB said! On our way to the Clinic every morning, we had to pass the Dormitory, and we'd see the big girls there on their hands and knees with scrubbin' brushes. There were ten to fifteen of them just working for the Mission, cleanin' the Manager's house and the Clinic, cooking, washing and ironing, no wages. I think they might have accumulated a bit of money but they didn't have it, not in their own hands.

One Mission Manager had sons and daughters, and if the Aboriginal girls in the Dormitory didn't sleep with one of

the sons when he said to, the whole Mission suffered for
it. If the girl got pregnant to that white boy, the Manager
would send her to the Aboriginal Girls' Home at Cootamundra. It wouldn't have mattered to her parents if she
was carryin' a white baby, they still loved their daughter
and they'd have looked after her. But that Mission Manager
and his wife didn't want the people in the town to know
that they had sons who fathered the babies the Aboriginal
girls were carryin'. I guess that's how some of the creamy
ones came about on the Mission. Girls who were about twelve
or thirteen were very wary of this. If the Mission Manager's
son said, "You wait down there by that tree to-night and
I'll be there," and the girl wasn't there, then he'd tell some
cock-and-bull story to his father to get her into trouble and
everybody was chopped back on rations.

In every Aboriginal family, all your life your parents'd
say, "You be home here before dark." If you weren't home
in time you were in for a hidin' unless you had a very good
excuse. On the Mission it was no different. And it was
more strict for us girls than it was for the boys.

The Mission Manager's daughters had no way of gettin'
into town to meet white boys, so if they fancied a black
boy he'd have to go down the creek with them, otherwise
they'd tell some cock-and-bull story to their father about
him attackin' them, and he'd get punished – belted or starved
or sent to the Boys' Home at Kinchega.

There was hell to pay when one of the white girls fell
pregnant. She was kept in the house all the time, and when
the baby was born, it wasn't the Clinic Sister that was there
to tend her. It was an old Aboriginal woman, and when
the baby was born and the girl fixed up, the midwife left –
with the creamy baby. Then the Clinic Sister came. When
the doctor came out from the town to check on the girl
they said she'd had a miscarriage. He asked no more questions.
Maybe he thought it would make things worse for the Aboriginal people if he made a fuss. That doctor was real good

to the Aboriginal people. He used to give 'em a lot of attention in the hospital in town. The Aboriginal people were in a part separate from the white patients – still were in the 1980s.

That midwife happened to be the mother of the boy who'd fathered the baby, so she was very lucky, she had her own grandchild. He was always kept inside, and no one could say he was the Manager's grandson.

No drink was allowed on the Mission so drunkenness didn't cause any hassles but with the harsh Managers and strict rules a lot of aggression built up, especially with the different tribal groups. One family used to fight a lot, but they weren't punished because they lived right down the back of the Mission away from the Manager's house.

The Mission Manager came over one day and gathered up all the full-blood men. Us kids were listening, to see what the white man wanted all these real black blackfellers for. He told them there was goin' to be a re-enactment of the landing of Captain Cook, 150 years since he came, so it must've been at the start of 1938. He asked if anybody wanted to be part of it. They never answered him – just stood there. So he explained about how the Aboriginal people were on the shore when Captain Cook came in his boat, how he was the first white man Aborigines had seen. They still just stood there. He told 'em they'd travel on the train to Sydney, and I don't think anyone had an idea how far away Sydney was. The younger blokes – curiosity would've got the best of them – they wanted to go just to have a look at Sydney, or to ride in a train. Most of the men on the Mission would never've been on anything but a horse and buggy or an old truck.

Some of the old fellers were a little bit dubious about goin'. My mother's uncle, Grandfather Hero Black, went, and his son, Paddy, old Archie Boney, young Archie Boney, the two Barton fellers, Dickie Leonard, Alfie Shillingsworth – others too. I remember us kids standin' there watchin' them pack 'em all in the truck. Everybody cried because we didn't think we'd ever see 'em again, because whenever a black person was taken away from the Mission on a truck they never came back. These ones did come back but we'd cleared off before then so we didn't see Grandfather Hero Black again, but we heard afterwards they were told there'd be no tucker unless they did what they were told and acted like the white fellers said. On the way back, Grandfather Hero and Paddy snuck off at Bourke, headin' for Wilcannia where they'd come from.

No Aboriginal person on the Mission would go willingly **anywhere** where there was a white person, they were so scared of them. The Mission Station part, where the Manager's house was, was off-limits, but no one ever had to tell us kids not to go near there. We just went to school and straight home again – couldn't get away quick enough. Us kids used to play games in the afternoons before sundown. The mums and dads played games too, with us or by themselves, a game like softball, we called it rounders. Sometimes they'd have claypan dances at night, but they needed the permission of the Manager.

There'd be a big fire, and the fellers would get a kangaroo or emu, so there'd be lots of rissoles. Can you imagine the job of mincin' the meat off a whole big emu or kangaroo with a hand mincer? Three or four women would start, then they'd call out, "Come on, you kids, turn the handle for a little while, Aunty's tired." So you'd be there, turnin' away with both hands. When they put the onions in, tears'd be runnin' down your cheeks.

Every kid did something. Some would be out on the claypan, pickin' up stones and bits of stick, some would be waterin' it – others helpin' to put up stools where the people could sit around. That way we was all involved. We were part of it all and enjoyed it, even the work gettin' ready.

For music they had an accordion and a mouth organ. One feller had an old violin with only two strings but he could play a lot of tunes on it. The gum leaf was a favourite instrument, all the boys played gum leaves. Girls weren't supposed to, makin' music was a man's thing. That's why I didn't play the accordion, at least not openly, till I grew up. When I'd have a go at home at night, the next day someone would say to Dad, "Who was playin' the accordion in your tent last night, Mullya?"

"Ah-h, the girls' mother was havin' a go."

They danced waltzes and barn dances, quicksteps – you should've seen the dust rise when the dancin' got goin'. Sometimes there were birthday parties, but just for the old people. We never knew about birthday parties for kids. I used to think, "When I get old, I'll have a birthday party." We didn't really understand what 'birthday' was. I think those parties were really a way to show the older people how they were appreciated, to show love for them. There were a lot of old people at the Mission who didn't have any of their own family there, so the grown-ups gave them a party.

Things were a little bit better when a new manager came. He said every family on the Mission had to make a garden to grow their own vegies and fruit. Some of the biggest turnips I've ever seen were grown on that Mission – those white turnips with purple tops. What so-and-so didn't grow, someone else did, so there was a lot of swopping – onions for cabbages, tomatoes for cucumbers, strawberries for almost anything. Not many had eggs, but you could swop vegies and fruit for eggs. Everybody had carrots. The Manager gave out piles of carrot seeds. He was a great believer in carrots. I suppose he wanted all bright-eyed people!

Then everybody had to grow orange trees, lemon trees and mandarin trees. There were some stone fruit trees too, peaches, apricots and plums, but citrus was the main kind.

The Manager's wife inspected the back yards where people had to grow vegies.

Old Granny Barnes had a lovely garden. She was growin'

74

strawberries and was so proud of them. She used to tell everybody she was goin' to make strawberry jam. She'd made all other kinds but she'd never had any strawberries. One day the Manager's wife inspected Granny Barnes's garden and saw this one big red strawberry, the very first ripe one. We'd all watched it, and Granny was so proud of it. We all were. That woman just stooped down and picked it, washed it under the tap and ate it, and said, "Mm-mm, very nice."

The old lady could've cried. We all could've.

We had Sunday School under a canegrass shed. The Sunday School teacher was a little old English feller with a goatee beard who came from Bourke. All the kids had to go to Sunday School, but Mum and Dad would've sent us anyway. Every now and then ministers came, and the priest came. They all said, "We're having Church," and everybody went, grown-ups and all. I suppose it was something to do.


We were just getting used to the Mission when they brought the people from Tibooburra. Then we seen another lot of Aboriginal people treated differently again. See, we'd come in a buggy ourselves, voluntarily, because we thought we wanted to be there, but these were just rounded up and brought there in three old red trucks one day, and the next day there were two more truck loads.

The APB fellers were cunning. They knew that most people, Aboriginal people too, like to be with their families at Christmas, and that most of the men who worked on Naryilco and other stations round would bring their wives and kids to Tibooburra then and people from other towns would be visiting. So that's when they grabbed 'em. Only one family escaped the round-up net. Sneider Brown was a boss drover and had his wife and kids with him, camped along the Cooper. So what's left of their family are the only *Wankamurrahs* at Tibooburra.

At the Mission no one knew anything was happening until

the Manager said, "You kids go and get a bale of straw each and bring it over to the school. Take all the desks and chairs out, stack them in the shed. Then cut the wire on the straw and spread it all over the school. Make it thick round the walls for people to sleep on." When we went home I said to Mum, "They're bringin' more black people 'ere tomorrow – from Tibooburra. We 'ad to put out all the straw. They got to sleep on it." When Dad came in he said, "Tibooburra's more than a couple o'hundred miles away. They must have been travellin' a long time. They're *Wankamurrah* people."

Next morning, about half-past-seven, we could hear trucks comin' across the plain, sounding like chaff cutters. And as they got closer towards the Mission boundary we could hear people cryin', cryin' really loud like Aboriginal people goin' to a funeral. I wondered what they were cryin' for. We went to look and all the other people were comin' out of their houses over to the fence where we were standin'. This cryin' made you come. It just went right through you, and pulled you.

There were three trucks, with three white fellers in the front of each truck and the back packed, jam-packed with black people, all cryin'. The Manager went round the back of the truck and shouted at 'em to shut up, he couldn't hear. Didn't even ask what was the matter, just yelled, "**Shut up!**" They slowed down to a little whimper. We could tell they were scared of him. Then he started takin' names of families, kids' ages, and things like that. They were left sittin' in the trucks for a long time. When those people had last had a feed I don't know. We were about fifty yards away and we could see the kids jump down and the young fellers, then they helped the old people get down. A few of the old women had dilly bags, but not one of the lot would've had a full swag.

The Manager called all the white fellers together and they herded them *Wankamurrahs* over to the school. I could hear some of our older people sayin', "They won't be able to fit in there... there's too many of 'em... place's not big enough." But they all went in, and the Manager banged the door, bang, click, clock, and locked it. Then he took all the white fellers over to his place, probably for a feed. A couple of hours after, he sent word that our people were to collect food from the stores and carry it over to the school. When the school door was opened the white fellers were hoverin' all round a long way back, watchin' to see if anyone would try to run away.

Those Tibooburra people were crowded in the doorway, and all we could see was the whites of their eyes. The only person inside who spoke was Walter Whyman. Now, him and his son, young Jim, had been in Tibooburra, at the time when they collected 'em, campin' out there, speckin' for gold. They roped them in too, even though they had nothin' to do with the Tibooburra people. The Whymans are *Baarkanji* from Wilcannia, but to the white man he was just another blackfeller.

Dad carried over a big basket of bread, yeast bread that they'd got in from the town, and a big voice from inside sung out, "Hey, g'day, Mallyer. What're you doin' over 'ere?" When the Manager found out that Walter Whyman and Dad knew each other, he started sayin', "Get Mallyer to tell 'em to do this... to do that."

They sat in the school all day, those people. Us kids were watchin', and we'd see a kid come out every now and then and get a pint of water and take it inside. People'd go to the toilet and straight back in again, didn't look at nobody. That night Mum saw some kids had come outside and she said to me, "Why don't you go and talk to those kids?" So me and my sister, and a couple of cousins, Aunty Violet's kids, went over to some girls our age, but they wouldn't talk to us. We tried for a while and then come home.

Next day, two more truck loads came, and there were more kids. So we thought, "Well, we'll talk to this lot," but the same thing happened. Our mothers started cookin' whatever they could to take over to the people, 'cos they didn't see 'em outside at the fires cookin'. We knew they must've been hungry. The Manager told the men to take some meat over to them, and we were beginnin' to think they were eatin' it raw because we never seen them out at the fireplaces. We found out they were cookin' at night when there was no one around, they were that scared.

By the time they were in the schoolhouse for about three weeks the straw must've been gettin' a little bit smelly. They started takin' bundles of it out every morning, spreadin' it out where the sun could get at it, and takin' it in at night to sleep on. There was straw blowin' everywhere. The schoolhouse must've been pretty full with those five truck-loads. There must've been well over sixty people, because the APB built houses for twenty families. All the time before the houses were built they stayed packed into the school, and we didn't have any school lessons.

Some of the old people died before the houses were built. I'm sure the conditions they were living under must have had a lot to do with it. There was diarrhoea and sore eyes, but they kept it hidden, never showed themselves. They were people who'd lived a long way from anyone. The kids used to come out and play in the late afternoon, but if anyone came around they all went back inside. So our mums and dads put restrictions on us, "Don't go anywhere near that place so them people can come outside." For the first nine days, not one kid out of all those *Wankamurrah* people would talk to us, even though all us kids tried every way we knew to make friends with them.

Dad said, "Well, they mightn't be able to understand. Try their own language." But those full bloods could speak English, and much better than we could! Their grammar was beautiful! They pronounced the H's and ING's and every-thing. I think it was because a lot of them went to school on Naryilco Station and they got good teachers from Adelaide.

The first one that spoke to us was a girl, Rita Hartnett. She was a bit younger than me, and the same colour as me. She come out the school door and called, "Where's your mother?"

I called back, "Home."

"You tell your mother to come. My mother got a little baby and it's **real** sick . . . won't drink no titty . . . just cries ye-ee-ee all the time."

So we ran right down to our camp and got Mum. The woman brought the baby out, and Mum said, "I'll take the baby to the Treatment Room to the Sister." It was about eight weeks old, only a little skinny baby and there was nothing they could do for it. It was too dehydrated and it died. The poor mother wasn't well herself. Her baby had been born out in the scrub, and she wasn't attended properly, so it was only about four days after they buried the baby that the woman herself died, a young woman still in her twenties, I think. Four more of that family died within a couple of months.

About six weeks after that big mob came the new houses were ready, and the Manager moved everyone out of the school. He had a big fence with barbed wire put all round those houses in case the Tibooburra people run away. Funny thing, they all wanted to get into the houses that were the furthest away from anybody, right up at the end of the rows. As time went on many of the *Wankamurrah* people managed to sneak off the Mission and headed back to Tibooburra, but they didn't make it all the way back. Lots of them didn't get further than Bourke – now there's more *Wankamurrah* people in Bourke than in Tibooburra.

Right from the day they cut our hair Mum hated the place. She never settled down at all. She was always the last one to go to bed, she'd be just sittin' at the fire-bucket, lookin' down the river – just sittin' there, thinkin'. She must've been lonely, too. At first the Zooch family had camped near us, but then they were given a house, because Charles had signed those papers, and we didn't see much of them after that. There were a lot of houses between where we were and their house and we didn't like goin' past strange people's places to get there. And their kids didn't come down to play with us for the same reason. It was even worse for Mum, Nellie being her closest friend.

I'd often hear her sayin' to Dad, "Jack, why did we ever come to this awful place? I can't stand it 'ere."

"I know, Annie. There's a lot of people here don't like it, but what can they do? They can't get away."

"We can. You never signed that paper and we've got the buggy and horses."

I don't know what finally decided them. When we were young, kids really were seen and not heard. There were a lot of things grown-ups never discussed with us. The old people would sit and yarn among themselves, and if you came anywhere within hearin' distance, you'd be told to go, and if you didn't you'd get a crack with a stick or anything handy. None of us were brave enough for that so we stayed away. Now when I think about it, I realize that I was gettin' older, and you never knew when the Manager would send a girl to live in the Girl's Dormitory, whether her parents wanted it or not. Any girls, especially the fair-skinned ones, could be sent away to Cootamundra to be trained as house-maids, or for work on stations. Their parents had no say in it, and wouldn't even know where they were. That could have influenced Mum and Dad too.

In the end my father said he'd had enough. It was in the summer after Christmas and school had started again. He just said to Mum, "We'll go."

Word got around that Mallyer was going. Every grown-up Aboriginal on the Mission knew, but of course us kids knew nothing about it. The white fellers never heard a word. We didn't trust **any** white person.

Then people who wanted to save their creamy kids came and said to my father, "Mullya, will you take our kids out with you?" Dad said he'd take as many as he could.

The fathers got together and built this big frame thing, a bit like a false floor, that they could put in the back of the buggy, so that the kids could get in under it, and Mum and Dad could pile all their stuff on top. They were even afraid the white fellers would come and wonder what it was for. It would be nothing to them to pull your buggy to pieces and just chuck everything on the ground, even if things got smashed.

It was kept quiet – from the kids, that is – right up to the night we were leavin'. We heard about the planning a long time after.

We come home from school that afternoon and went for a swim 'cos it was very hot. When we got back we noticed all our toys and things were picked up. We just thought Mum had been tidying up, and wondered if she'd go mad at us for leavin' them in a mess. Then we spotted Dad greasin' some harness, and greasin' the buggy wheels, and we knew what that meant. So, being the inquisitive one, I asked Aunty Violet, "Where's Dad goin' with the buggy? Is he goin' for wood?"

She said, "No, but I can't tell you what's to do. They'll tell you themselves. But whatever you do, don't go away from the camp. Don't you leave here – Gladys too."

There were kids playin' round that I'd never seen at our place before and I wondered what they were doin' here with their parents. It wasn't till about eleven o'clock that night that we knew what it was all about. We were leavin', Mum and Dad, me and Gladys, and takin' these other kids with us. Our family was going back to Yantabulla through Enngonia where some of the other kids were to be collected by relatives. Enngonia is about ninety miles in a straight line from Brewarrina, so they thought that was far enough away for us all to be safe. Of course we couldn't travel in anything like a straight line.

Mum had all our clothes and stuff packed up ready. The other kids and mums and dads were cryin' because they had to leave each other. There were eleven kids altogether, me and Gladys and nine others. Gladys was real dark and so were two of the others, so Mum sat them up on top of the load in full view. No white person wanted **black** kids. The other two kids on top were a bit older too, and understood better that Dad really meant "**No noise.**" They had to listen all the time that no one was following.

The rest of us were all pretty light-skinned, some fairer than me. They packed us away lyin' down under the frame. It was pretty cramped but we were only there that one night. There was a bit of "Move over, you got all the space..." just like kids in the same bed.

Dad waited till the moon was up and past its top so we could travel in the long shadow with the trees between us and the Mission Station. They couldn't use any lamps on the buggy so it must have been scary for Mum who was driving while Dad rode ahead to cut the fence wires, because he thought it would be safer going across country instead of by the road where the white fellers could pick up the buggy tracks. We had four dogs that were used to just walkin' quietly along under the buggy. Mum wouldn't go anywhere without her little bantams slung in their coop, but by the next morning when the chooks were crowin', we were well away from the Mission. We had to go along the creek, over grass so we wouldn't leave a track. The grass would have sprung up again before the white fellers thought of lookin' off the road.

Mum was driving along the creek bank and went over a stump in the dark, and all of us kids tried not to squeal. We'd been warned over and over to stay still and not make a sound. I though we were all going to be tipped out. Dad was singin' out in a funny sort of whisper, "Annie, look where you're bloody well goin'. You'll tip all the kids out and kill the lot!"

Early in the morning – it was still dark – Mum and Dad pulled up at the Cato Bridge and got all us kids out. We had a feed and they gave us each a little bundle of something to eat and some water because we had to split up. We were to be just each one by ourself, one kid to a tree, one kid to a stump. That way there'd be no crowdin' and pushin', and makin' a noise.

The smallest kid was Brucie, a real little almost-white feller, a five-year old. His mother was an Aboriginal girl out on a property, where she was livin' with her aunty and uncle. The uncle was a stockman and the aunty did the homestead laundry. The girl must have been sleepin' with the station owner's son, and got pregnant. Then her uncle died and the owner's missus said the aunty'd have to go.

"Go to the Mission, and take that pregnant one with you."

They'd never have admitted their son was responsible, no matter what the evidence, and nobody dared say anything. When that baby was born, it was a little white baby, and only the Aboriginal people knew he'd even been born. He was given an Aboriginal name, *Kuthloo*, but later on they called him Brucie. For five years Brucie was hidden away, from one house to another, when the Manager's wife and the Clinic Sister did their rounds. They always kept to a fixed time so it wasn't too hard, and those women wouldn't have been seen dead near the **blacks'** part, except it was their work! Brucie was only let out to play in the evenings among all us kids, so he was a fat, soft little feller. The big ones took turns looking after him. Iris Eulo from out at Engonnia took him first. The next one older than Brucie would have been about eight, so he had to take his chance by himself with his own little bundle of damper and meat and find a tree he could hide behind, or a log he could crawl under.

Dad had marked out a mud map for us before we left, showin' us the lie of the land between Brewarrina and Enngonia, a river here and a creek there. We had to go from the Cato Creek towards the Bokhara, across the back of Mitchell Vale Station.

Dad told us to follow the creek a bit and hide till dark. The plan was that we were to travel only in the dark and hide during the day, each of us under our own bush. That turned out to be the hardest time – the daytime – because it was such very hot weather. Gladys and two other kids, much, much darker than her, stayed with Mum and Dad. I suppose you could say they were the decoys.

I felt terrible. Mum was sayin', "Hurry up and go now, Ev, quick, because it's gettin' daylight," I thought to meself, "Will I ever see Mum and Dad and Gladys again?" 'cos that would have been the first time in my whole life that the family had been split up. The eight of us kids separated and cleared off down the Cato Creek towards Quantambone Station.

My old ginger sheep dog used to follow me everywhere, so they had to tie him up, and the last thing I could hear from right down the creek was this old dog still playin' up, barkin' and pullin' on the chain. A couple of times I was sure I heard him get hit to try and shut him up. Dad had wanted to leave him behind at the Mission but I'd kept sayin', "He'll be alright." Dad knew how much he'd miss one of his own dogs so he let him come. I'm sure he wished he hadn't because he told me afterwards that he caused a lot of hassles lookin' for me. They had to hide all me clothes and anything I'd touched so he lost the scent of me altogether. Then he gave up on me and became Gladys's friend.

When I got away from hearin' the dog, it was gettin' daylight, and I couldn't see any of the other kids. I didn't know if they were in front of me or behind me or where. Course, in our grey Mission clothes it was easy to blend in with the trees. If they'd thought of that I suppose they would have dressed us in red!

What we had to do then was walk along and listen for noises, or listen to the birds. If there's anyone about that wasn't supposed to be there, birds let you know, singin' out and soundin' excited.

Dad had told us, "When you get to Quantambone Station,

stay on the far side of the homestead, or the dogs'll start barkin'. It'll only need the boss to come down and see a heap of kids to know you're from the Mission."

When it got real daylight I thought, "The first big bush I come to, that's where I'll camp." All that day I didn't see any of the other kids. That didn't bother me during the day but when it got sundown I was worried bein' by meself. I wanted to get up on a bit of a rise so I could look out across the Cato Plain, because Dad had said that each night they'd make a big campfire just to let us know where they were. We were not to come near them. He carried wood in the buggy 'cos there's no trees on that Cato Plain. Talk about the Nullarbor – the Cato's just the same, flat and bare, with just patches of saltbush. You can burn saltbush, but it doesn't last for a fire.

When it was real dark I climbed up in a big bush lookin' for Dad's fire. I was still pretty close to the station and there were trees and fruit trees round the homestead blockin' the view, so I had to find a bigger tree. It must've taken me an hour to find one and get up it, and all I could see was a little fire way off. It could have been a drover's fire, but I was satisfied it was Mum and Dad.

Dad told us afterwards that they'd only gone a little distance in the buggy that day. In the afternoon there were heaps of white fellers riding round looking for us. They'd missed us kids from the school, 'cos, remember, the Mission Manager was the teacher. He used to stand at the door and count us as we went in, so of course he'd miss eleven kids. The other kids said we were sick. But if we were too sick to go to school we had to go to the treatment room, and the nurse said none of us had been there. That's when they all started rushin' round. The call went out to see if anyone was travellin', and they got onto the search real quick. Every time the APB fellers went lookin' for people they always took a policeman with them, and the one they picked always seemed to be a brute of a person, almost a sadist, a feller with no feelings.

That first afternoon at the Cato Mum and Dad spotted them out on horseback way across the Plain, looking for us. They could see the sun flashin' off the policeman's leggings. Stockmen wore leggings too, but the policeman's were part of his uniform so he kept them real shiny. The sun would shine on 'em, and you could see them through the trees or anywhere. Late in the afternoon APB people had pulled Dad up and questioned him. He told 'em something was wrong with the buggy and he had to fix it. Lucky it was no one who knew him well from the Mission, and to most white fellers one blackfeller was the same as another, and they thought the three real dark kids were all his.

All that second day while I camped up, I didn't see anyone. It was only the second night when I started travellin' again that I heard a kid cryin'. I listened, then I thought, "Nah, that's a native bear." You know how koalas sound like a baby cryin'. But I walked along and followed the noise, and there was Iris with little Brucie. We were real glad to see each other, and I said, "Where's the other kids?"

"I dunno. We been camped 'ere all day and I never seen nobody, just us two. And it's John's turn to take Brucie."

John, the biggest boy, was about thirteen. What had happened was that he'd stumbled onto two of the eight-year-old kids just walkin' along lost. One was cryin' so he took 'em under his wing. That slowed him down, but he knew he had to take Brucie from Iris and he was lookin' for her. Every second night was his turn to walk with the little feller, or soon, mostly carry 'im. By the third day we were supposed to be between Mitchell Vale and a station called Coolah. That day we met up with the other two kids about my size, so we were all together.

We had to sit quiet all the blazin' hot day in the lignum scrub above the creek. To get a drink we had to stand on hard-baked ground or lie on a log not to leave a footmark.

I sat there under my bush wonderin' if I'd ever play in a river again, or if I'd ever be singin' and laughin' with my parents and sister again.

We were very, very hungry. We'd all run out of the tucker Mum had given us, so we had to manage on the bits of bush tucker any of us could find. We'd give the best bits to the little kids. We never thought that maybe we should have eaten more of the berries and tucker so we'd have the strength to carry the little kids. We just knew their bellies were empty and forgot that we were hungry ourselves.

Burrs were startin' to worry me, my feet were so sore. All day while I was hidin' I'd try to pick them out, but I only made things worse. We were on a white clay and sand area – the kind of country the most terrible burrs love. Galvanised burrs grow on a grey bush, very sharp with orange points, very painful. They'll give you blood poisoning very smartly. There's another one called the cat-head, very bad burr, **very bad**. It could blood poison you in about twenty-four hours.

John said, " 'ow're we gonna git through there?"

We had nothing we could put on our feet, except the bit of clothes we had on our backs, and we needed them for the daytime 'cos the sun was burnin' hot. We couldn't strip bark, because the white fellers'd notice freshly-barked trees. The only thing we could do then was to climb into the middle of the hop-bush and pick the leaves. Hop leaves are long but narrow, so you can imagine how many we had to pick and tie together with grass to put on our feet to walk through – must have been fifteen – miles of burrs. We could only walk three or four miles before we'd have to pick and tie more leaves. But in a way it was a good thing, because we never left no tracks. Then one of the boys found a dead fox that'd been there for ages so we emptied out the old bones, cut the skin up and tied that on Brucie's feet. He had very stinkin' feet from that filthy skin, but he didn't have burrs in 'em and that was the main thing.

That night when it got dark we could still hear men singin'
out and whistlin' to dogs, so we waited till we thought
people were asleep or settled down. We'd just got going
when one of the bigger kids said, "I c'n smell fresh meat.
Someone must've been killin'." So we hid in the scrub,
'n John and Iris went to check. They saw two Aboriginal
fellers killin' a sheep down at the cowyard. In summer you
don't kill till dark when the flies go. They musta got a
bad shock when two black kids came out of the dark. They
came back with John and Iris and found there was a pack
of us.

"What're you kids doin' here?"

"Goin' to Enngonia."

"Who you travellin' with? Where's your parents?"

"We gittin' away from the Bre Mission ... Her mum and
dad are on the road over there ... My Dad said not to go
near the road."

They looked at each other real worried-like then, they
were afraid of being implicated too. We didn't know them
but it turned out that they had been kids on the Mission
too, and been sent to Coolah as stockmen when they were
old enough, without havin' no say in it themselves, or their
parents. So they had another good reason to help us, besides
the best reason – us all bein' Aboriginals.

One feller said, "What you been eatin'?"

"Mum gave us some tucker, but it's all gone. We got
nothin' – we're **hungry**."

"You kids stay here quiet, and we'll go and cook some
meat. We'll bring it back to you."

They were livin' in a hut and cookin' for themselves so
they went back and cooked the liver and the heart, all the
parts white people didn't use, and we waited there for what
seemed hours. The night was gettin' on and we knew we
had a long way still to go, but we were that hungry we
waited. Then they brought the cooked meat and damper
down to us.

"Now, you kids, sit down and eat real careful. Don't you don't leave any specks for the ants to find. If they're trackin' you, the white fellers'll want to know what the ants is eatin'. If they see ants with a load they'll pick 'em up to see what they're carryin'. If it's a bit of cooked meat or fat they'll know somethin's wrong, and we'll all be in trouble."

They stayed there with us in the dark while we had a feed. I was sittin' on the ground with my dress spread out to catch any bits, then I felt all over the skirt to find them. When we couldn't eat any more we packed up what we had left to take with us. It was gettin' real late, so they said, "You kids go on, we'll clean up the ground." They probably raked it all over with bushes. I don't ever remember seein' those two fellers again in my life, but they certainly were good to us.

From there we walked all of what was left of that night. It didn't seem long before it was daylight and we had to sit down again, and we had no water this time. I felt real sorry for the littler kids. Soon as we got to a place where we could stop they'd just lie down and go straight to sleep. I used to shake 'em sometimes to see if they were still alive. That would wake them up and break their sleep and they'd start crying. That was dangerous for us all, so I left 'em alone and just worried to meself.

We missed seein' Dad's fire that night because we were walkin' in a hollow. We couldn't get anywhere high in case someone saw us, and we couldn't walk on the creek bank because of burrs again. So we walked along on the creek beds, and the last kid comin' along was always draggin' a bush, and we took turns at that too. Dad had said, "Walk on grass or hard ground as much as you can," but we couldn't, 'cos by this time our feet were that sore.

Well, we got off Coolah, with enough meat to keep us goin', and half a damper, and we only ate when we thought we were **really** hungry. The bread got rock hard, and the meat a bit smelly. We didn't give it to the little kids, 'cos we knew they easily got bellyache, so we just gave them the dry bread. We found some berries along the gullies, but we filled ourselves up mainly on water.

Then we had to leave the creek and there was a big stretch of very dry plain between the Birrie and the Culgoa. We hid during the day under *moogeealla* bushes, or got up in 'em. One kid to a bush you wouldn't see. You could even ride past close and you wouldn't know he was there.

The bigger kids were sayin' to us, "You gotta hurry up. We don't know 'ow wide this plain is... 'urry up, it'll be daylight 'fore we git to the next creek... 'urry up, we'll 'ave no place to 'ide." The *moogeealla* bushes were thinning out as we got further towards the sandhill country.

Just on daylight we saw the line of trees, and that was the Culgoa River. We hid there, some in bushes, some up in big trees. Everyone was tired, wantin' to sleep. We had a big drink of water, did what we had to do, and settled down to sleep. We waited there all that day until a long time after dark, but the big ones still didn't start. We kept askin', "Why can't we move?... We need to get goin'... What you waitin' for?"

They didn't tell us, but John had gone prowling and he'd heard fellers ahead. They must've been workin' on the road – the road from Bourke to Weilmoringle follows the Culgoa – and he could hear motor cars too. So we stayed there that night as well, and that night was good. We could walk about at our own leisure and sleep, relax a bit. The only thing was the mosquitoes were so bad and by this time most of us had bad lumps all over us – hands and eyes and the tummies of the little ones 'cos they were wearin' only little short shirts. I wore that one dress and pair of pants all the time we walked. We didn't carry a change of clothes, just what we had on. We all had scratches and sores that started to get infected.

We hid at the Culgoa all the next day and when it got

dark we crossed the river. It wasn't too big for us to swim across – John had Brucie on his back. We crossed the road without leavin' any tracks because it's all dry claypan country there, and were goin' towards what we thought was a big hill. As we got closer we could feel the sand gettin' softer so we had to backtrack and walk right round, followin' the hard ground all the time. John went up to have a look. Actually it was a ground tank on the side of the sandhill, which made it look bigger. We had a couple of Camp Pie tins that John used goin' backwards and forwards to bring us all a drink. We spent the rest of that night near the tank, because John and Iris said we'd have to see in daylight which way we should be travellin'.

Across the plain on the other side of that tank, hop bush and brunda bush country started and the real thick mulga scrub that's growing all round Enngonia. When it got dark we headed into it and felt safe 'cos after that we could walk in the daytime. It was so thick you could walk for miles and nobody'd know you were there unless you stood on a stick and they heard the crack. We walked a bit that night then John said, " 'old up, we're goin' the wrong way." We were crossing the dry plain and there was no creek to guide us. It seems we were goin' towards Bourke, south-west instead of north-west, so he turned us back. We knew something was wrong because we couldn't see any sign of Dad's fire. You know, if the white fellers had a think about it, they should have wondered why those blackfellers made such a big fire in summertime instead of just a little cooking fire.

Mum used to play her old accordion real loud too in case we could hear her. When we did hear it, I felt like cryin' and sometimes I did. That was my mum and dad out there and I couldn't get to them. I suppose the other kids wanted to cry because it **wasn't** their mum and dad. All next day we had no water. The little bit we had was for the smallest kids, and I tell you, I was thirsty. I was chewing anything that was green to stop me from dryin' up altogether.

Next night we saw the fire! We thought it was a long way off, but actually it wasn't far – just a small fire. John said, "I'll go and see who it is." Off he went and we waited, hittin' mosquitoes and tryin' to keep the little ones quiet. Then the rest of us started, "'e's a long time gone... we shoulda gone with 'im... John's got lost, 'e's not comin' back...." Morbid mob we was by then!

John had got close to the camp. He lay down and he waited and he waited till the fire burned down real low. Then he whistled to the dogs. Dad heard him and saw the dogs wagging their tails, and knew it must be us. He walked towards the bushes and there was John huddled down behind a tree.

"Where's all the kids? How come you're this late? You should've been here ages ago. We've been camped here two days now."

"We had to stay by water two days, Uncle Jack – and the daylight caught us and we couldn't move. Eileen keeps cryin' all the time she wants Aunty Annie."

"Where's Eileen now?"

"She's back with the others, and no one can make 'er be quiet. Most of the kids is sick, got bites and sore eyes."

So Dad come back with John, got Eileen, put her on his back and took her to their camp. I wished it was me he was carryin' back. Then he came back again with food and medicines for the rest of us.

When Dad and Mum got movin' again, Eileen had to be hidden under the gear in the buggy. She was that fair it would have endangered us all. By that time everyone would have known that the APB were looking for kids. I for one was glad she wasn't with us because she'd been crying that much, saying, "I'm frightened" that she sort of scared us all and none of us could settle down. She was only a little kid, small and bony even though she was about eight. Dad told us to stay hidden there the next day, and told John we were to move as soon as the sun got behind the trees. That way we could stay in their shadow, then travel all night.

While we were waiting Brucie cut his foot. Mum gave us Vicks and some rags and some Aspros for him, and we took him with us. They knew they could make Eileen keep quiet if white fellers stopped them, but they couldn't trust Brucie, he was too young. That night we got into the real sandhill country. Walkin' along we'd run into wild bullocks layin' down. We'd frighten them and they'd jump up and frighten **us**.

The very next morning Brucie started to get bad sick. The cut on his foot must have got infected. From then on, every little bit of water we come to, we'd wash his foot and put him in the water and splash him all over, he was that hot. That was all we could do for him. His little lips were all cracked. Then he started vomitin' everything we'd give him, and he'd go to sleep and yell out and scream and cry in his sleep. We didn't know what we could do for him. Of course I know now he was delirious with blood poisoning in his foot.

The other small kids were sick too. We'd give 'em a bit of the tucker Mum had given us, and they'd bring it straight up again. The hardest part for us was that we could do nothing for them, except give 'em a cuddle or a nurse, and then carry whatever little kid had just been sick. We drug brunda bushes behind ourselves and never walked in a bunch. John kept remindin' us not to.

You know, without that feller John none of us would have survived, we relied on him so much. I don't know what his other name was, we just met him that last night at the Mission. I've only seen him once since, at Thargominda. He was married with a family then. He knew me when he seen me too, you know. He came and cuddled me and cried. I said, "I'm the one should be cryin' to see you. Only for you we'd have been dead."

As we got closer to Enngonia, we had to cross the gravel Bourke to Cunnamulla road and not leave tracks each side or across it. John said, "One at a time now, and cover your tracks." So one kid went across, and another kid, till the last small one was over. Then he said, "I'll go across now. Evelyn, you rub out my track." So I was feelin' in the dark for his track, which was deep in the sand with Brucie's weight as well, and smoothin' out his track and my own.

We walked for two more nights before we got anywhere near where we could hear dogs and fowls and kids. We knew then we must be near some camps, so we stayed all day at the side of a dry creek. By that time we'd been a whole day and a night with no water. All we had was a bit of damper that the little kids were eatin', but then John said not to give it to them because it made them more thirsty. We looked for fruit on the trees. Quondongs weren't ripe, *mooley* apples weren't ripe, nearly everything we picked just wasn't ripe, but we kept hopin'.

That night we went on walkin' again. We thought we must find Dad soon. We could hear dogs barkin', and someone said, "That's them."

"Nah, that's station dogs. There's too many, and that's a white feller whistlin' them. We not goin' near no station."

We really needed water so we listened for windmills. Now all the windmills in the bush squeak, so we listened for that squeak. When we did hear it a rabbiter was camped right there, an old white feller who made a livin' from skins and pickin' up dead wool. Years after we found out he was a friendly old feller, but to us he was just a **white man**. So we didn't go near the windmill. We listened to hear where the water was runnin' in the trough, and went to the end of the trough, way down in the back of the paddock. We seemed to get nowhere that night, first circlin' round the station, then goin' to get water, then thinkin' we heard noises so we went back to hide in the thick scrub, then daylight came on us, and that was another day we had to stay without water.

If we climbed up a bushy tree we could see into the old feller's camp. We were safe because there was no way in the world he'd be lookin' up trees for kids. He was too busy lookin' on the ground for dead sheep. There we were, and there he was with his big fire goin', havin' a wash early in the morning, throwin' the water out. We could smell his tucker, and when he fed his dogs they were all eatin' up and we were perched up in these big *mooley* apple trees starvin'.

As soon as it began to get dark John said, "You girls wait 'ere and mind the little fellers, and I'll look for Uncle Jack."

Joanie said, "No, we'll walk 'em along slow."

Away he went, stridin' it out, while we hobbled along with the kids, takin' turns to carry Brucie who was very, very sick by then. When we come to a big old gum tree that had fallen down we said, "We'll wait 'ere for John." A big worry then was snakes in the fallen logs. Then we heard a low coo-ee-ing. I thought it was still someone lookin' to catch us, we'd been scared for that long, but Joanie was callin' out, "He-ey-ey!"

Next thing, we could 'ear John runnin' back in the dark, callin' in a whisper, "Don't be singin' out. They might be white fellers. You listen hard, Ev, is it Uncle Jack?"

"I'm listenin', but I can't make out if it's Dad's voice or not."

John said, "Git those kids now and we'll go straight to that coo-ee-in', but keep 'em quiet. We might 'ave to come back." Every now and then we could hear it, and when we got round a bend in the creek – it was all dry of course – we could see a fire way down ahead along the bed of the creek. Iris said, "That must be them!"

But John wanted to be sure. "It might just be someone died and they're burnin' the camp. Wait 'ere." and he sneaked off. Then he come back and he was **singin' out** to us, namin' the lot of us, runnin', and his arms was goin'.

"Evelyn! Joanie! Iris! It's Aunty Annie and Uncle Jack's camp! Come on, I've found 'em!"

We were runnin' along the creek to meet him, forgettin' our sore feet, and I heard Dad callin' out, "You there, Ev?"

"Yeah, we all 'ere, Dad."

When Dad got to us, he took Brucie from Joanie who'd been carrying him. I said, "Dad, that little feller's real sick. He don't even lift up his head, not for days." By then we were standin' by their fire, and Mum was there, sayin', "Oh-h, Jack, look at her – just look at her."

We must 'ave looked done from walking – we were eleven days on the track, see. Mum come over and she cuddled me, crying, and Dad was sayin, "Don't stand there cryin'! Take her and give her a feed and a drink." He had two kids under his arm, and others huggin' his legs, 'cos my father was a big man.

That night we all had a feed, but Dad said, "Only eat a little bit now and have a sleep. Don't eat too much 'cos you'll get sick, your bellies aren't used to it. You can fill up when you wake up."

While Mum was feeding us, Dad got on his horse and took Brucie in to the Clinic Sister in Enngonia, because they were camped about two miles out of the town. When he got there he found that the Sister was the policeman's wife! She knew Dad because once he'd fixed the windmill at the back of the old jail.

Soon as Dad rode in with that very sick kid she was curious. "Where'd you get this little boy from, Jack?"

"Met some people travellin' on their way to the Bre Mission. Their buggy wheel got broke, and they're fixin' it, but the boy seemed real bad so I said I'd bring 'im back and see if you'd give 'im some medicine."

"Medicine won't do him any good, Jack. We'll have to send him to Bourke Hospital."

So that was the last we seen of Brucie. He had a poisoned foot, dysentery and sore eyes, he was dehydrated and infected from mosquito bites, and a high fever with it all. It took a long time but he got better. Of course no one was able to trace the people he was supposed to belong to and we found out later that some station people adopted him.

Most of the next day they were pickin' burrs out of my feet and it was hard for me to walk about, but it didn't matter a bit. We played in the gully and we swam in the creek and we shouted and yelled to each other while we played. We could play in the daytime, sleep at night and Mum and Dad and Gladys were there. All those bad eleven days just disappeared.

One lot of parents from the Mission were already in Enngonia. They'd got permission to visit relatives in Bourke, and I guess the APB had already checked that the missing kids weren't there. We had to wait for a few days for the other kids' relations to pick them up, then we went off to Yantabulla by ourselves, just the four of us, a family again.

# MOVING ON

*'That's when my whole*

*world changed'*

I never thought our life'd be any more than livin'
at Yantabulla, bein' at the Mission and back to
Yantabulla. There was nothing else, just that for
us. There didn't seem to be another world. If
anyone mentioned goin' somewhere you said
straightaway, "I don't want to go." After the
Mission time, we were always afraid there were
people waitin' to grab us and take us away. If
we saw a strange person on a horse, or a policeman,
we'd run for the scrub. If you saw a white person
before he saw you, then he **didn't** see you. I
suppose I thought I'd be doing that all my life,
because I never thought that one day they'd let
us be ourselves, just blackfellers wantin' to live
on the creek without any bother.

As we were gettin' close to Yantabulla Gladys
and me were standin' up in the buggy ready to
sing out, "We're back", but the first camp we

come to was empty. We looked at each other and wondered, because those people were there when we'd left. A bit further on was the Edwards' camp, a big one, and it was empty.

Dad said, "Everyone must've left, Annie. Might've gone to the Mission."

"We never seen 'em there."

"Might be on their way."

Then the worry came on their faces, because the first thing they wanted to do when they got back was to tell people definitely not to go to the Brewarrina Mission, or any Mission.

By the time we were up in the sandhills where we'd lived, we found only three left out of the twenty-seven families that had been there. Dad rode down to ask the publican what had happened.

"Things've been bad, Mullya. The Depression's worse than ever. Most people are on the move lookin' for work."

We were livin' on virtually nothin' by then, just what we found in the scrub. Like all kids, we took it for granted that we were never short of a feed, that we always had a bed, and shelter over us. We never realized how hard it was to provide these things for a family. There wasn't all the government assistance in them days. If you really had nothing, you could get a ration order from the Police Station for tea, sugar, salt and pepper, potatoes and onions, a bag of flour – and a bottle of black sauce, always a bottle of Holbrook's sauce. You never got butter or honey or jam, them things were luxuries.

Dad decided to go on to Willara Station where he'd often worked. The boss there was real good, and would give anyone a few days' work so they could at least git some tucker at the store for their family.

Dad had about eleven days' work, so he got two killers, a bag of flour, half a bag of sugar and other things we needed. We killed and salted the sheep, hung the woolly skins on the rails to be cured for rugs.

Not long after we got back to Yantabulla from Willara, the old tribal people who lived at Mootawingee sent the message along that the special ceremonial time for kids of a certain age to be initiated was coming. They'd tell you a long, long time ahead because for lots of people it was a hell of a long way. It took us months, workin' on the way as Dad mostly did.

People said to Dad, "Why do you want to go there, Mullya? There's nothing there."

"I want my kids to finish their Aboriginal learning. It's a special place that they should know."

If you wanted your kids to have the full Aboriginal training, you took them. Just like the white man doesn't have to send his kids to University or College if he doesn't want to, it was like that for us. I could say that our lessons on the sandhills at Yantabulla were our primary schooling, and so our time at Mootawingee was our Aboriginal 'College'.

We went across the stony hills to Clifton Downs, camped there and at Willara Station, then right down the Paroo to Wanaaring.

After three days on the track we came to Tinapagee Station. There was no Aboriginal people livin' there then, but a few years before, there'd been heaps. We'd lived there once for a couple of weeks so Tinapagee held a lot of small kid memories for Gladys and me. We wanted to have a look around, but Mum said, "No! If you go down where them old camps were, you could be dreamin' all night, see."

Mum really believed that if you walked round where people had died, they'd follow you home and torment you while you slept, because you'd disturbed where they used to live. The impression was so strong that I even say it to my kids these days, when we're livin' in the 1990s. You never go near old camps – a white man's old camp, yes, but not another Aboriginal's, whether they died there or not. You just don't do these things.

We went on to Yarrawonga Station where Aunty Rose

and Uncle Ted Elwood lived. Across the river was Backwood Station, where Uncle Albert Knight and Mum's oldest brother, Uncle Harry, lived for years.

Further down the Paroo is Glenroy Station. We didn't pull in to the homestead, just camped at the fence. Roy Green owned the place, and he rode up and was sittin' at the fire talkin' with dad for a long time. He was a great friend of my father. I think they went to school together at Ford's Bridge.

Next morning Dad rode up to the homestead and came back with meat and more food. We were very appreciative of all the good things Roy Green gave us, because we'd been livin' on not too much since we'd left the Mission. There was jars of fruit too, because them days, the old *wudjiins* on the stations preserved their own fruits and pickles, sauces and jams and chutneys. Every station had big cellars where they'd store all the stuff they'd bottled.

Then we moved on to Wanaaring Station where the owner, Jack Gibbons, had decided to build new yards. Mulga rails had to be cut and carted in, so Dad had months of work.

While we were there, Gladys and me went to the school. It was a neat little school, tucked in the shelter of thick hop bush, and big shady currajongs in the playground with mulga rails on forky sticks for seats under 'em.

That was the first time I ever seen a toothbrush! I was handed this thing and in the little side room where all the taps were, there was a row of nails each with a kid's name at it. I looked at this little brush and said to meself, "What's this?" I knew about hair-brushes, and boot-brushes, and brushes you groomed horses with, but I didn't know what this little feller was for, with its long handle. So I said nothin', just watched a white kid near me squeeze white stuff out and hand the tube to me. So I did the same and went on copyin' him, like I'd done it all me life. I didn't like it at first, kind of soap runnin' out me mouth, and it felt funny spittin' it out! Colgate's, it was, not a bad taste. I wasn't too good at it at first, and ripped me gums to pieces with the bristles till I made 'em sore.

Next day I told the teacher, "Can't use that – all me mouth is sore."

He said, "Just clean the bottom teeth till your mouth gets better."

We used to take our dinners to school. We each had a white enamel pint with a blue rim that hung on our own nail and stayed at school. Once a week each kid would bring a little jar of sugar and a little jar of tea-leaves, and we'd empty them into big jars. The big boys would boil the billy for dinner each day in the fire-place under the cane-grass shelter, and the big girls would dip the tea out. Each family had a spoon to stir with, and a tin plate, 'cos sometimes you'd take a tin of Camp Pie. Course Gladys and me couldn't eat a whole tin, so we'd hand it round to any kid who wanted some more.

When we told Dad you had to hang your spoon up with your pint, he growled, "Just fancy 'avin' to put a hole in the 'andle of a spoon!"

"Ya gotta do that, Dad, everybody's gotta hang their spoon."

We grew vegies at that school. There was only one tap and no hose, so we all carried water in billies to the patch. The vegies were shared out. Like, the teacher would say, "You can all take a soup bunch home today." That teacher was good. He wasn't an old feller, had a big moustache, wore glasses. He was English, so he sounded funny to us, and if someone fell over and went up to him, he go "Tut-tut-tut," and patch 'em up. In the classroom he'd sing for us – no music, just songs.

I just loved that little bush school. We'd be up in the mornin', dip in the river, school clothes on, couldn't git there quick enough – there were brand-new mates there, so there was always a lot of talkin' and laughin'.

Some of the bigger kids we knew had been on a Government

Mission in Queensland, and been sent out to work on stations at eleven years of age if they had no mums or dads. If they didn't like it where they were sent they'd run away, just go bush. The station owners let 'em go, 'cos no way you could find kids in country where they'd grown up, not if they didn't want you to find 'em. They lived in gullies in the lignum, 'n come out at night for a feed. Stole when they couldn't git tucker any other way. Like the street kids today. Aboriginal people knew they were there, but no one said anything. They were scared if the police caught the kids they'd be sent back. When we were playin', if anyone said somethin' like, "They did that on the Mission," straight-away one of those big kids would jump on ya. "Shut up talkin' about the Mission. Who wants to talk about that rotten place!" Their Mission must've been just as bad as ours. That was taboo, so there was nothin' hangin' over us. It helped us to put that sadness to the back of us.

When Dad's work finished we moved on to Wilcannia, still travellin' to Mootawingee. Steamers were still comin' up to Wilcannia in the 1930s. Gladys and me never went to school there. We used to do bits of jobs on the steamers. The boys cleaned out the space for the wood that fired the boat, and stacked the cords of wood for the next trip, and us girls chucked water on the decks and swept 'em with big push brooms.

I remember the cook on the steamer – Tom Lo, a sun-burnt Chinaman, 'cos 'is skin wasn't yellow. P'raps it was, under his shirt! He used to make soft toffee for us, and show us how to pull it. The captain was a short fat feller, smoked a pipe, but all you could see was the smoke sieving out through his thick bushy moustache. He had a big Lassie collie called Jonesy, used to let us take 'im for a walk. He taught us to write his name – Isaac McMillan. We'd sit down and write it in the sand. Real proud of ourselves we were, to spell that big name. Freddie even cut it into a tree. One day me and Gladys painted it on the side of our buggy with some paint we found at the tip. Dad said, "Who the 'ell's this Isaac McMillan?"

Mr Matthews, the bloke in the booking office, had a tin like a baby petrol tin, with a little round lid in the top, fitted real tight, **full** of boiled lollies. He'd give us a handful for runnin' messages for him, like from the wharf to the warehouse, with lists of when the next steamer was comin' and what its load was. The Afghans camped at the warehouse with all their camels, waitin' for a load to take to Broken Hill.

The steamers carried supplies for all the stations – from syrup and sauce to shoes and saddles. Wagons brought the bales of wool to the river and took back supplies. Properties along the river had their own jetties. It was a busy old river in them days. From Wilcannia we went to White Cliffs, then to Mootawingee, still in the old buggy.

Mootawingee Station was a big property them days. There were a few white people workin' there, but for the big corroboree time Aboriginal people had come from everywhere, some much further than us, and camps were all over the place, along the creeks and back up in the hills. Whatever little hollow there was, there were camps. Lots of Mum's family were there too. We knew Syd Windsor's family from Cobar, some people from Hungerford, Tibooburra, all over.

The camps were at least fifty yards away from each other, but people would be sittin' on logs and rocks at their own fires, all laughin' and talkin' at the top of their voice from one camp to another, passin' news on.

This is something we grew up with. We did it even with white people. We stood at their front gate, they stood at their front door. We stood at their back gate, they stood at their back door. If someone else came along, maybe on a horse, you had a big conversation, it just went round and round.

Only when there was serious things to be discussed the

grown-ups sat down and talked in low voices, but most of the time it was a 'yellin'-out' party. Whatever one person told, the people a hundred yards away heard, and could join in. I don't ever remember hearing anyone say, "Mind your own business!"

The corroboree would start about three o'clock in the afternoon. A man would stand on the hill and he'd sing. His voice would go right down the hill and all round. It was so strong it would carry way, way off.

Then you'd see the dancers comin' from way down the end of the creek, all done up in their paint and feathers and leaves. I don't know who they were – probably fellers we seen every day in the camp. They weren't meant to be themselves. They were dressed as all sorts of animals and birds, dressed to dance stories. You know, hundreds of years ago all the animals were really **huge**, like that big wombat out at Lake Mungo.

One feller was dressed in black and white feathers, a magpie of course, and he was struttin' along just like them. On very special occasions they'd have a goanna, and if you were up on the hill watchin', you'd swear it was a real goanna, huge like in the Dreamtime. They got all the right coloured kangaroo skins, sewed 'em together, and there was a group of young men under him. Four young fellers'd be his legs, and six or more would hold up his body – frightening big thing it was. It moved just like a goanna, but to a man's singing, the corroboree caller's singing.

No didgeridoos down here in New South Wales, they're really from way up north. We had clap sticks and boomerangs. There was one thing a bit like a didgeridoo, a piece of timber. They'd clean it out, wax it in and make one little hole. You blew in it and it sounded like a bass drum. You could conjure up emus with it – emu drum, they called it. Sometimes they used that for corroboree, but mostly it was the tapping.

There were very clever people who could hit special

boomerangs together for hours and hours, makin' the little quick tapping noise. You'd hear a light sound, then it'd go into a deep tone and out again, just like waves in the water. Corroboree clap sticks were one big flat one and one little round one, not like the ones you see now that people just hit together.

With that instrument they could make different sounds, heavy tones or light tones, depending on whether they hit the big one with the little one or the other way round, or what end they used. It was just like runnin' the scales on a piano if they tapped from one end of the flat stick to the other. It was the special wood they used and the way they made 'em. If you watched the hands of those boomerang fellers they'd be goin' just like they had the shakes, and they could keep it up for hours. They did too!

Corroboree would go on till way into the night. Small kids were allowed to stay until about nine o'clock, us middlin' ones a bit longer, and the oldest kids stayed nearly the whole time. We'd be told to go back to camp and go to bed, and we'd be happy to go. We were pretty tired because we'd had lessons all day and then we'd been sittin' watchin' since about three o'clock. We had our usual sort of beds at Mootawingee, slung on the forky sticks, but Dad had a hell of a time gettin' the sticks in the ground, because Mootawingee is all rocks.

It's a very beautiful place, Mootawingee, very beautiful – a very eerie place too. I've never seen a place like it – gum trees growing out of bare flat rock, and they seem to go up to the sky.

Even today, in the 1990s, in Aboriginal families rearing their kids traditional, there's special plans for boys. Thirteen-year-old boys still go to live with their maternal uncle, even if the uncle lives in another State. His uncle treats him exactly as if he was his father. There's got to be a lot of trust both ways. Like, the uncle might drop the boy at the YMCA

Club. He'll never say, "Don't you leave here till I come back" or "I'll come back for you in two hours time." He'll trust the boy to stay at the Club, and will ask, "What time do you want me to pick you up?" If the boy's trusted to act as a responsible person, he's more likely to act that way. And when the uncle goes back to get him, he won't go to the door to see where he is, or if he's ready, because you can't shame him in front of his friends by treating him as a child. The kid becomes so proud and thinks, "My Uncle cares about me ... there he is, waitin' like I told the kids he would be."

While the boys' initiation programme was on, us girls weren't allowed to leave the camp, none of the women were. There were limits around the camp we weren't allowed to pass. But we talked among ourselves, and wondered what the boys were doin' and what they were learning.

Girls' big learning was about childbirth, so the women must've made sure there were some pregnant ones there. They taught us how to help and none of us liked it much! As soon as someone was going to have a baby we'd be called over and told, "You've got to do this, you've got to do that." Mostly there was plenty of rags and a lot of hot water, but – so we could learn the old ways! – for one poor woman there was no water or rags, just heaps of bushes. No scissors to cut the cord, that was done with a grey piece of flint, not too sharp either! One girl had to hold the cord stretched tight and another sawed away at it. There was a special piece of string that tied the cord in two places for them to cut between.

The cleanin' up was done with the brunda bush, the one we used for brooms. It's got very fine leaves, with some shiny substance on them. I think that substance acted as an antiseptic. The old women did things very quick and I thought, "Gord, that poor girl's legs'll never be the same again, bein' scratched with bushes like that!"

That birth was more tricky than those with the water

and rags, but it was something we had to learn. It was
deliberately to teach us how to help and survive in a situation
like that. Even livin' in the white man's world, you could
be a long way from a hospital and you could be in the
buggy comin' in from a bush camp and the baby could arrive.

If there was a sick baby in the camp, cryin' all the time,
that would be brought to the young girls' attention. The
women'd say, "What do you think's wrong with that baby?"

"I dunno. Must be hungry."

They'd strip it down and let you look at it. "Feel it,"
they'd say, so you'd feel it all over. And still today, if a
kid's sick, the first place I'll feel is not his forehead, but
his tummy, and if that's hot, I know he's sick. I remember
feeling this skinny little baby's belly and it was hot, too
warm for a little baby that small. It was cuttin' teeth and
of course it had a bit of diarrhoea, and that was the warm
in its stomach.

We learnt too about patchin' up cuts and curin' sores.
Gum leaves have a lot of oil so you warmed the leaf near
a fire till it went real green and greasy – not too hot or
it'd burn the skin. You put the warm leaf on with a substance
you'd made by crushing dried quondongs and mixing them
with emu or goanna fat. You could make a very good ointment
with dried and crushed *gweeyuhmuddah* seeds mixed with
animal fat. You piled it on and tied it up with whatever
you had. We always carried strips of young kangaroo hide.

The *gweeyuhmuddah* as we knew it doesn't grow at Mootawingee, because there's no river there. But there is a tree
just like it. The white man calls it 'emu bush'. It's got
berries and a white flower, and if you boil the leaves the
smell is exactly the same, and the medicine it makes is just
as good.

For sandy blight we used the *gweeyuhmuddah* leaves, and
bark from the butt of the tree. You boiled it all up together
to make it stronger. The women'd make you lie flat on
your back so the liquid could go well in and it'd become

like a green scum over your eyes. It was like dark glasses, you could open your eyes and see through it and everything looked green. It took away the glare and helped you see. They would put cold tea leaves in a piece of cloth or mosquito net and tie it wet over your eyes every night, or in the daytime if you were sittin' in the camp or in the buggy travellin'. You could feel it coolin' down your burning eyes.

A girl would be told that she was to feed the class the next day, sixteen of us and the old lady who was our special teacher and went everywhere with us. Early in the morning she'd go hunting for whatever she could gather, and cadge kangaroo or emu meat from whoever had a fresh kill. Feeding the group with plenty of good tucker would be your test as a food gatherer and cook.

We weren't allowed to use camp ovens, because they were white feller things, and we had to do everything the traditional way. I cooked in the sand in the bed of the creek. I just made a fire, moved it aside, dug a hole in the sand, made a bed of leaves, put the food in, covered it with more leaves and sand. It was pretty easy for me because Mum had taught us.

We cooked nearly everything we got – a real 'mixed grill'. If you found eggs you put them in too. The only eggs we couldn't use were the Green Hawk's eggs. He lives at Mootawingee, and nowhere else outside Kakadu, so they tell us. No one seems to know how he got from Kakadu to Mootawingee. He's a very pretty hawk, and his eggs were taboo. Even if you found a feather of his under a tree where he was preening himself, you couldn't take it. He's protected by the white man too.

Our teachers showed us how to find native wells. We'd look for tufts of grass that seemed to be growing out of bare rock, or an acacia tree – *marpoo* – that has a very sweet green berry. It doesn't grow anywhere but near that kind of water. The opening to the well could be quite small, about the size of a saucepan, or quite big, that you could fit your head and shoulders down to dip the water. But mainly you'd have a billycan on a piece of rope, and dipped like from a well. The water's very clear and sweet, and very, very cool. It's great to have clear water. Mostly the water we had outback was muddy. You'd get a bucket of it and let it stand overnight and pour off the clearer water from the top into another bucket. Then you tipped out the mud and got another lot to let it settle, and went on and on like that. You couldn't just dip it out of the creeks and make damper with it. It would be like eatin' cement!

Mootawingee has lots of sand creeks where you could dig soakages. All you had to do was dig a hole in the sand and wait. The water just slowly comes into the hole if you dig it deep enough. The sand there wasn't fine like we would expect to see in a creek. The grains were big, and they made a swishin' noise under your foot, so if you had tender feet it would tear the soles off. That sand was as white as anything, whiter than any sand I've seen on a beach.

The only other sand I've seen as white is at Mungo, but of course Mungo sand is fine, very **fine**. It gets in your teeth, your eyes, and fills up the roof of your hat.

There's ochres at Mootawingee, twenty to sixty feet .in the air, just straight up, big orange slabs of rock, white, yellow, dark-red and some blood-red – beautiful ochres, just like organ pipes in the sky. If you rub your hand on it it feels like talcum powder. In the caves where whole families lived there are paintings on the walls.

There was a special teacher who just did bark painting. He showed us how to get the colours we wanted, not to take a great big stone but just to scrape off a little onto a piece of bark, or a mussel shell if we had it. He told us never to scrape off more than we needed, because when it was mixed with water and left over it couldn't be used again and that was waste. There's little bits of a sticky substance like tiny glass beads at the roots of the spinifex grass. We soaked them in the water to mix the ochres, and it made the paintings permanent. Mostly we picked up bark the trees had shed and shaped it with a pocket knife. If a big piece of bark was curved we flattened it on a flat rock and loaded it with more rocks – turned it over a few times to dry clean. Our 'brushes' were green sticks. Some we cut with a sharp point to make a thin line, and if we wanted the lines wider we'd chew or hammer the end of the stick so it became a brush. You couldn't use a proper hair paintbrush with ochre, because it's sand. That spreads the brush right out so it becomes hard and ruined. When the stick brush got scruffy we'd cut off that end and chew the next bit. To start off, the stick would be about eight inches, and we'd work 'em down to about two inches, like kids in school with pencils.

The first traditional things we were taught to paint were animals, not X-ray animals like they do up north, but covered-in animals, with their skin on. Then we'd make marks where we thought the ribs were. Fish was the only thing we drew like the X-ray style because you gotta see the bones to know it's a fish. We didn't use a lot of spots either, we mainly used lines, thick lines, thin ones, squiggles and esses. Nowadays we put in a few spots to fancy it up, but it's those Top End people who use X-ray and spots.

We did a lot of paintings while we were there, but we only took our favourite pieces when we left. I had so many favourite pieces that Dad was worried where we were going to put them. Course, while we were at Mootawingee with a beautiful place all round us, and bark paintings all over the ground and so many people doing them, mine were just pieces, but by the time we were back at Waverley Downs Station where it was just stony hills, dry sticks and no water, we seen those paintings were very pretty things, so they sat up in the tent. I used to look at them all the time.

From then on, all I ever did was look for bark and ochres to paint with. Little did I know that my father had collected some at Mootawingee and put it in the shrimp can in the buggy. He said to me one day, "There's some stone there, Ev, if you want to paint."

I couldn't believe it. "Where'd you get it, Dad?"

All he said was, "Just picked it up."

Gladys and I used to paint with it then. I'd say to her, "Don't scrape too much off, Sister. There's only one piece of stone." I didn't know Dad had more.

While we were at Waverley Downs, Gladys and I did the story of our trip back from Mootawingee. We painted it together on a piece of bark that had fallen off a box tree. Mum put that tough bark through the ashes and softened it for us, then we put stones on it and flattened it out. Gladys's job was to mark every camp, how many times we camped on the way to White Cliffs, Wanaaring, Hungerford, then back to Waverley Downs. We tried to remember all the things that happened and put them in in our own little style of painting.

Mum would ask, "What's this little squiggly bit here... what's that bit there?" and what I couldn't answer Gladys would, because they were parts she'd put in. We used the traditional symbols we'd been taught. There's hundreds of traditional symbols and with them you can tell any story you want. There's symbols for birds, fish, animals, trees, mountains, flat plains, stony hills, sandy hills, people doing every kind of action – there's no end to them.

Concentric circles were camps. The bigger the camp, the more concentric circles.

The same symbol as 'camp' but with just three half-circles means three wise men making decisions.

There were never more than three Aboriginal men who made the decisions, so it would be two to one all the time, and they'd get somewhere. There'd be no arguing all the time like in the Shire or Parliament now. Those fellers are worse than old women – can't make up their minds what to do.

Four half circles round a fire with four lines coming out like spokes were women cooking at a fire, using their yam sticks.

These sticks were used for everything – to whack kids if they needed it, fight, poke the old feller out of bed, dig holes to get goannas or rabbits out, stir the fire up, turn the meat over, measure the water if you were walking across a creek. It was like an extension of your arm, so the women were never without them. They were made of the hardest wood that wouldn't burn in the fire. A gidgee one would last forever, but it was hard to cut and heavy to carry everywhere. Ironwood was very good, but mulga was the most popular wood for everything. It was easy to cut and light to carry.

Mootawingee has stayed a very special place to me all my life. I was sad when that time ended, but I didn't know that something bigger was ended.

On our way home Dad got work again at Willara Station. He could turn his hand to anything – patch up tractors, old motor cars, windmills, shearing engines – there was nothing he couldn't mend, and he worked hard.

There was a big camp of Aboriginal people on Willara, mostly *Wankamurrahs* who had cleared off from the Bre Mission after we'd left. I think when Dad went it must've given others the push to risk it. On their way back to Tibooburra they'd gone up the Paroo to Willara to get work.

Then it was gettin' on Christmas and the shearin' was cuttin' out so everyone was thinkin' of goin' home. Four buggy loads – Mum's first cousins, the Clarkes from Wilcannia, Granny Moysey's kids – left to go home, and Gladys and Mum just went with 'em.

And that's when my whole world, the world of living with my Mum and Dad and my sister, the world that I'd known all my life and cried for on those terrible eleven days walkin' to Enngonia, changed.

I didn't know there was any little differences between Dad and Mum, I always thought they were good mates because they never let us see them arguing. I was too wrapped up in my own little world to notice if anything was wrong. In the bush us kids were always busy doin' our own things. Big people's business never concerned us. We always seemed contented being together, just the four of us, with our dogs. There never was a place I liked more than being with my mother and father and Gladys. We didn't fight, me and Gladys, 'cos we wasn't allowed to. We had our little arguments, but she was the only mate I had because we weren't allowed to go to other kids' places to play. Dad always made us our own cubby house, and carts, and Mum made us rag dolls.

My mother was a very happy person, a very jolly, noisy person. She used to laugh and joke, sing and dance, and play Dad's old accordion. She'd play jokes on me and Gladys, and Dad, and she'd laugh the loudest! You could hear her all round the camps. People livin' round would say, "Wonder what Annie's doin' to them kids and Mullya up there. Hear her laughin'?" If we went swimmin' with the other kids, Mum would be there, divin' under the water, grabbin' legs, throwin' water on the ones on the bank that didn't want to come in, bad as the worst kid.

I used to look at Mum sometimes when she was sound asleep, and think it was strange to see her there, asleep and still, and not laughing or smiling all the time. I used to feel real good in the chest that she was my mother, with her real happy ways. Bein' with your own mum and dad is something special. You never tell your mum and dad that you're proud of 'em, that you like the way they are, that you love them, and how much you appreciate them. You know the love's there, but you never think about tellin' 'em.

Mum said to me, "I'm goin' to live in Wilcannia, Ev, and Gladys's comin' with me."

"What're ya goin' away for? How long're you goin' for? Why can't I go too?"

"Someone's got to stop with your father – I can't leave him on his own. He's gotta have someone to talk to."

But I thought to meself, "No one likes me, 'ere's Mum goin' to leave me."

I didn't know that Mum had met someone she liked better than Dad. So they went.

That world I'd always known was sort of behind me. I had to start a new one. When you are together – a family – everything in the world that's important to you is there, and as a kid you think it's **always** going to be like that, but that's not the way it is. Things change. You wonder then – will good things come to you, or bad things? It's certainly not a good feeling, being left behind. But I still asked myself, "Why did she leave **me**? She could've taken me and left Gladys. I must 'ave done something really **bad**." I knew I wasn't a model kid, but I couldn't think of anything that I'd done that was really bad enough for her to leave me behind.

I even said to Dad later on, "Why did Mum take Gladys and not take me?"

"What did she say to you, Evelyn?"

"She said I had to stay 'ere for company for you."

"Yeah, well, I'm glad you stayed, because you are company for me, good company."

So that made me feel a bit good, and I didn't want to

hurt his feelings by saying, "I don't want to stay with you. I want Mum and Gladys." I loved my old Dad too. Dad was like a mate to me. He'd taught me to do a lot of things that I knew he'd teach a son if he'd had one. There were times I'd say, "Gee, I'm sick of diggin' with this crowbar... I'm sick of borin' holes in this mulga stump with an old blunt bit..." Dad would just say, "Well, get the three-cornered file, and sharpen the bit."

I'd think to meself, "I'm not a boy. Why don't he realize I'm not a boy." I remember askin' him one day, "What if you traded me for a boy?... What if I went and lived with Aunty Eva and you got Cousin Freddie?"

"Freddie'd be alright, but I'd keep lookin' for you. I'd be sayin', 'Where's Ev?' See, it wouldn't work. I'd want **you**."

It was things like that that made me feel good, because I knew someone loved me very, very much.

But I wouldn't have Gladys to talk to and to play with. I wouldn't have Mum to talk to and to show me how to do things. Dad was a good mate and showed me how to drive an old motor car, how to pull nuts and bolts off machinery, how to bore holes in posts, how to build a camp and cook a bush feed. I liked what both taught me, and I've used what both taught me, over the years. All that knowledge became very valuable assets to me. But there's a difference, a big difference. I loved them **both** and I wanted them **both**. Sometimes I'd think that if I'd told 'em I loved 'em they wouldn't have split up, or I wouldn't have been left.

After mum went, and Dad moved on from Willara, he sent me to live with Aunty Rose Ellwood on Mooleyarrah Station not far down from Willara. That was the first Aunty I lived with.

When I was still a kid, my Mum's family, all my aunties in Bourke, were sort of sorry for me, because I was an unwanted kid. I hated people feelin' sorry for me. I didn't want to be near anybody that said, "Poor old Ev. You come and stay with me." When someone does you a good turn, you owe that person all your life, and I felt that if I owed a lot of people for a lot of things I'd end up with nothing for meself. If I went out on me own, I wouldn't owe nobody nothing, only just me.

I don't think Mum ever realised how much I missed her and Gladys. I never seen my mother for I don't know how long after that. I used to wonder, "Will I see my mother again?" But I never got cranky inside me with her, or wild with her. I never said to myself, "I'll never speak to her again for leavin' me." But I was cold inside for a long time. Dad tried his best to smooth it over for me. He never actually said anything, neither did I, but he used to do things for me, and talk about Mum. I learned from him how things you say can hurt, and nobody wants to hurt someone they love.

All I ever wanted to know was **WHY**, why I was left. And I still do.

# WORKING

*'If I'm on my own from
start to finish, that's it!'*

As a young teenager I always seemed to be living
with my aunties. In those days when you were
left with people you didn't expect anything from
them. I had to look after the kids – always mobs
of 'em, it seemed, do the washin', clean round
the camp, just for bed and tucker – no cash pay.
That had gone on for a year or more, and I'd
had enough of working hard for nothing. My chance
came when the boss on Mooleyarra wanted horses
taken in to Bourke for a Rodeo. I said I'd be
one of the drovers, but I didn't tell Aunty Rose
I wasn't comin' back.

Almost the first person I seen when we rode
into North Bourke was my cousin, Freddie Leppert – hadn't seen him for years. He sung out to
me in the lingo, "What're you doin' up there
on that horse, Cousin?" Now the lingo was like
our secret weapon. We could say what we liked,

even cheek the white feller right under his nose and not one of them could understand.

I yelled back to Freddie, "Bringin' in these 'orses for the Rodeo, but I'm not goin' back – ever."

When we yarded the horses he told me that Mum was livin' on the Reserve in Bourke. I walked the two miles in through the lagoons and swamps, swam the river over to the Reserve and found my way to Mum's camp. She was bakin' bread and came out, flour all over her hands and gave me a big cuddle. I couldn't say anything.

I stayed with Mum for a little while until one of the Sisters from the Convent got me a job working for Alan Bloxham, a Stock and Station Agent. This was the first town job I ever had. I'd have been about fourteen or fifteen, I dunno. They had two little girls, six and eight, and I was a sort of housemaid-nursemaid. Mrs Bloxham had to go to Sydney for a goitre operation, so she asked if I'd go with her to look after the children.

So off I went – never been in a train in me life. All I'd done was help put sheep and cattle on trains. The little box carriages held about six or eight people. The Bloxhams were in another carriage, and they were all white people in the one I was in, so of course there was nothing I could say to them. The further the train got away from home, the more I missed Bourke, and the more afraid I got. And going so fast – well, to me it was fast because I'd travelled all me life on a horse or in a buggy. But I still enjoyed lookin' out the window at the country round Oxley Mountain.

Then we stopped and someone said, "We're at Byrock – there's time for a cup of tea." I had no money, so I'm standin' there, stayin' close to the train so it couldn't go off without me, but lookin' at everything. People were gettin' tea and sandwiches. In those days you got real cups, thick white cups, sort of flat and round, and not just a cup, but a saucer and a spoon to go with it. Old fellers in their big boots and big hats trotted across to the pub, pretty flowers were growin' everywhere, the guard in his uniform was wheelin' trollies with bags and bottles and big cans. I wondered what them great big cans were for, till I seen the word 'milk' on 'em. Mrs Bloxham used to help me to read more. In fact she bought me a dictionary that was a great help.

Then we went on again and there was more country to see. Most of the people settled down for a bit of a rest, but I was too excited. I must have dozed a bit about Narramine, because it was gettin' dark when I opened my eyes. We were comin' down hill and I seen all these lights! I thought to meself, "This is it. This is Sydney." When the train pulled up I saw the big sign DUBBO, and I'd met people from Dubbo, so I knew the word. Everybody in the carriage was gettin' out but I was scared to move, so I'm sittin' up in the carriage all by myself when Mrs Bloxham come along.

"Ah, there you are, Ev! Come on, we'll go to the cafeteria and have some supper."

I'd never eaten with these people in all the months I'd worked for them. They'd eat in the dining room and I ate in the kitchen, and here we were, all sittin' around the same table. I felt awful.

Mr Bloxham was a very nice feller, grey-headed, with glasses, and two bits of real white hair stickin' up the top of his baldy patch. He had a crippled leg – a sulky had run over his foot. He was fussin' round, tryin' to make me feel good. "Come on, girl, don't be shy. There's a cup of tea. Do you want a pie – or some sandwiches. Do you want tomato sauce?"

I was mustering up me good manners, "No, thank you ... yes, please."

Their younger girl, Pam, was a spoilt kid when she was with her parents. Like so many kids she knew she had them where she wanted 'em!

"I don't want this ... I want a corned beef sandwich

with mustard on it." She kept it up even when her father said, "You can't have mustard – it'll burn your tongue like it did last time."

I thought, "At least, **I'll** behave meself!"

Her older sister, Jill, said she wanted to go to the lavatory, and the missus said, "Ev will take you."

"Yes, alright," and I stood up. "Where is it?"

"There, look, right behind you." The word was written on the door, but I couldn't spell the damn thing at that time!

It was the first time I'd ever been in a toilet with a lot of women, some doing their faces, some straightening the seams on their stockings, putting coats on, brushing their hair, putting more lippy on – it really fascinated me. The toilets I'd been used to were just one-person-at-a-time things, and here was a whole bunch of women.

Back on the train again, Mr Bloxham give me a rug and a pillow, and said, "We'll be travellin' all night, Ev, so go to sleep. It'll be six o'clock in the morning when we get to Sydney."

It was still dark when I woke up, and there were more lights, but we were still movin'. I said to meself, "Gee, I wish I never come! I'll never git home again." For the rest of the train time I was awake with those miserable thoughts. "If this woman dies down 'ere, this man'll stay 'ere with his family, then 'ow'll I git back 'ome?" I was a sad and sorry girl, and made up me mind I'd never do anything stupid like goin' away from home again. I'd thought Sydney was just 'over there', and you could pop home when you wanted to. But here I'd travelled a whole day and a whole night, in something that moved so fast. I'd gone to another world, not my world, and not a world I wanted to fit into.

Into Central Station – six o'clock in the morning. I looked out the window, and there was PEOPLE all over the place, more people than I'd ever seen in my whole life, and I didn't know one of them. I decided then that I wasn't goin' to shift out of that train. It had to go back to Bourke, and I was gonna be in it! Mrs Bloxham came along again, leading one kid by the hand. "Come on, Ev, we're here." There was no escape. I folded up the blanket and grabbed the pillow and me bag, and walked out. I dunno how me legs carried me, they were that shaky.

"Come on now. My sister'll be here to pick us up and take us out to Mum's place. Here, you take Pam's hand and hold the strap on my suitcase."

So we went along through this mob of people. I didn't feel a big half-grown fool hangin' onto that strap – I felt very secure. I wasn't goin' to let that woman out of my sight, and in that crowd, two steps would have been out of sight. And she was sick, poor thing, with a big bandage round her neck, and her husband coming along behind with the cases, limping and leading the other kid – and me, 'frightened' wasn't the word!

Mrs Bloxham's sister, Jo, was at the station to meet us and drove us out to her place at Dolls Point. Her Mum and Dad, Mr and Mrs Grace, were there and two more sisters. There were six girls in this family, English people, to make it worse for me. Their speech was so English I was flat out understanding what they were sayin'.

We had a nice breakfast, then they took us to Kogarah where we were to live with another sister, Mrs Brennan, who had a husband in a wheel chair and two little girls. They lived in Weeney Street, and where the golf course is now there were just paddocks that made me feel homesick. The little house was full as anything, so I was worrying where I was gonna sleep. Sleepin' in a house with white people, that just wasn't right, I couldn't do that.

I was a bit relieved when they said, "We've fixed up a place for you to have for yourself. We'll show you."

Out the back they had a garage and a work shed and another shed. They'd cleared that one out, and put a piece of carpet on the floor, and a bed with a nice bedspread on it, a table with a wireless and a lamp, and a cupboard and chair.

One of my jobs was to take the four kids on the bus to school, then pick them up in the afternoon. I don't know how I managed to do it. Mrs Brennan took me the first day, and after that I had to do it by myself. I watched for the number on the bus, because even if KOGARAH had been written on it, I wouldn't have been able to read a word like that. I'd take 'em into the school yard, catch another bus back, work all day in the house, then go and pick 'em up. I was terrified, not of losing the kids, but of losing ME! Every day, I said to meself, "I wish I didn't come to this place. I should've stayed home."

One Saturday, late in the afternoon, I was sittin' out in the back yard, polishin' the kids' school shoes, and I noticed this big thing runnin' backwards and forwards near the house. I knew they didn't have a cat, so I thought, "I'll just sit real still, and if he doesn't come back, I'll go into the shed and look through a hole in the wall." When it came back, me eyes popped. "They sure grow big mice down 'ere!" I thought, "When I git 'ome I'll tell 'em about these giant mice – and they won't believe me." Mr Brennan told me what they were and after that I was scared sleepin' out there, because I knew rats could bite you.

Mrs Brennan was a nice lady, told me to call her 'Winnie' and her husband 'Jim'. When I'd be workin' round the house, he'd wheel his chair round and talk to me, do the potatoes for me – things like that. They treated me like family. If they went out in the car I was always included, for the outing, not to mind the kids.

Jo was a doctor, and she said to me one day, "You can use my bike if you want to go for a ride." I'd learnt on old bikes we'd put together from bits at the tip in Bourke, ridin' round the gullies, no tyres or tubes, just on the rims. She gave me a little map, but I couldn't read it and anyway

I'd stand at the gate lookin' down the road and think, "Gee, if I go out there, I'll be lost for sure."

It was Christmastime when we were in Sydney so it was hot. They took me to this place, Sand something, for a swim. Later on I found out it was Sans Souci, where there was a Baths with a great big nettin' fence right round it. I wondered what it was there for, and they said it was because of sharks. I didn't know what a shark was. I didn't even know sea water was salty. In fresh water, in rivers and lagoons, you swim with your mouth open. You don't drink the water, but it's in your mouth when you're blowin' water round. So, I did that, playin', and oh-h-h . . . I spat it out real quick! I'd scratched my leg on a rose bush the day before, gettin' a ball for the kids. Into this sea water I went, and my leg started to sting. I thought, "Wonder what's 'appenin' now," and it just wouldn't stop stingin'. I'm standin' there rubbin' it, and they're all singin' out, "Water's nice, isn't it, Ev?"

"Yeah . . . lovely . . ." but I'm not too sure, all the same. When I'd stand straight in the water, it'd move me, rock me, lift me up off the bottom! I said to meself, "This's no water like I know. This feller's **alive!**" You can stand in fresh water, even runnin' water, and it just goes past you. But not this stuff. So I decided I wasn't safe in that kind of water. If it got me and took me away I wouldn't be able to git back, even though I was a good swimmer. It'd hang onto me, 'cos it seemed to be heavy around me. And all this time my leg was stingin'. I got out and they said, "There's showers in there," and when I had a shower my leg stopped stingin'. I didn't like to ask any of the women about it, but I did ask Jim when we were workin' round the house, "How come my leg got sore in the water?"

He explained, so I asked him about sharks. He tried to tell me about them but he didn't have a picture, and I didn't know what he meant.

One afternoon I decided to go on the bike to the beach at Dolls Point before I went to pick up the kids. I was gittin' a bit brave by then! People were walkin' round in the water just up to their waists, and I went in again just to get the feel of this strange water, when all of a sudden there was this bell ringin' and people runnin' everywhere. I was standin' in the water, watchin' 'em all runnin' like crazy ants. Some were singin' out, "Get out, girl, get out." I was sayin' to meself, "I'm not in your spot . . . I'm not gettin' out for you . . ."

A bloke come along in a boat and said, "Jump in, girlie, and quick about it !"

He took me to the beach and I thought, "Blow you! Yous can keep your water! I'm goin' 'ome." I went over to the bike and pulled on me dress and was gettin' ready to leave, and I saw these blokes in boats and they seemed to be very busy, grabbin' and hittin', then they were comin' back to the bank, or sand or whatever you call it – the beach – draggin' this thing.

"Wonder what that is?" I thought, and people were crowdin' round it, so I put the bike back against the wall and walked down to 'ave a look too.

"By gee, that's the biggest catfish I've ever seen in my life – he must be a saltwater catfish. If we could catch 'em back home like that, one fish would feed everybody for I don't know how long!" Just as well I only said it to meself or people would have thought, "Who's this stupid bunny?"

One of the fellers pulled its mouth open and propped sticks in. I stood back when I seen all them teeth, too many even to fit inside.

When I got home Jim said, "How was your swim, Ev?"

"Good, but they got a big thing out of the water, like a big catfish."

He swung his chair round. "Where were you?" he said, real sharp.

"In the water . . ."

"That was a shark. Don't you go down there any more.

They'll eat you, grab your legs off, break you in half, anything . . .''

That was the end of the sea for me. I wouldn't even go in the water at Sans Souci where the wire netting was. If they went in, I'd be sittin' there watchin' the net, waitin' for it to shake. I'd think, "I'll never get safe home to Bourke away from them things."

When Mrs Bloxham came home from hospital we all had a trip to the Zoo. That was a ride on the Ferry, but the water looked so dark and deep, and now that I knew there were **sharks** in it, it terrified me.

I'd never seen animals and birds locked up before, so I asked, "What are they in cages for? Can't they just let 'em loose?"

"Oh, no, this is a zoo. This is what you do with them here."

I felt bad when I seen the emu, because across the front part of his cage he had a pad that was worn deep from him walkin' up and down. If I'd had a pair of cutters I would've opened a gap for him. He looked so sad, and when he went to have a bit of a pick another emu sort of took over, walkin' and walkin' nowhere.

The cockies and hawks that are used to flyin' high were right up in the roof of their cage. I reckoned they shouldn't have been there because they had their own livin' to do, and couldn't do it. The poor old galahs were sittin' watchin' everybody, not sayin' anything. I was sad for the little water hens too because in the bush, when they see people, they just take off and fly, and here they didn't have any sky to fly to, just a wire roof over that great big cage. The old lazy kangaroos was laying in the sun, one scratchin' his ribs, another scratchin' his belly. I thought to meself, "Wonder if you've ever been out under a big tree on a sandhill."

Mr Bloxham came over to me and said, "What are you thinking about, Ev?"

"Wonderin' what this feller'd do if he was on the sandhills at North Bourke. They 'aven't even got red sand in there for 'im, to make 'im feel a bit at 'ome, no grass, nothin'."

The penguins seemed to be enjoyin' themselves, jumpin' in and out of the water and showin' off for the people, then goin' into a little hole. I would've liked to sit there all day and watched them. The young monkeys played and jumped around but the older monkeys just sat there very sad. It made me think of the old people on the Bre Mission. It was the first time I'd been close to a giraffe – just couldn't get over it, his yellow skin and brown patches, and his head at the end of that real long neck, and little short horns on top. I would've loved to be able to rub my hand on his head, and to feel his skin, whether he had coarse hair on him, or soft fur or what. One was drinkin' water, with his legs stiff right out sideways. I was waitin' all the time for him to do the splits and flop down.

We went to see the fish being fed, and those sharks! The men threw in long fish and the sharks went chomp! and cut 'em in half as neat as any axe. Then I knew what Jim had been sayin', and I was real glad I hadn't gone back into the sea swimmin'.

The peacock had his beautiful tail up, walkin' and struttin' around – looking so pleased with himself, as if he was sayin', "Hey, you, look at me. You're not as pretty as I am." Then we saw the hippopotamus – great big thing, in a pool.

I said to them, "What sort of water does this feller live in?" 'cos I knew all about salt water and fresh water by then – clever me!

"He lives in fresh water, Ev, in rivers."

I thought to meself, "Wonder if there's any in the Paroo – nah, that river wouldn't be deep enough to hold a big thing like that. We'd see it for sure, there wouldn't be enough water to cover 'im."

I didn't like that zoo at all. But I do like Dubbo Zoo. Animals there have got a bit of a chance to live their own life. I don't think Mrs Bloxham was too pleased when I said I didn't like it, and asked her how white people would like it if they were all locked up for animals to come and look at them. But I didn't want to get into a hassle with her, so usually I kept my opinions to meself. But she heard me talkin' to Jim about it.

They took us to Luna Park too. Soon as we got in, we met station people from Wanaaring, the Middletons. Old Grandfather Ted Middleton, who grew up with my dad, had come with them when they came to pick up their teenage kids from school in Sydney. Big voice he had, and talked very sl-o-o-w. When they'd all stopped sayin' Hello, Mrs Middleton said, "We were just going on the Ghost Train. Let's all go together." So they mixed the two families all up and in we went. Of all places to take a frightened little Aboriginal person – the Ghost Train!

I was in the front seat with old Ted and one of his grandsons – and off it went, into the **dark**!

When we got out the other end I felt as if I'd been runnin' and dodgin' things for a full night, I was that done. My throat was so dry, I must have been screamin' all the time I was in there. Sweat was runnin' out of both of us.

"You alright, Dad?" asked Mrs Middleton.

"Ye-ah, I think so. Don't put me through that bloody thing again."

"I don't want to get in there again either," I croaked.

Mrs Middleton wanted to be sure we were havin' a good time.

"There's another ride you can have. It's the Big Dipper."

"You gettin' in there, Ted?" I asked him.

"No bloody fear, girl. I'll sit down and watch the Merry-Go-Round. That's more my style."

The Merry-Go-Round was my style too. I rode on it, and went into other places that I liked. I think if I'd been on other things first I might have almost liked the Ghost Train, but to go there straight off, when you don't know about things like that, that it's just a put-on – it wasn't good.

By the time we were getting ready to leave Sydney I was game to go out on the bike and rode over Tom Ugly's Bridge to Cronulla. I liked walkin' in the sand without shoes, and lookin' at **all that water**. Didn't know if I'd ever see it again.

Mrs Bloxham said, "Do you want to do some shopping before you go home, Ev?"

"What's 'shopping'?"

She explained, and they took me 'into town'. I didn't know what I wanted to buy, everything looked so nice, and there was so much of it, and the big shops were so full of people. I wanted to buy things for the people at home, for me Mum and everyone. I bought bangles and hair clips and scarves and hankies.

We'd been in Sydney for months, and while I was there I'd put on weight, and I'd learned to look after my hair. I used to brush it and feel all the waves in it, real nice. I put cream on my skin, little bit of lipstick and rouge, and all that sort of stuff. So I bought myself some pretty dresses, some nice underwear, sandals, and shorts – very daring in them days – and I had these nice tan legs that had sort of filled out, not 'stick-legged' any more! I never got round to painting my toenails or fingernails. I always wanted to buy a ring with a blue stone, but I could never afford it till I bought myself one in 1986. I was anxious to see what people would say when I got home, filled out and everything. I looked like a girl then.

At last they said, "We're going home on Sunday night's train. We'll get home at five o'clock Monday."

We got everything packed up, hot water bottles full, 'cos it was chilly at night goin' through the Blue Mountains, even though it was summertime. This time I was pretty game in the train. We were in a carriage where you could walk from one little compartment to another, so the kids could sit in one with me, and walk along to their parents when they wanted to. So I wasn't by myself with strangers. It was good comin' home. The family sounded happy and I know I was. The kids kept goin' back into their mother and father, and I could hear 'em saying, "Evelyn wants to know how many hours now before we get home." I hadn't sent them but I sure wanted to know. The hours got shorter and shorter but it still seemed like forever for me.

We come to Byrock and I knew then the next stop was HOME – Bourke. From there on, I didn't want to talk, just sat lookin' out the window thinkin' how nice it would be to see everybody, and how they'd all look, and all I had to tell. I looked across the big plain and could just see the top of Oxley Mountain, and I felt great. Then I could see the old town and the smoke comin' out the chimney at the Meatworks, and from the dynamo for the power. Then we were at the railway station. Nobody knew that I was comin' – I didn't write any letters. Another Stock and Station Agent who picked the Bloxhams up said, "You'll be able to find your way home, won't ya?"

I had nearly three miles to go, me case was heavy, and I had another heavy bag because I'd bought bits of crockery and photo frames at a second-hand shop in Kogarah. But I didn't notice the weight – I was home.

I started off to the Reserve where Mum lived. An old white bloke was goin' along in his sulky. I knew him, so I asked for a ride to the corner where I could walk straight in to the camps.

"Where're you comin' from, girl?

"Sydney – went there with Alan Bloxham and his family."

When I got down he said, "Those cases heavy?"

"No, I'm right."

So I walked in my new shoes and my new dress with my new hair, and my new ME. I couldn't wait for people to see me, to see how much I'd changed, to hear what they'd say.

Mum and them were still camped under the same big gumtrees. I could see dogs playin' with a real little feller and a stick. The oldest dog lifted his head up, I could see his tail movin', then all of a sudden, he ran – flat out! Jumped all over me, and I was pushin' him down because I had this pretty dress on, and stockings and sandals.

I heard Mum call out, "Lie down!"

Then she came out of the tent.

I'm walkin' up singin' out, "I'm back. It's me."

Mum didn't say 'G'day' but "Gee, Ev, you look good," and that was what I wanted to hear. "You've got a bit fatter at last," and she's feelin' me arms, lookin' me up and down!

So I was the big conversation for a couple of weeks around the camp. "Seen Evelyn Mallyer, how she come 'ome from Sydney? Hair done and all dressed up..." and all I had was three new dresses!

Of course in them days none of the girls wore shorts about Bourke, and my green shorts with a cream top and green pocket and green buttons, green sandals to go with it – was the very latest! I was probably seen as a Paris Model, I know I felt like one.

I had the latest swimmers, too. We usually swam in our clothes and sat on the roots of the gumtrees to dry out. I didn't sit on just the gumtree any more, did I? I spread a **towel** on the roots and sat on it, a proper lady. I was beginning to get the attention of a lot of people and I really liked it. For the first time in my life I could think, "People are takin' notice of **me**. They know I'm 'ere, Evelyn Mallyer's 'ere." It was nice for the little while it lasted.

Now that Mrs Bloxham was better Mum asked me what I was going to do.

"I'll tell 'em to-morrow that I'm finishin' up."

So I told Mrs Bloxham, "I'm glad you're better, and now you are all back 'ere safe together, I'm goin' away."

"Where're you going, Ev? You've been with us a long time now. We don't want you to leave. We'll miss you."

"Just goin' away to see if I can get another job somewhere."

"But you've got a job here. Alan was going to get one end of the verandah fixed up so you could have your own room, and you could live here with us."

But after that stint in Sydney I'd had enough of living in close quarters with white people. I wanted to get out where I could stretch me legs, I suppose, and go back to some of the places where I'd lived as a skinny bony kid, and show 'em I was a young lady, a partly-grown-up person.

When I left her house Mrs Bloxham had a little bit of a cry. She said, "We'll miss you, Ev, and I don't think I'll be able to manage without you."

"Yeah, you will. The kids are big now, and you're better. But if you get sick again you go down to Mum. She'll know where I am, and I'll come back, I promise." And I meant it.

For a while I was just around at mum's camp, but I needed a job to get a bit of cash, and one of the Sisters at the Convent told me that the butcher's wife needed someone to do the housework and look after her three small kids while she worked in the shop. But doin' the same kind of thing again – that was no use to me.

I got a job on Mooculta Station, just out of Bourke on the way to Brewarrina. Alan Bloxham told me they were lookin' for musterers. I was able to buy two young horses and Mum gave me a pup for company.

When Mooculta cut out, I went to Kahmoo Station where Dad was workin' as handyman, thinkin' I'd maybe get work there. Dad didn't know me – this young lady! – even in me workin' togs. He kept commenting all the time how nice my hair looked, 'cos it was real thick, with waves in it. I was so proud of that hair – washed it every night with the shampoo stuff I'd bought in Sydney, but after a dust storm I'd have to wash all the sand out first and then use shampoo, or it just clogged up.

Then a drover, Les Girdler from Thargomindah, come through to pick up a mob of sheep. Girdlers always had over forty horses, and he was lookin' for a horse tailer, so I said to Dad that I'd like to go with them. At that time I was a bony little thing – still had to stand on a stump to get on a horse! This drover always had his wife with him, and his little kids. She said, "She'll be right with us, Jack. I'll look after her." She did, too, and I was a fully fledged drover by the time I left them.

I got very proud of bein' able to count stock in mobs, because in the droving camp, it didn't matter who you were, boy or girl, black or white, if you could count stock within the period of time you were allocated, say, an hour, you were a **genius**. Even though I'd found it real hard in school, there were no hassles if it was stock. You'd sit on your horse, and the person on the other side of you had a stick and a pocket knife. Every time you called, "Hundred", he'd cut a nick in the stick, and you knew that when you had ten hundred you had a thousand. It didn't matter if they came through in tens or twelves, I could still count 'em. There was a feller a bit further on doin' a double check, and most of the time my countin' would tally with what he had. I felt good.

From Girdlers I went to Cunnamulla to be near Dad who was workin' on Charlotte Plains near there.

All us young people waitin' for jobs were camped on the Warrego River above the town. Most had families with young brothers and sisters and knew if they stayed home they'd be eatin' food needed for the young ones, so they moved out to try to fend for themselves. The police encouraged us to camp together, 'cos that way they could easily let us know when there was work. There wasn't much work around, and the policeman was one of the first to know when anyone needed stockmen. The police sergeant at Cunnamulla was a good bloke. He'd ride up, "Come on, Joe . . . or whoever, I've got work for you," and Joe'd roll his swag and jump on his horse, glad to get it. So we were happy to stay in numbers where he could find us.

Livin' just down below us were two Irishmen, real Irishmen, that talked funny. We could hardly understand 'em. The oldest feller used to come along to our camp with a big silver pot of Irish stew. We thought, "That's only natural. Irishmen should cook Irish stew, Indians should cook curry. We eat kangaroos and emus 'cos we're Aboriginals." He'd give us this Irish stew, and it was beautiful. We were there a long time before we found out the meat in it was galahs! We were knockin' galahs down ourselves with sticks and stewin' them and curryin' them, but when we had a bit of money we'd go into the town and buy pig's trotters. We were just mad on pig's trotters.

One day I was in the town with a mob of the other kids. Mr Wiggins had the Drapery Store and I could spell his name because it was in big letters right across the middle window. The last window of his shop was clothes, and there was a beautiful pink dress with pleats all round it. Us girls were commentin' how nice those dresses looked. There were a couple of young fellers in Cunnamulla that started to look pretty good to me. I thought to meself, "Mmm-mm, I got the wavy hair, and the good legs, but I don't have anything special to wear. I need an extra nice dress to draw their attention."

The pink dress was seven pounds – almost a week's wages for a stockman, seven pounds that I didn't have. We were lucky havin' seven bob among the lot of us. [Before decimal currency, 20 shillings (a bob) made one pound.]

That afternoon I was layin' down under a tree, and heard horses slippin' down the high bank so I got up to have a look. All our horses were there havin' a drink at the soak we'd dug in the sandy bed, and a strange horse was with 'em, a big brown horse with a baldy face, four white feet, half-draught it was, and fat too. I waited till they'd had a drink, then I went down and was pattin' our horses who knew me. The new feller was real quiet, so I just slipped a bridle on him and led him back up to the camp. Along the river bank was thick ti-tree and we were camped in its shelter. I tied him up and thought to meself, "Mm-mm, I need a dress for seven quid. I'll sell this horse." I felt all over him till I found a brand – a wine glass and a bar underneath it.

I went down to the Irishmen, and asked, "You fellers got a horse?"

"No, burrs got him and poisoned him."

"Well, how c'n ya use that nice black sulky there when you got no horse. I got a horse I c'n sell ya."

"How much you wantin' for him, girlie?"

"Seven quid."

"Bring it down so we can see it."

Just on sundown I took the horse to their yard and I got the seven quid. Next mornin' I couldn't git up quick enough, off to Wiggins, bought the pink dress, and went to visit Dad's sister, Aunty Kate McCarthy, who lived on the Aboriginal Reserve at Cunnamulla. Aunty Kate knew I was camped up the creek and was glad to see me.

"We're 'avin' a claypan dance t'night, Ev. Stay and come with us."

"That'd be good," said I, as if I didn't know.

"You got a dress to wear?"

"Yeah, I got a dress." Didn't say it was a new dress, or how I got it!

There was one single tap where everyone got their water, carried it five, six hundred yards to the camps. That tap was at the cemetery fence, and everyone got their water **before sundown**. We carted water to the boiler on the fire so we could have baths for the dance, even though we were only dancin' on the claypan and ended up full of dust anyway. Off we went, me all dressed up in my pink dress. But that new dress didn't do any good for me. There was a couple of nibbles, but that was it – nothing

I could sort of git the hook into. So much for the pink dress.

About two o'clock in the morning I went back to Aunty Kate's, took off the dress, rolled it in a bit of brown paper, put it in my saddlebag and rode back to our camp at the soak.

About half-past-eight the next morning, when we were havin' a feed, someone said, " 'ere comes the *gunjabul*." The policeman was ridin' a big black high-steppin' horse, and smokin' the longest-stemmed pipe you ever seen.

"G'day, you lot. Eating pig's trotters again! You were eating them last time I was here. You'll be trotting too if you keep that up."

I was sittin' there chewin', sayin' nothin', thinkin', "Any minute now he'll say, 'Anyone seen a brown baldy-faced horse around?'"

But no. He said, "Got jobs for five of you."

When he named the places I said, "I'll take that one. My dad's workin' there."

"I reckoned you would. Right, you can have it."

I was glad to put space between me and that baldy-faced horse.

It was a real long time before I saw my mother again after I left Bourke, years it was. I was working in a contract mustering team on Talyealye Station on the Paroo. I didn't know it, but she was with Willie Dutton who worked there and they had two little boys, Lionel, who was about four and Trevor, a toddler.

It was the funniest thing, you know, the way I met Lionel that time. I was leadin' my horse towards the yard where they had some cattle penned. There was this little fat boy sittin' on the top rail. I said, "G'day!" He chirped, "G'day."

"What're you doin' there?"

"Lookin' at the cows."

"You'll fall in, and they'll walk on ya."

"Nah, they won't."

Just then I heard a woman's voice singin' out, "Come on, Lionel. Come and 'ave some dinner." So he climbed down and away he went. It never dawned on me that it was my mother, never recognised the voice, 'cos I wasn't thinkin about her. Before the little kid got to the camp she called out again, "'urry up, come on." An old dog ran out to find him, one of the dogs we'd had all our lives. I knew him straight away, even though he was pretty old and grey and limping. I sung out, "Red!" and patted me knee, and he come over and jumped all over me. I could hear my mother's voice sayin' "Who's that feller the dog's jumpin' all over? The dog must know him."

I called out, "Yeah, he knows me alright."

"Ev! Where'd you come from? . . . what're you doin' up 'ere? . . . 'ow long've you been 'ere?" All these questions . . . and in one breath!

I had no answers. I just looked at her. Lionel was talkin' up too, "What's your name? . . . who are you?" and Trevor was there, just hangin' on to her.

She said, "Where're you comin' from? Where you been?"

"Oh, just workin' around, all over."

"Still by yourself? . . . on your own, like a Mad Hatter?"

"Yeah, got a couple of dogs but."

It was awful, that feelin' I couldn't talk. I hadn't wanted to depend on anyone for anything. I didn't want to make friends because I thought, "What's the good of bein' friends with people, then all of a sudden they're gone and I'm back on me own again! If I'm on me own from start to finish, that's it."

I suppose I was afraid of being hurt again – more, I was afraid of bein' left behind again. I felt more secure with just me two horses and me dogs.

I worked in that mustering camp six weeks. We were way out in the back paddocks but we'd ride in at the weekends and I'd stay at the hut where Mum and the boys and their father lived. I made up me mind that I'd get to know the boys' father, what sort of a person he was. Willie Dutton was a full-blood *Wankamurrah* – the most likeable, friendliest man I've ever met. I got on real well with him. Gladys did later on too. When Mum was first with him, Gladys had thought she wouldn't like him before she even gave him a chance, so she went to live with an Aboriginal family at Tibooburra. We both had children before we seen each other again.

A couple of days before we finished musterin', a six-year old kid got lost, a little white boy. His dad worked on the station, lived there with his wife and three kids. This little boy was everlasting swingin' on the gates in the stockyards and sheepyards. It was shearing time, so the yards became very, very dusty, real thick in the air, almost like bull-dust. There was one very big gate, solid, not just rails, made of heavy beefwood. The kid was swingin' away by himself on the gate and somehow it must've fell on top of him. Us musterers were keepin' the yards full, so of course, with the dust, you didn't notice the gate had fallen down.

All the sheep we brought in that day – could've been sixteen, seventeen hundred of 'em, draggin' their feet and raisin' more dust – would've walked into the holding pens over that gate with the little kid lyin' underneath it. Nobody missed him until teatime. Then they were singin' out for him everywhere. People went along the river, and up in the paddocks. He had a dog, this kid, but the dog was on his chain while we were pennin' up because it was only young and like chasin' sheep. All that night they looked and never thought to let the dog go so **it** could find him.

All the next day everyone searched. The travellin' shearin' plant just turned the engine off and went lookin' for him. We looked everywhere.

On the second day, early in the morning, the kid's dog was howlin' and the father went over to give it a drink.

Then he thought, "I'll just let it loose. It can go to the
river and get its own drink." When he let the dog go –
even though it hadn't had a drink for a couple of days and
nights, everyone had been thinkin' only about the little boy –
it headed straight for the sheepyards. Uncle Willie Dutton
was near on his horse and he said, "Is that the boy's dog?"

"Yeah."

"This dog might be able to tell us where that kid is."

With that, he cantered off and followed the dog over to
the sheepyards. The dog jumped over the rails into the yard
and was sniffin' under that big old gate that was all covered
in sheep dung by then. Looked as if it had been layin' there
for ever. When Uncle Willie got off his horse and went to
see what the dog was sniffin' at, all he could see was a blue
shirt. By that time the little feller was pretty well flattened.
Uncle Willie yelled out to the man that he'd found him.

"What d'ya mean 'You've found 'im'? We've looked all
through these bloody yards for two days and nights."

"The little feller's here, mate, under the gate. I'm sorry."

The man couldn't go over to the gate. He went off in
a sort of staggery walkin' run back to the house to tell
his wife and stop her from comin' up. She must've been
on the verandah and seen him comin', or she seen all the
action and wondered what it was. I was sittin' on my horse
near the yard and by this time my heart was beatin' fast
too. The man hadn't got to the house when he just fell
on the ground – fainted, I suppose. The woman ran out,
then back into the house and come out again with a jug
of water, took her apron off, and was wipin' his face, talkin'
to him. I was too far away to hear the words. Uncle Willie
waited till the shearers came and they lifted the big gate
off. What stuck in my heart was that little boy had been
so close to us all the time, it was unreal. I don't know
if I walked on that gate while we were lookin'. I do know
I sat on the rail near it. And that was where I'd seen Lionel
when I come to Talyealye – he always played there too.

The travelling nursing sister came down from Hungerford and said the little boy would have died at once from the head injuries. They buried him on the property.

From Talyealye I went on down the Paroo to Mooleyarrah Station. Jack Scott who owned it was pretty sick so his son, young Jack, had leave from the army – it was war time of course – to put the shearing through. The shearing contractor was a feller called Danny Ryan. They were all nice people in that shed, no swearing, everybody had respect for everybody. But we all worked bloody hard, from the boss down.

He employed anybody he could git, so I got a job as part of the shed crew, not as a musterer. We camped near the yards, not far from the sheds – myself, Freddie Leppert, his sister Eileen and her husband, Roy Hunt, and old Jimmy Galton. Another Aboriginal feller was Syd Windsor, who lived at Cobar. He'd been at Mootawingee when we were there.

They taught me to pen up and draft sheep, to be a tar-boy, to pick up wool and throw fleeces for the wool classer – the whole works. I remember, after being shown about fifteen times, when I picked the first fleece up and threw it. The classer was a little white feller, very short, not much higher than the woolclassing table. I threw the fleece right over him!

He sang out, "Vat you doing, girl?" This little feller, they called him Nugget, was Jewish, and always smoked a big cigar... well, he'd have it in his mouth, but I can't ever remember seein' smoke comin' out of it.

I went from there to Wanaaring. They wanted a housemaid at the pub and I took the job. It was a change – found meself makin' beds, clearin' the tables, washin' pots, mainly sweepin' dust out.

It was near Christmas and we got a terrible lot of rain,

and there was rain up in Queensland too. The floods come down all the little rivers, then the Paroo got very, very high – the water was right up to the pub verandah. Wanaaring Station homestead was pisé, rammed mud like sandstone. It was on a little hill that floods had never reached before, but this time, when the water came and got about a foot up the homestead walls, they just collapsed on everything the poor people owned.

We ate whatever vegies were in the gardens, then we run out of potatoes. The only thing Bob Bent seemed to have plenty of in his new store was haricot beans. We used to soak 'em overnight, then boil up pots and pots of these beans, and mash 'em like potatoes, with salt and pepper and butter. They tasted quite good. We were like on an island so we couldn't get sheep for meat. There were goats on the hill with us, so we ate them and set traps for rabbits in the hop bushes.

Then New Year time came, and everybody was thinkin' about the New Year's party, which is a very traditional thing outback. Behind the hall were big coppers for boiling water, and tables made of bush timber. We decorated the place with all the bits of crepe paper we could git, and what gum leaves we could git, not much because most of the gumtrees were in the water.

New Year's Eve day, about two o'clock, everyone was hot from helpin' decorate. The shearers were swimming out the front, diving off the pub's verandah onto where the main road was under the water. Syd Windsor was there too, and he was drunk. I heard the others sayin' to him, "Don't go too far, Syd!" The Paroo is really just a creek, but in flood and runnin', it's a dangerous thing. Syd took no notice and kept walkin' on, past where the road had been. They yelled, "That's far enough . . . come back!" but he kept goin' and kept goin'. Then he wasn't there any more. He must've stepped off the bank into the main stream where the bank would normally have been six or eight feet high, and just went straight down.

Some of the shearers went and tried to feel for him, some ran to the Police Station, downstream about fifty yards. The policeman went in in his clothes, others went to where the town waterpump is, hopin' to catch him when the stream washed him past. But he wasn't anywhere to be felt. They dived in, but you can't see anything through muddy flood water.

I stood there, holdin' onto the windmill. I'd never seen anyone go into the water and just sink out of sight and never come up again. I just stood, thinkin', "How could that man just disappear like that? . . . not bob up and down where they could save him?" I'd got to know the old feller and become friends with him. He'd been tellin' me what he was goin' to buy his family when he got home, because he'd have money. He'd told me about the house he lived in, what Cobar was like. It took the shine off the New Year's Eve dance then, well, it did for me. I didn't even go. I think the only ones that went were those who would've gone just to get really drunk anyway. But the music played on until late.

Next morning, New Year's Day, we all followed the edge of the water – it was still rising – looking for any sign of him. All he'd had on was shorts, and by that time he would've been all muddy, same colour as the water. We walked right around the 'island' – no sign of him. It really saddened everybody, you could feel it in that tiny little town. It was fourteen days before the river started to go down.

Two white fellers found Syd's body while they were lookin' for stock. He'd been washed down right past the town, and his body was caught in the fork of a tree. There it was wedged and there it stayed till the water went down. The police went with them and got him down, dug a hole in the nearest part of the sandhill, and buried him there.

I moved on again. I was alright because I had a bit of money in me pocket. When you worked on a station you were paid at the end of the job. There was always a station store where you could buy anything you wanted, tucker, clothes, boots, hats. You bought your own gear and tucker, like tea and flour and sugar, salt and baking powder – no self-raisin' flour out there in them days – potatoes and onions, bottle of black sauce, tin of jam or syrup, couple of tins of meat. You didn't buy much meat 'cos you could always cadge a bit off the musterers' cook. Lots of station stores were better stocked than General Stores in many small towns.

When your work was finished on a property, they'd make up your account. All the money you'd spent on groceries, boots, hats, saddles or whatever, they'd dock from your pay and you got what was left.

I only spent on necessities, but if we were goin' to a Rodeo we'd all buy flash sort of things – fancy shirt, fancy hat, trousers that had a crease in 'em that would slice butter, and boots you could see your face in!

At that age, if you were well-dressed and could ride a buckin' horse, or any decent horse, that was the way to attract young Aboriginal males. When we started roamin' around as teenagers, it wasn't important to boys or young men, or to yourself, that you had a pretty dress or beautiful hair. Pretty dresses and hair-dos, lipstick and powder and ear-rings, fancy shoes and all that sort of thing – even a nice figure! – wasn't what got you a boy. My pink dress hadn't caught me one. What you could do as a horseman, that was the thing. I'd grown up around horses, and on the big properties there were always horses to be broken in. I could ride pretty good by then. So we went all out. Some of us nearly killed ourselves, literally killed ourselves, tryin' to prove that we could do these things. When I see the young girls today prettying themselves up, I think, "Gee, if it had only been as easy as that when I was tryin' to catch meself a boy!"

I was with Lizzie Bradley at Nuriootpa down in the Barossa Valley with a drovin' plant, havin' a look at that kind of country, so very different from the land I knew. There was a Rodeo on while we were there and you could win money. Our mustering job was finished so Lizzie and me took on ridin' with Tex Morton's Show.

One of the best riders there was a feller they called Gong. He was with the Australian Rough Riders Association. I didn't get to talk to him, but I knew he was good 'cos we watched him ridin' the buckjumpers out of the chute, and I knew I wasn't the only girl sittin' on the rails that day thinkin' he was pretty good. His real name was Raymond Crawford, and Gong was his Aboriginal name, that means 'very serious person'. He was a very quiet person, but he had the greatest sense of humour. But I didn't find that out till later. There was no thought of him as special at that time. He was just one of the boys we met.

Then I discovered other girls were sayin' he looked good, and I started lookin' at him through someone else's eyes and saw he **did** look good! That was why I stayed with the Rodeo, to follow, but not too close, just close enough to trip anyone who got in the way.

That went on for a long time and there was times when I wished I was as brave as the other girls, to go up to him and say, "Gee, that was a good ride . . . I thought you was gone when your boot slipped . . . you were great," but I never ever done it. I wondered what he'd say if I did, but I still stayed a bit back. And all the time I hung back, my mates seemed to be gittin' braver and closer, so I got to thinkin', "I'll have to make a bid here somewhere," 'cos it seemed I was leavin' the runnin' too late.

While we were with the Tex Morton Show I had some bad goes, one time hit up against the rails, another time a horse rolled on me. But you get up, achin' and painin' all over, but walkin' straight and as stiff as you can, pretending that it didn't hurt! And all the time you're thinkin', "I'll drop dead any minute. I wish I **was** dead and I wouldn't be feelin' all this pain!" That was to prove you could take as much as anyone. But I bet people knew how you really felt by the colour of your face. As teenagers we were too stupid to think of that! The code in the Rodeo was you didn't let anyone carry you off, or even see you limpin'. You'd get back up again and not even blink in case the tears started and washed you out of the saddle!

I guess that was another world I was tryin' to fit into, to become part of, from bein' on me own for so long. It was a wild world to want to be part of too, 'cos a lot of 'em drank and they fought... yeah, they were tough. But nobody seemed to be really hurt in the fights, and everybody looked after anyone hurt in a fall. What finished me with that Tex Morton camp was the cook. One day we saw him 'aving a real good wash in the big tin dish, latherin' up soap and all. Then he chucked out the water, just filled it up again, and put the corned meat in it to cook! So we headed back north.

It was shearing time again and Lizzie and me got work on Brindingabba Station, a huge property about thirty miles out of Hungerford towards Bourke. Lizzie was in the mustering camp and I was working the far back paddocks, a couple of days' ride out from the sheds. My job was to round up the sheep and drive them in towards the station so the musterers could bring 'em on to the sheds. You'd get goin' before daylight, because you had to keep feeding in sheep.

I was camped by myself in a boundary rider's hut. I had a real bad cold and nothing for it. No *gweeyuhmuddah* grows in that part. I got that sick I couldn't even pull me boots on – just managed to drag meself to the toilet, more than fifty yards away from the hut, outside in the cold. I'd eaten all the food I had, but I was too crook to cook anything even if I'd had it, and certainly too crook to eat it. Couldn't even make a fire for tea, just drank water. All I had to talk to was me dogs. All you could hear was the crows and a few birds, a dog barking every now and then.

I was on that bunk for four days. I could have done with some care from my mother, or my father, but at that particular time I didn't even know where they were. I never felt that bad that I'd die of sickness, but I certainly thought I'd die of loneliness.

When there were no more sheep heading in towards the station from my part of the run the musterers knew something must be wrong and someone came looking for me.

We rode back in to the station. My mother's aunty, Granny Moysey, with her daughter, Big Emily – the hugest woman I've ever seen – and her little grandson Badger, was living there so she took over the doctorin' of me. It was about five days before I hit the saddle again.

When we were out of work, we just unrolled our swags on the river bank, hobbled the horses and camped. Your swag had just about everything anyone would really need. You had a tarpaulin and blankets – four blankets were the limit you'd have in a swag, and they'd make a big one. Then your clothes, and if you were lucky, you had a pillow. If you didn't, you'd get a flour bag and stuff your good clothes in it, and when you got 'em out they were pressed because you'd had your head on 'em for weeks.

It was the cook's job to load everyone's swag on the truck before he moved on to set up the next camp. He'd growl something fierce about untidily-rolled swags, or bulky ones that were hard to throw up. It had to be real neat, so he could put his two hands under the straps and pitch it straight up onto the load. If anything fell out, some cooks were just as likely to leave the whole swag on the ground, and that night when you came into the new camp after workin' all day you'd have to ride all the way back to pick up your swag.

So you packed carefully, tarpaulin spread on the ground, with blankets and pillow in position, just as if you were gettin' into bed. Then clothes spread flat, hair brush, soap, towel – everything you owned went into that swag. Fold down the extra tarpaulin over the pillow part, fold in the two long sides, then roll it up like a sausage from the pillow end. Buckle two straps round it, and that's it. A spare coat could be tucked under the straps, and spare boots tied on, easy to get at. All your gear was safe in the one place then. Not that anyone in your camp would shake things, but if you lost something, you didn't know when you'd get money to buy another.

You slept on the ground. You'd have the tarp under you, but if it rained your blankets got damp, then when you rolled your swag, everything inside got damp, and the clothes you'd been ridin' in all day might be wet from the rain too. If you were lucky, if the cook was sociable and didn't mind you standin' round dryin' trousers and shirts while he was cookin', you could dry 'em at the fire, otherwise, those yesterday's clothes made your swag damp. Stupid mob we must've been – we never thought of makin' another fire just for dryin' our gear.

You couldn't say to the cook, "Look, mate, when you set up camp will you unroll my swag to dry out?" because nobody ever touched anybody's swag, or their saddlebag, the small one that was buckled on the back of your saddle. It hung on the left side of the horse's flank, and your quart pot, with your pint inside it, on the right. When you were away workin' all day you carried your own lunch and water with you. You had a canvas water bag that could hold about two gallons. It buckled round the horse's neck and hung down in front. On a quiet horse you just left it hang, but if you had one that jumped about, you hooked a strap onto the bottom of the bag, brought it between his front legs and buckled it to the surcingle under his belly. Then you could gallop and the bag wouldn't move. Bigger waterbags went on the pack horses. They were five gallon cans with big buckles that went onto special hooks on the pack saddle. Then a strap went right over them and fastened underneath so they wouldn't flap and move about. I tell you those filled cans were real heavy to lift onto the hooks. Everything was done with leather, so you took good care of all your harness.

You took on any sort of work. If you didn't have anything to do you felt out on your own, but if you had work there was always someone to talk to and you were part of things.

One day I was sitting on me horse in the street in Brewarrina and a feller came along and said, "We want a kitchenmaid at the pub. Interested?"

I needed a job so I said, "Yeah, I'll take it. When do I start?"

"In the morning."

I got off the horse and said to a mate, "What's a kitchenmaid?"

"Dunno, Ev, but you're it!"

So that was it. I got up early next day, fed me horses, took 'em along the creek, hobbled 'em out and went to work.

The cook there was an Aboriginal person, Aunty Ada. She said, "You gotta wash up the pots, and peel the vegies, and all that kind of thing." I thought, "This is great. No workin' in the hot sun." But after a while I didn't like workin' in that hot kitchen either! I learned a lot from Aunty Ada – how to make custard without it bein' all lumps, how to make pastry. She was a marvellous cook and she taught me well.

# PAIRING UP

*'Who's gonna marry **me**?'*

Everyone around me seemed to be getting married, and when one of the other girls workin' at the pub got married too I thought, "Gee, it must be about time for me."

People started askin', "You got a boyfriend, Ev?"

"Nah, I haven't got a boyfriend. I got a lot of mates."

They were the fellers I worked with. They shared your boots, hats and things like that. If one was goin' into town he might say, "You've got new boots, Ev. Lend 'em to me, I'm takin' a girl to the pictures." So I'd put the holey boots on and he'd take the new ones. It was only sometimes you never got them boots back!

"Isn't it about time you got a boyfriend?" they'd say.

"Yeah," I'd say to shut 'em up, but I'd be thinkin', "What the hell would I do with a boyfriend?"

Now, there's a code in a drover's camp. You're not girls and boys – just working men together. They were people who'd grown up to respect that way of livin' so you become like a big family. They're like your brothers and sisters, because you're workin' with them all day and every day. Some of the boys would have a go, joking-like, at the white girls in the camp. If you had to ride in to a homestead to ask permission to travel through, they'd be sayin' things like, "Ah-h-h, we seen that bloke winkin' at you . . . he's the station owner's son!"

At that time during the war there was heaps of work drovin' for anyone who wanted it, boy or girl, man or woman. The meatworks at Bourke canned meat for the army, and needed stock brought in.

After I left the pub job I went back to where Dad was working and one day he said to me, "When're you gittin' married, Ev?" I just laughed. "Who's gonna marry **me**?" I was beginning to think I was gettin' left behind, especially as all me cousins were gettin' married, and I was older than some of them.

A white man had wanted me to marry him. We were very good friends, and we could have been more than friends, if I'd've just let meself go and forgotten I was an Aboriginal. But we'd been brought up strict in Aboriginal law, and it's the whole support for your life. But just sometimes it becomes like a steel band around you, 'n you feel like it's chokin' you off from things you'd like to do. You'd try to say to yourself, "There's no 'arm in doin' it," but because I was punished as a kid for doin' the wrong thing, – the 'not-Aboriginal' thing – I just couldn't break the Aboriginal laws set down for marriage and family. I knew it would be a wrong thing for **me** to do. It seemed that the only person who wanted me I couldn't have because he was a white feller! It wasn't that I didn't like him. I really did, and thought a lot of him. I thought, "There's no 'ope for me.

I'll end up a dried-up stick out in a paddock somewhere, with the crows sittin' on me."

In families like ours, that reared their kids in the traditional Aboriginal way, when the old ones in your family arranged that you were to marry a particular person, it was a **well-kept secret**. Nobody was to know till you was told about it, by the right person at the right time. Kids weren't told till they were considered old enough to be able to handle that sort of news. And because both of us – me and the feller they'd planned for me to marry – were droving all over the country we were both older than the age when we should have been told.

Well, that day when I said, "Who's gonna marry **me**?" Dad said, "You know, Ev – that feller who wins at all the Rodeos – you know Gong Crawford."

Until now, in the 1990s, I've never even wondered about how my family got to know Gong's family. It was just a fact of my life. We're different tribes – I'm *Baarkanji* and Gong's *Camilleroi*. He was born on the Cato Creek at Brewarrina, on Armstice Day, 11th of November, 1920, but his people came from near Warren, on the Macquarie River. I guess they must have planned it while we were on the Mission, because the Crawfords lived on Quantambone Station and Dad worked there, walkin' four miles each way every day from the Mission.

Like every other young person, I didn't believe a lot of things people told me, and so I said, "Dad, you must be jokin'! Not me! I'm not marryin' a person I don't really know!" I couldn't see myself married to Gong because he was a much different person to me. When I was in a drovin' camp, everyone knew I was there – I inherited that off my mum – and he was so quiet. I thought, "How could I live with a feller like that – wonder if he'd even answer if I spoke to him." After Dad dropped that bomb I wondered over and over why Mum hadn't told me before she went away, but I suppose she thought I was still too young. But she still didn't say anything even when I met her years later.

I waited around at the trucking yards after that, thinking there'd sure to be a drover who was goin' way up to buggery. "I'll go with him," I thought, "and git well away from this marryin' business."

But I kept crossing that Crawford boy's tracks.

I remember once working in a camp when we ran out of salt. They'd killed a bullock and needed it, so they said, "Ev, you ride back to the next camp and get some." When I got there, I sung out, "Who's here?" and the person who came round, hobblin' on a forky stick, was this Gong Crawford.

I asked, "Where's the cook?"

"Ridin' instead of me. I had a bad buster, brute of a horse crushed me leg against a tree. There's only me 'ere."

"I've come for some salt."

"Alright," he says. "Aren't ya goin' to get off the horse?"

Grannies always tell you, because you're a girl, "Don't speak to anybody you don't know. If you go to a strange place, stay on your horse."

"No, I'm right." I knew what kind of a rider he was, I didn't know what kind of a **person** he was.

"Well, I can't climb up in the buggy and get the salt. You'll have to get it yourself. The billy's on, and there's some brownie there."

"I'll be breakin' a rule." What those grannies told you stuck for life!

"You're alright. Don't worry about me."

I thought, "Yeah, I'll be alright with this feller, he's got a limpy leg . . . I could git away from 'im easy."

So I got down and had some tea.

He said, "What's your dog's name?"

I told him and said, "What's your horse's name?" I always laugh about that – what a silly conversation, eh! Then I heaved the bag of salt onto the tailgate of the buggy, got on my horse, dragged the bag across the saddle, said, "Thanks very much," and off I went.

I used to think about him a lot after that, wonder if the poor bugger was alright. I ran into him later at Blackall, when he could walk but was still limping badly. There was only just time to say G'day, 'cos I was in the truck with the drovers' cook and we'd come in for food, and were off again.

On another drovin' trip when we were out three days on the road the boss said, "We've got some more men comin' out. We'll need 'em with fourteen hundred head to take, and they're all big bullocks." And who should turn up as one of the new hands but that feller, Gong Crawford! One night we were all sittin' round the fire and Gong said to me, but everyone could hear, "One of these days I'm gonna marry you." The drover's cook was there, and they're real jokers, those fellers. So he chipped in. "What d'ya mean, you're gonna marry Ev?"

"Well, our law says she's gotta be my wife."

"Dunno what Ev'll have to say about that, mate. She's as wild as a March Hare."

I got my bit in then! "I know what Ev'll have to say. I'm not marryin' anyone!"

Gong didn't say anything to that.

I couldn't believe it. I admired Gong, because he was a good buckjump rider, and a nice-lookin' person, but I didn't know him real close, not like you'd want to know the feller you're goin' to marry!

It was unbelievable, to pass this one person so many times, and I got that way that I was sort of lookin' forward to seein' him. When anyone would say, "There's drovers up the road," I'd think, "Wonder if that boy's with 'em?" Then I'd find myself bein' disappointed if he wasn't, and wonder why the hell I was disappointed not seein' this feller I said I wasn't goin' to marry anyway!

We got then that when our tracks crossed we got real

close, **real close**! We camped together, and Maree was born in 1946.

We took work wherever we could get it, together or in different places.

When we were both on Charlton Downs Station, out of Charleville, I was on a horse that played up all the time. One morning it danced around and swung itself against the fence of the horse-yard and jammed my leg. I got a bad gash over ten inches long right down the front of my shin. In my boot I could feel all this warmth – it was full of blood. I was cut to the bone literally and the bone itself was split. There were a couple of young horsebreakers with me but they didn't know what to do. They went up to the homestead and the missus gave them an old sheet and some metho. She thought it was just another cut, I didn't go near her myself.

As carefully as I could with the point of me pocket knife I poked out chips of bone, and with a big needle picked out splinters and splinters and splinters off the rails. It was that sore I didn't really feel meself pokin' round in it. Ruined me good pocket knife, it did, burnin' the point black. Burnt the temper out of it, so I couldn't sharpen it after that. That leg wouldn't heal up. The cook at the station said to wash it with plenty of bore water. When I did I thought my head would bust with the pain. Sleep – there was no such thing.

That injury really got at me because I lost a terrible lot of weight. I was lucky I hadn't got blood poisoning, but I'd used the *gweeyuhmuddah*. I still went to work. Gong kept sayin' to me, "Look, stop home. You'll fall off the horse and away by yourself no one'll know where you are." But I hung in though someone had to throw the saddle up for me and tighten the girth. I think I only missed work three days, when it first happened. The Aboriginal woman who did the homestead washing minded Maree. She was very little, just crawling.

*Chris during a 'recording' session with Evelyn near Brewarrina*

*Evelyn Crawford, 1990*

Above: Gong at West Bre. 'All his life sat on a horse.'

Right: 'I wasn't the only girl thinkin' Gong Crawford looked pretty good.'

*Bill Rose with Jess. 'That white man played a very important role in my life.'*

*'I took Cousin Freddie fishin' not long before his death.'*

Granny Moysey – 'keeper of the knowledge and enforcer of the law'
Photo courtesy of Bob Wilson, Wilcannia

Evelyn telling Jess about ancient
Aboriginal artefacts. Lake Wilcannia,
1979

From left: Jess, Dinty, Raymond and Paul
Baker and Roxanne, on Dinty's white
horse, Prince

*Grandfather Hero Black at the opening of Aboriginal housing, Wilcannia, 1950*
*Photo courtesy of Bob Wilson, Wilcannia*

*On the swing outside the 'do-it-yourself'*
*house. Guy, Verina, Dinty, Bimbo and*
*Chooby*

*Evelyn with sister Gladys, and brothers Trevor, Neville and Lionel, c.1985*

*From left: Maree, Lesley, Ev, Cheryl (Dinty), Evelyn Jnr (Tiny), Rebecca (Tilly), Diane (Bimbo) Verina (inset) took the photograph*

*Smiley (Guy)*

*Alan*

*Jack (Raymond)*

*Jess*

*Rocco (Rodney)*

*Chooby (Val)*

*Aboriginal fisheries at Brewarrina. 'Our kids caught big fish with their hands so we could eat.'*

*'I've always like drawing, and to think you could draw on bark with mud!'*
*One of Ev's paintings, donated to the Broken Hill City Art Gallery*

When our job on Charlton Downs cut out we camped at the Cato on Quantambone Station where Gong got a job mustering. One day at dark he still hadn't turned up back at our camp. He'd left his black Kelpie, Jock, at home, so I let him go to track his boss. I put Maree on my saddle, and we followed Jock. It was pretty tough followin' a black dog in the dark!

We found Gong lyin' on the ground. His horse had shied at a snake, got tangled up in some barbed wire and had fallen.

I said, "C'n ya git up?"

"Nah, I'm pinned on this thing – can't move or turn." What I couldn't see in the dark was that he'd fallen sideways onto a stump that was split off about a handspan above ground. It went right into his hip and made a hole in the bone.

The poor horse was still down, squealin' and strugglin', because the wire was round his legs, and the more he struggled the tighter the wire become. Maybe it was just as well, or he could've kicked Gong to death.

I got two sticks the size of crowbars and put them under Gong's ribs and levered him up. When he was off the stump I felt the warm blood gush over my hand. He slithered over onto the ground and I felt the stump against my boot. The sharp point was much thicker than my thumb.

Gong said, "Roll me over on me side and stuff something in to stop the bleedin', then ya c'n go and git help."

I tore off my shirt-tail and rolled it up, put it in, and it was too small. Had to pull it out, put more on – it seemed like half my shirt and half of his – made a plug and sort of pushed it in. The doctor told me I did damage by pushing more wood into the wound, but he wasn't there to see the bleeding. I had to stop that first. I dragged Gong away from where the trapped horse was goin' mad, thrashin' around still tangled up in the wire.

"I think I c'n get on the horse now."

"Don't you move! You might bleed to death before we get you to the station."

I put Maree on the ground, and told Jock to mind her. He was a working dog, and hadn't had much to do with her, but there were times when he'd walk past and give her a bit of a lick. I put her hand in his collar and told him to 'stay', so I could let him know that he was to look after her. Then I lit out in the dark for the station. They all got in the trucks and we came back, heaps of us. They put Gong on the truck, and some attended to the horse that was bleedin' so bad they had to shoot it. Jock hadn't moved from the baby. They took Gong on to the hospital while I rode with Maree down to our camp, left the horse, walked out to the road and the other truck picked me up and took me into town. By the time I got to the hospital Gong was unconscious from loss of blood. They looked after him in that hospital for nine weeks. Delirious he was, callin', whistlin' to his dogs, then all of a sudden he'd recognise me.

I moved into Bre and camped over at the Fisheries, near Gong's sister, Priscilla and her husband, Dummy Smith. They wanted me to stay with them but I was determined to be independent. Gong's brother Tom and Dummy set up the tent for me in our own spot. I had no money, but Gong had good working dogs. A station owner hired them out, weeks at a time, especially at mustering. He'd use 'em to bring sheep in to Brewarrina, and those stockmen-dogs would bring their cheques home. Jock would work well for anyone, but the best of them was Peter, a black and tan Kelpie, and that feller wouldn't work for nobody, only just me and Gong. So there was times I'd go out working Peter, so the three of us were earnin', not just Jock.

I'd take Maree with me, and we'd camp by ourselves, even though the station owners' wives would be wantin' me to camp on their verandah, or offerin' to mind Maree for me. When Gong was out of hospital, but still not able to work, I'd leave her with him, but if I was near enough I'd ride home for the weekend.

We managed.

In 1948, about November, Gong and me had an Aboriginal marriage.

There was a big ceremony meeting, three days of it, and late into each night. We didn't go to Mootawingee or anything, but we met up on the reserve at Bourke with Mum and Dad and my three brothers and their father, Willie Dutton, and all my aunties and uncles left in the family. The special elder in my family was my mother's oldest sister, Auntie Eva, Fred Leppert's mother. Gong's mum was dead and his old white dad said he didn't want to mess around with blackfeller things, neither did his brother, Swinger, or his sisters. His other brothers, Tom and Dickens, really loved Gong, but they were away working.

Gong told me, "I was shivering in me boots. I jist wanted to git married and git away, not be swarmed over by the whole mob." But it wasn't as bad as he'd expected. In the old traditional Aboriginal marriages you gotta cut your head with a boomerang so you bleed. Even at that time his hair was fallin' out and he thought they might've cut more than they should! It wasn't like that at all. It was more like the white man's ceremony when someone gets up and welcomes this new bride or groom into the family as a new son or daughter, or a new brother or sister. It was him spending a lot of time away with my uncles, men's talk – them tellin' him about our *Baarkinji* part of it, and what was expected of him. I never knew what they talked about, and I never asked him, just waited for him to tell me what he could – and he never did! When we meet up in heaven, I might be brave enough to ask him, along with a few other questions.

After all that long time of talkin', we both had to stand up together and the parents and the special elder said things like, "Evelyn, you look after Gong," and "Gong, you look after Evelyn".

My family were disappointed that there was nobody from his family to talk to me, and so was Gong. That day he said to me, "Looks like you're the only mate I've got." I said, "Yeah," but I was young and didn't really understand till a lot later how hurt he must've been.

There was so much about Gong's culture I should have been told at that time but didn't learn till well into our life together, as Gong passed it on to our kids. Those boys of mine, right from when they were little toddlers, if they want to give me anything, they don't put it in my hand. They put it on the table for me, or give it to somebody else to give me. I do the same to them. I can be standing there and one of them'll say, "Give this to Mum." Someone who's maybe visiting 'll say, "You c'n give it to her yourself. She's just there. You blind or somethin'?" But if his sisters are there they'll just take it from him and give it to me. That's their father's culture. I don't know the reason for it.

After our marriage we both took a droving job with Girdlers.

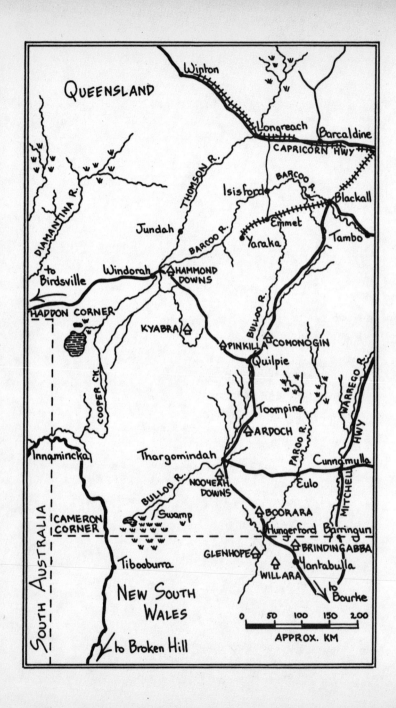

# ON THE TRACK

*'I never thought*

*I'd make it back'*

Les Girdler had a contract to bring over two thousand cattle from the railhead at Yaraka in Queensland to the meatworks at Bourke. I was horse tailer, along with bandy-legged old Aboriginal Jimmy Galton and a young red-headed white feller, taking forty-two horses ahead of the main plant. Girdler had an army truck, so old they had to keep workin' on it as they travelled so they needed all the strong people with them to help. Gong and four other drovers had ridden ahead to take delivery of the cattle and load 'em at the start of the branch line.

Maree was about two and she could talk like anything. She got into all the strife you could imagine – and some you couldn't – because I was only a brand-new mum, and I didn't know how to look after a brand-new baby. I had to find out the hard way, and poor old Maree must have suffered. I wouldn't leave her with anyone except Gong. I'd be thinkin', "What if we come back and she's not there . . . what if we can't find her . . ." Kids are too precious to lose.

Before he left Gong had said, "Whatever you do, don't put that kid in the saddlebag, because the horse could run away with her. You wouldn't know where she'd end up." Now the saddlebag on the pack-horse was a good place for the kid. It's pretty big, you could put toys in with her, a bit of bread, a titty-bottle. She could have stretched out easily to sleep. But I said, "No, I won't do that." South of Yantabulla we went into a bore to water the horses, and with the mob of 'em it was a pretty long job. It was hot! I said to Maree, "We're in the paddock now. You sit in the bag and play while we water the horses, then I'll get you out and chuck you in the trough, and you can have a swim."

The first horses watered quietly, but then a couple reared up – a snake slithered from near the trough! Off round the tank went the lot, **and** the pack-horse, with Maree sittin' up in that bag, cryin'!

There was this kid in the bag, only the head and one arm stickin' out, singin' out, "Mu-u-u-m-m! Mu-u-u-m-m!" The more the kid screamed, the more the bloody horse went silly.

Jimmy Galton was singin' out too. He had a very, very loud voice, this Aboriginal feller, 'cos since he was a little boy he was trained to be a singer of songs for Corroborees. There was horse bells clangin', Maree cryin', Jimmy singin' out, me yellin', "Grab the horse, grab the horse," and all the cattle dogs barkin' just for the fun of it! Bedlam!

The pack-horse got into a corner and the other horses hemmed it in. I jumped off my horse and ran in among them, grabbed Maree by the collar of her shirt to lift her out, and the horse pulled and got away. I was left standin' there, the kid still in the saddlebag cryin', and all I had was the collar! While I was runnin' after the horse, I was sayin' to myself, "Gong'll kill me, for sure. I won't tell him about this, I won't tell him." But Maree could tell him for herself, even though she was still small. Anyway, Jimmy caught the horse and got her out. After that, she wouldn't go near the saddle bag, even when it was on the ground, not even to get something she wanted.

When we got to Yantabulla, we needed meat. The only meat they had at the little store – still leanin' there – was bully beef in tins. We camped a couple of days to make dampers, so we wouldn't have to keep pullin' up to cook. In the night we just ate while we rode along.

Ahjune, the Afghan hawker, was at Yantabulla when we got there. I bought a pretty dress for Maree. She liked it, and in the morning when we were packing up she said, "What I do with my *gumbi* (dress)?" I was busy and not really lookin' at her, and said, "Throw it in the fire if you like!" And she did! I didn't know then that little kids took literally what you said to them. I could have kicked myself. Ten and sixpence it cost, and that was a **lot** of money – half a day's pay for me. I really couldn't afford even the sixpence, but I suppose I bought it after the fright we'd had a few days before.

Past Yantabulla, the Cutterburra was just a few damp holes, so we had to scout up and down for water. Many a time I said to meself, "What the bloody hell am I doin' here, when I could be back at Bourke sittin' under a tree!"

At Waroo Station just short of the Queensland border they gave us a lot of fruit. We weren't used to fresh fruit, so you know what that did to our insides! We had to keep stoppin', and it really slowed us down till we got to Hungerford. They kept old Jimmy at the pub because he was really sick. I went to the Police Station and asked if we could put the horses in the police paddock. His wife asked me where I was campin'.

"I camp where the horses are."

"They'll be alright shut in the paddock. You can come up and sleep with the little one in the bed on the verandah."

That night we had a great time – the lady fed us, and played the piano for us.

The next morning when I woke up it was real late. I went in to her kitchen. "You should've woke me up."

"No, Dan said you looked so tired I was to let you sleep."

"Where's me little girl?"

"Oh, they went down to the shop in the old car. Dan took her for the ride."

She came back beaming, two packets of Arrowroot biscuits under her arm. We stayed there a couple of days waiting for Jimmy's belly to settle down, but then he said, "I'm too sick to go on with you, Ev. I'll wait here for a while, then I'll catch you up." The young feller, Bluey, said, "I'm goin' back to Bourke. This kind of life is no good to me." I was thinkin', "And you're not much good to it, mate," but all I said was, "That's a sensible idea." Jimmy said, "You better have two, three days more here, Ev, and get a good rest. From here on, you're in dingo country, and them wild dogs'll frighten the horses. Hobble the horses and camp a long way off, near a big tree. That way, if the dingoes start 'em up you can get behind the tree, 'n they'll go round ya."

I had my two sheep dogs and Girdler's five cattle dogs, Queensland Heelers. Girdler's dogs were well known for driving horses by themselves, he trained them specially. They were as good as any man on horseback, and the horses knew them, so I felt I could cope by myself.

I left Hungerford, crossed the Paroo, and set off in a pretty straight line for Thargomindah, about 150 miles. About three days on I came to Boorara, a real big sheep station. They had a **big** market garden and, like many properties in them days, had Chinamen working as gardeners and cooks – whole families of Chinamen.

I said to Maree – 'cos I had to talk to someone – "We'll find the creek and camp." There was a deep waterhole so the horses filled up, had a swim, then started feeding. Maree had a swim, and I made a bed for her under a tree in the shade and she went to sleep. My old dog Susie was there with her, and I knew I could trust her. So I thought, "I'll have a swim too." But it didn't turn out like that.

That waterhole was only about five hundred yards from the homestead, but thick scrub all round. So I went in to swim with nothing on – all I had on was me hair, and on the track that was pretty short, like a boy's. It was great in the lagoon, then I could hear the dogs barkin', and when I looked, there was this young white feller, a jackeroo, sittin' on a horse! I was sinkin' right down in the muddy water, thinkin', "How the hell am I goin' to get out of this? His horse is standin' right near my clothes."

He said, "Hello, what're you doin'?"

"Swimmin'," I said in a big deep voice.

"Good idea. I might have a swim too." Then he looked and said, "Oh, you're a girl."

I growled, "No, I'm not."

"I'll have a swim with you, mate." So he got down off his horse, took his hat off and started strippin'.

I thought, "What am I gonna do?"

He come into the water and I swum across to the other side, and **ran!** He must've been able to swim like a bloody duck 'cos he was right behind me! When I looked, there was this young naked white feller runnin', flat to the boards! And here was me headin' for the Chinaman's kitchen at the homestead.

I tore into the kitchen – nothing on – the old Chinaman was wiping a dish and he's singin' out, "Where you go, girl? Where you go?" and he threw his teatowel over me chest. Then his wife called out, "Here, look, comin' in here . . ." and here's this young white feller runnin'. Just then the boss's missus come around and shouted, "Where're you going, Bert, without your clothes?" He went green, red and all colours, he did, all over. There I was, crouching behind this big meatsafe with the cook's teatowel over me front!

The Chinaman ran out to her, yellin', "He chasee girl, he chasee black girl!"

"What black girl? There's no black girls here."

"Yeah, yeah – in my kitchen – naked black girl in my kitchen!"

She came in and saw me. "What're you doing?"

"Hidin', missus."

"Where's your clothes?"

"Back on the other side of the creek where that cheeky white feller chased me."

"What were you doing, swimming without your clothes?"

"There wasn't nobody around. How was I s'pposed to know he'd come along and do a thing like that?"

So she hunted him down to the lagoon to get his clothes. The old Chinese woman, big as I am now, come out with a green dress that smelt like garlic. The missus asked me to stay for a feed, but I said I had to go straight back, because I remembered Maree asleep under the tree. So she said, "Come on up when you're ready to leave."

I went back, barefoot, of course. I think I trod on every bloody burr goin' back, but I'd been runnin' too fast to feel 'em on the way in. I had to swim the lagoon, and when I got back Maree was still asleep, and **all** the dogs were mindin' her! While I was gettin' dressed, I said to meself, "That's the end of you swimmin' with no clothes on! The next time you get under the overflow of the bores, my girl, you stay dressed, even if you think there's no one for hundreds of miles."

When Maree woke up, I did go up to the homestead and stayed a couple of days. They helped me put the horses in the paddock so I didn't have to hobble them. Thank God for that break, I needed it. Maybe that young white feller did me a good turn, but I didn't see him again – he kept well out of my way. The Chinaman fed us well, good fresh tucker after all that bully beef.

I went on then to Priora Station. I left the horses down

at the bore and rode up to the homestead, with Maree on the front of my saddle, to ask leave to travel through. The boss had an old spinster sister who used to be a Welfare Officer. In them days the Welfare people were pretty strict and seemed to pop up everywhere, like bad pennies. I was always scared they'd try to take Maree, even though she was a fat, well-cared-for little baby, with nice dresses and clothes.

The first thing that woman said was, "What're you doing with that baby on your saddle?"

"She's my baby."

"Are you married?"

"No, I'm not married." Well, not the way she meant, anyway.

"Where's the baby's father?"

"At Thargomindah, where I'm goin'."

She thought there was just me and the baby, the dogs and my one horse. She'd have had a fit if she'd seen the mob of horses. All these questions, and she'd never seen me before. And I answered her, because I'd grown up thinkin' white people had a right to question me about anything.

"Well, we'll see what we can do. What's your name?"

"I haven't got a name," I snapped at her. I'd had enough.

Her brother said, "Look, just leave her alone. She's got work to do, hard work. They rang me from Boorara this morning to say you were coming through, and that you were travelling alone. Do you want some hands? We've got a couple of blokes here I can spare."

I thought to meself, "No way in the world do I want any more white blokes!" but I just said, "No, thanks, I've got dogs, Girdler's dogs. I'm right."

He gave me a sugarbag of cold meat, tomatoes and stuff and I went back to the bore, boiled the billy and we had a feed. I said to Maree, "We'll push off now and keep goin' till we get to your dad."

Two more days and nights it took to get to Thargomindah.

I think I dozed on the horse, hardly lay down. I took the mob up to the horse yards near where Girdlers lived and heard someone yell out, "Here's Ev with the horses." It had taken us about five weeks to get to Thargomindah from Bourke. It was early afternoon when I went to sleep. I had no worries about Maree – didn't wake up until six o'clock the next morning! While we were at Thargomindah I had plenty to do, the horses still to look after, and Mary Girdler was five or six weeks off a new baby, with four kids and Maree in the house. I was always that tired I could go to sleep standing up.

We stayed there about a week while they finished getting all the gear ready. But I had to get on ahead with the horses, so Les said, "Leave Maree here with Mary and our kids."

I said, "I don't know about that, she's got enough to do."

"And so have you, and one kid more won't make any difference here."

So I let him persuade me, but I missed her. We travelled so many miles together, me and that kid, just the two of us. She was like the best of me, I think.

I was really by my own self, because I was still waitin' for Jimmy to get better. I'd only camp at dinner time. In the middle of the day when it's real hot, horses pull up to sleep, so I'd sleep too, and as soon as they started pokin' about, their bells would ring and I'd wake up and get goin'. All night they could walk, so I wasn't havin' much more than a couple of hours' sleep each day.

At Ardoch Station, about fifty miles up the Bulloo, they were waiting for the Flying Doctor. At the back of Ardoch there's big canegrass lakes that go right back and there were still bloody wild Aborigines livin' out there. The boss and the overseer had gone out there, and were speared in the legs, I don't know why. They'd been lying out in the open for days before they were found, and the hot sun had got to them. One of them was all puffed up, looked terrible, I thought he was already dead.

I followed up the Bulloo then, goin' to Quilpie. On the way I passed a boundary rider's hut across on a hill, with a big red blanket hangin' on the clothes line – you could see it for miles. I'd like to have gone across to see if there was a woman there to have a bit of a yarn, but I couldn't take my eyes off the horses because the scrub was so thick. So I kept pushing right on to Quilpie and waited for the rest to catch me up.

My next halt was on stony hill country at Pinkilla Station. The creeks were all dry, so I had to look for native wells. Good thing I'd learnt that at Mootawingee!

All day and half the night it took me to water those forty-two horses, with just a billycan to draw it up with. I dug a kind of little channel from the mouth of the well to a big hollow and poured can after can after can of water into it. I filled the mob right up because I didn't know where the next water would be. When we moved on I could only walk the mob, couldn't let 'em work up a sweat. Even the dogs were slowin' down. Everybody was gettin' dehydrated.

The sandy ground was hot as a stove plate so the fellers had made little leather boots for the dogs – like mittens with holes to let the toenails stick through. I laced them on, and I had seven dogs! Dogs'll pull things to pieces, chew off a bandage, but not one of them ever attempted to pull the laces out of those leather boots. They must've felt good to them, and protected them from burrs as well. Sometimes a burr would get between their foot and the boot and you'd see 'em limping, so you'd get down and help them. Off would come the boot and you'd clear it out for them. I really depended on my dogs.

I was getting into parts where I'd never been before, tellin' meself, "I'm gettin' into country where the wild blackfellers are." So I'd sleep in the day, and ride all night. While the horse bells were ringin', everything was right, but if I didn't hear that, the quietness would make me prick me ears and think, "What's goin' on? There's somethin' wrong somewhere."

I kept ridin' the same couple of horses, 'cos one I didn't know so well could've thrown me, and I could have been lyin' there for days. I always had a fear of ants gettin' all over me if I had a buster, 'cos if you bleed, the first thing that finds you is ants. I talked to those two horses a lot, 'specially old Bet. I'd give 'em a bit of johnny cake, even a potato now and then, which I shouldn't, 'cos they were precious. Those two old horses were company, like my own two dogs. The other five dogs were really just workers.

A couple of days before I got to Yaraka, I come to a creek, 'n it was **full** of water, runnin' so fast I couldn't swim the horses. I was gettin' a bit pushed for time to meet that cattle train but I still had to camp on the wrong side of that creek. It was a flash flood – comes so fast and goes just as fast. Blackfellers know that, so they'd never try to cross a flooded creek. They just sit down till the water goes. It's the white feller that gets himself drowned, like that Harry Dale, the Drover, in the poem. If he'd been an Aborigine, he'd have got home to marry his girl.

The next morning I woke up and – no water! I took the horses on to the little town where the railhead is. Bad drought time and hardly any grass.

All the people there must have been tall people. I bought myself trousers and a shirt, but the only shirt I could get was big and baggy, and the trousers – they fitted around the waist, but the legs were about ten inches away from my foot along the ground! All I had to hack 'em off with was a pocket knife!

I was talkin' to the store keeper outside the shop and I could see the top of a cowboy hat near the cowyard, and his wife come around the corner, this ta-ll-ll woman in long trousers and big high-heeled cowboy boots . The only other woman I've spoken to as tall as her was Margaret Whitlam. That store lady wore the biggest glasses and I thought, "You poor woman! You must be nearly blind." When she took them off her eyes looked real small.

"Where you going, girl?" she asked me.

"I just brought horses up from Thargomindah. I'm waitin' for Les Girdler."

"Oh, yeah. That'll be for those cattle they're bringin' down from Winton in the train – about two thousand, I hear. You just want to hope Girdler gets here first, girl, or you'll have all them wild bullocks to look after.

"Some of our blokes are travellin' with them. I'll be right."

"There's no water here and the tanks are goin' dry."

"Yeah, well, I can only wait."

"Have you had a feed?"

"Yeah."

"What did you have?"

"Bit of tinned meat and some johnny cake."

"Bloody johnny cake! Come in, girl, and I'll give you some yeast bread."

She must have baked that morning. It was lovely and fresh, and home-made butter.

"What do you reckon about that butter, girl?" I kept telling her my name was Evelyn, but she didn't seem to take it in.

"It's real good – but different."

"I made it, and it's goat's milk. You gotta make your own stuff here, otherwise you'll starve to death."

I had a good yarn with her, and she sat and smoked a pipe, this white woman. She said to me,

"There's a place down near the ground tank where you can camp, unless you're frightened of ghosts, girl. I know Aboriginal people are frightened of ghosts."

"I'm always too tired to worry about ghosts. I been more afraid of wild blackfellers!"

"Come up and sleep on the end of the verandah if you like. Our old dog sleeps under it. He'll look after you."

"Yeah, that'll be real good. Thanks."

So I brought me swag up, thinking what a nice lady she was. But what she didn't tell me was that she had a cocky that started talkin' and whistlin' at five o'clock in the morning and he was at the other end of the verandah. Gee, he give me a fright! It was people talk, but it wasn't a people voice! I was at Yaraka for three nights, but after that first morning I slept down at the ground tank, and there, where I was sittin', there was opal **everywhere**. When they dug out that tank, they just threw the dirt out all around the hole. I could pick up bits of opal that were just lying around. They looked real pretty, especially when the sun caught them.

The store lady came down to the tank to see why I'd moved. She laughed and said, "Look, girl, we're having a Christmas party up at the goods shed. You can come if you like."

"Yeah, I'd like that. Thanks."

"Come on up to the house with me. My daughter left some clothes when she went away, and they'll fit you."

"Nah, I don't want a dress."

"But you've got to have a pretty dress. All the young fellers'll be there. We're having a big feed and a dance and everything."

I loved dancing, so I said, "Mm-m-m-m. I'll come, but I'll just look on."

That night I went up, in me new hacked-off trousers and baggy shirt, and there was this big old mulga tree with balloons and all kinds of shiny coloured things hanging on it. I'd never seen anything like it – never been to a Christmas party ever in my life. I just sat there on a bale of straw, and looked at everyone. Someone said, "There's plenty of cool drinks, and plenty of stuff to eat. Help yourself." Kids were running everywhere, with pretty dresses and bows.

Then it went all silent and you could hear this horn blowin' down the creek, and a car pulled up, and there was Santa, sittin' on top of the car. He climbed down into the middle of the kids and came into the hall. I'd seen Santa, you know, in Bourke when I was a kid, but I didn't know he would come to a party. There he was with his big bag and everyone in the room was handed a parcel. I was even handed a parcel, a nice parcel with pretty paper. When I opened it up I just sat there and sort of...I couldn't talk. One lady said, "What did Santa give you, girl?"

I said to myself, "Here's another white woman who doesn't know my name's Evelyn."

I looked inside the parcel again. I just couldn't believe it. It was a brush and comb set. It had a peacock on the back of it, silver edge right round it, and silver handles – silver handle on the comb, silver handle on the brush.

"Ain't you gonna talk, girl?" and the store lady was shaking me.

I said, "Yeah... yeah." I didn't know what to say. I think if I'd said anything I would've cried. Nobody'd ever given me anything like that, not even in my dreams. I'd seen things like that on flash white women's dressing tables and in the catalogues and never thought that anyone would ever give **me** a thing like that in all my life. I couldn't believe it. I thought, "Here's something that must have cost a lot of money," but to me it was worth more than money. I kept thinking it was a mistake, 'cos there were other girls there, white girls, and that parcel might have been meant for one of them, so I asked the old long-legged cook, "Look, that parcel I got, you sure it wasn't meant for one of them white girls?"

"No, 'cos they all got the same sort of gift. It's for you, all right, girlie."

I treasured it. Everywhere I went I put it in my saddle bag. They were the nicest lot of white people I'd ever met, those people there at Yaraka. Not just one or two of them, but everybody. They were so friendly.

"Come on and have a dance."

"Nah. I got no dress – can't dance like this."

"You're alright. Dance anyway. Come on."

So we was dancin', and an old white feller was sittin' up on a bale of hay playing his accordion, and they kept goin' over to him with jugs of beer, and he was drinkin' with his hat on his head, then his hat was sittin' back, and in the end he had **no** hat on! The accordion was gettin' slower and slower, and he'd just get a squeak out of it now and then. The boys'd call out, "Come on, Bert, give us a waltz." But the old bloke was gettin' sleepier and sleepier. I went over to him and said, "How're you goin'?"

"Alright. But I'm gettin' tired, you know, girl."

No wonder. It must have been about two o'clock in the morning by then. I said, "Sit over there. Gimme that thing." So he moved over to another bale of hay and I played. We went on till daylight. I couldn't get down off that bale. They kept coming over, saying, "Have a cup of tea . . . D'ya want a jug of beer? . . . Here, have a feed."

"No, thanks, I don't drink, but I'll have a feed."

The old bloke went to sleep and didn't stir even with all the noise. The next morning he saw me near the store and drawled,

"How did that bloody dance finish, girl?

"Alright. We went till daylight this mornin'."

"They danced? What did they use for bloody music?"

One of the young fellers who'd come in from a station said, "Ev played your accordion for us for the rest of the night."

"You can play it!"

"Yeah."

"Well, you got to come over to my camp and let me hear ya. I was too bloody drunk to listen last night."

So I went over to that old white feller's camp. He had bundles and bundles of polished opals, heaps of them. But opal to me was just a pretty stone. I didn't know you could sell it for money. I played the accordion for him, so he ended up giving me an old one he had. I had that till I got married, and it just fell to pieces. Gong bought me another one, which I've still got. It's very worn but I still play it.

Right then, Girdlers and the rest of the plant came along in the old truck.

They'd just unpacked to set up camp when we heard the train whistlin' in the hills! So by half-past-eleven, after I'd been dancin' and playin' all night, we were helpin' Gong and the other drovers unload over two thousand bullocks. When they got out of the train their legs were almost locked from tryin' to keep their footing on the steep grades over the ranges between Blackall and Yaraka. You could see too that they'd had no water because they were all hollow and tucked up. They were only little fellers too. The bloke who owned them was hoping the drover would be able to fatten them up a bit on the road to the meatworks at Bourke so he'd get a better price for them.

If cattle looked good when they got to the saleyards the boss of the droving plant got a bonus, but the men he employed were on a fixed price agreed on at the start of the trip. A real good boss'd share some of the bonus with the plant, so he'd always be sure of good workers. Distance came into the price fixed by the owner and boss drover, but it made no difference to the men. You travel bullocks about nine miles a day, and six miles a day with sheep.

My pay was eight quid a week, a working week that started at four o'clock in the morning. If you lost a horse and spent three days looking for it you didn't get anything extra and you still had to have everything done on time.

Les said, "We can't water that many bullocks here – the town won't have any water left. Ev, you'll have to go on ahead and look for water." Seven miles I went before I found a spread of real sloppy stinkin' mud in the lignum. I worked my way round it and over further was a creek. I had to go back and tell them water was nearly nine miles away.

Waterin' that mob was a nightmare. We tried to hold them back, but when they smelt the water they just went. Even the lead dogs, who could grab a bullock by the nose and throw it, couldn't turn 'em. Three of our best dogs were run over and hurt. When the mob came to that first swampy mud in the lignum, the front ones all crammed in together, stirred it all up solid. That stuffed their nose holes up and they smothered – too weak to do anything about it. It must have been near morning before we got 'em off the water and back together. When it was light we rode around and found dead bullocks – lost about fifty there altogether.

We camped for the next three days, with plenty of water, and lignum for the cattle to eat. They needed to loosen up a bit for the next part of the trip. By this time it was really close to Christmas. We had no meat because there'd been no time to stock up in Yaraka, so the men killed what they thought was a nice-lookin' steer. That was a terrible mistake. He'd been so long without water the meat was affected. We all ended up with upset stomachs. It nearly killed some of the kids with diarrhoea. So we had to camp another couple of days

When the kids started to get the bellyache, Gong rode up onto a hill where he'd seen something shining way off in the distance. He guessed it must have been a house and it was. He got some stuff off the lady there, 'cos the Flying Doctor had dropped it off for diarrhoea or dysentery. He was gone all day gettin' it. We dosed everyone up and they started gettin' better.

Me and Gong didn't need it, 'cos we used bush medicine. We found *gweeyuhmuddah* on the sandhills and boiled up some leaves. It's rather bitter so we put some sugar in it for Maree.

Wherever we'd run into water we'd camp. We'd just set up camp at one place and it was all cloudy and hot – an electric storm was brewin' up between the hills. The cattle were very restless, dogs fightin', kids fightin', just like everyone was waitin' for somethin' to happen. We had the cattle all bunched in a corner between the creek and the fence. We always bedded the bullocks down as close as we could get them to the campfire, almost breathin' on it. Then, if they jumped up and scattered, they'd always run away from the fire and not over it, and over us.

This night they wouldn't lay down, so there was two people on watch instead of one. Les Girdler said to me, "Ev, you'd better go and get us all a horse each. We're gonna need them." The men were all callin' out, "Git Joe . . . I want Tommy . . ." because these were the horses they knew they could ride in a bad storm. Everyone saddled up and waited. Then there was this big clap of thunder and the lightnin' flashed, and you could see the blue sparks on the bullocks' backs just as if their hair was all 'lectrified. They ran up against the fence, and you could hear the wire goin' WHEE-EE-EE, it was that tight. Then it went TRCK-CK-CK, then a twang as the wire broke. Rain was pourin' down like it was solid. Then the horses went mad, the dogs run under the truck, the kids were in the tent screamin', and everyone singin' out. I was worried about Mary Girdler because of that baby she was expecting. I think it would have hurried it along too, that little mishap.

It was morning before we got all the bullocks settled down a long way from the camp. I'd only rounded up ten altogether, saddle cloth hangin' off, horse covered in sweat and burrs. I had no hat, sticks in me hair, mud all over me, soaked to the skin. Someone came along with a few more, someone with a couple of hundred. Finally we got them nearly all together. Time was runnin' out on us because Mary's baby was so close. We had no radio, so we had to get to an area out in the open where we could signal the Flying Doctor plane. Whenever the pilot saw a fire away from a camp they'd land 'cos that was the signal something was wrong.

Every time we'd sit down to have a feed, Les'd say, "How close now, old woman, is that bloody baby?"

"Ah, not far, Les."

He said to a couple of the boys, "You blokes'll have to move along in a circle about ten miles out from the camp. You might just happen to hear the Flying Doctor, and you can light a fire straight away."

Those boys rode all day, so that was two less to help muster up the rest of the missin' bullocks. I had to keep comin' back to check up on Mary and see that the kids were fed 'cos she was feeling so crook, then I had go back to look for bullocks as well as keep my mob of horses together. Yet at the time it didn't seem unfair, everyone had his own job to do, but gee, I was tired and I was only a skinny little thing in those days.

The boys came back that night. "No sign of anything at all, no Flying Doctor, no station planes."

The boss was worried about his wife, so when I went on ahead with the spare horses the next morning he said, "You make sure you listen for the Flying Doctor. They must be around here somewhere. Be ready to give them a signal."

I said, "Alright. But you'd better stay at camp with Mary. You can't leave her there by herself." The kids weren't big enough to do anything, they just played around and seemed to enjoy the trip. They were all fat little kids too, though they were living on hard tack – corned beef, damper, potatoes in their jackets.

I came to a big sandhill, and thought, "I'll get up there and have a look round." And just on the other side of the sandhill near a creek was a station homestead. They had a radio so they got in touch with the Flying Doctor for me. It was dark when I got back to camp. The boss wanted to leave his wife at the station so the Flying Doctor could pick her up and take her to the Bush Hospital at Junda – a tiny little town where most people live underground in dug-outs. She said, "**No-o-o-o!** I'll go when it's time to go and not before. I'm not sitting round no one's station waitin'." I suppose she was thinkin', "Who's gonna look after the other kids?'' But all the fellers were good to them, and the cook would've made sure they got good tucker.

She gave in in the end and went to the station. We moved off that night, and the next morning they'd picked her up and flown her to Junda. She only just got to the hospital . . . another ten minutes and the baby would have been born in the plane.

We had Christmas without her just up from Hammond Downs station. It rained all day Christmas Eve, rained and rained. It's all black ground along the Barcoo so we couldn't move the bullocks. That mud's worse than Superglue.

One of the stockmen went to the homestead to see if we could buy some milk and custard powder so we could have custard for our pudding. He came back with a station pack-horse loaded up with all the goodies for Christmas Day.

I can unpack those saddle-bags still. There was a Christmas cake, a couple of plum puddings and a packet of the custard he'd gone to buy, six tins of condensed milk, packets of peanuts in the shell, great long pieces of licorice, marble lollies, balloons, paper caps. There was even lolly stockings for the kids with those little things you blow and they roll out and make a noise. Les kept sayin', ''Don't let the kids blow them things! See those bullocks runnin' everywhere now.'' But they couldn't go far – that mud clogged their feet. We had a lot of vegies too from the station garden. He didn't bring any meat so we just had the corned beef we'd been livin' on. By this time it was jerky, dry like strips of leather. At that time of year you could only keep meat as jerky.

I was sittin' at the fire when I got me dinner, rain pourin' down. The cook had a bit of a shelter rigged up to protect just the fire, not him or us. The dint in the top of me hat was full of water, and when I looked down to eat, water ran down onto the brim and spilled over like a waterfall onto me plate so the green peas were floatin'! I said to the cook, ''There must be easier ways of makin' a livin'!

Look at this – Christmas Day and the rainwater's in me Christmas dinner!" I got no sympathy from him! All he said was, "Well, tip the water out!" I was hungry 'cos we were ridin' round them wet bullocks all day, tryin' to keep 'em together, so I tipped the water out – the gravy went with it – put me plate by the fire till it dried up a bit, put it back on me lap and finished me Christmas dinner.

Most of the time on that trip we had to carry water in cans on the pack-horses for the horses and dogs. Whenever I went to look for water for the horses I'd take all the dogs too. They'd drink till they had a skinful, and that'd do them till the next night. They'd work hard all day on that one drink. Blackfellers used to do that, you know, because they didn't have much to carry water in easily. Each person carried his own water inside himself, and that way you didn't spill any!

We all washed in the one dish. Someone would sing out, "Who had first wash last time?" At the time you don't notice those things as hard. It was just your life. The only thing I'd complain about was I never got enough sleep. I'd say, "When we finish this trip I'll sleep for a week." 'Course, I never did. Just one good sleep, when you're young, and you're up again and ready to go.

We stayed there long enough for the ground to dry out. We let the cattle feed in the mallee, but then we had to go in to round them up, gettin' ourselves scratched to pieces, trousers and shirts torn and big scratches up the sides of our horses, it was so thick. Acacia bushes in the mallee have very big thorns. We were patching the horses up for weeks, puttin' tar on them to stop the flies makin' sores.

We went in to Hammond Downs to wait for the Flying Doctor to drop off Mary with the new baby, a girl. Where the Thompson and the Barcoo meet and go on as Cooper Creek there's a great big hole washed down deep into the rock from water goin' round and round in flood time. It's like a big bowl with the lip curvin' in over the water like a lid, and all slippery. If you wanted to fish – and there's **big** fish in there – you'd have to stand back at least twenty feet from the edge. If you fell in there's no way you could get out unless someone threw you a rope. There were graves of people who'd been drowned there – all white people. They named it well when they called it Dead Man's Crossing.

At the Crossing the station people had cleared a landing stretch of flat ground, leaving little sandhills of loose sand all round. My Maree and one of the Girdler kids were sittin' up on one of these playin' with a doll. Someone backed the truck up and round, and the front wheel went right over the top of them!

I saw it happening but I was way over by the fire. I cooee-ed and ran. As I ran I couldn't see the kids anywhere. I had pictures in my mind of them being squashed, their heads flat. But the sand was piled up so high and they were on the loose top of it, that the truck wheel went right over them and pushed them down into the sand. As I got there, they were coming up out of the sand like they was swimmin', goin' 'pouff-pouff-pouff', blowin' out sand! They had a mouthful of sand and a noseful of sand. Everyone else in the camp was runnin' up and yellin', "What happened?"

"The truck run over them two kids!"

Gong had grabbed up Maree and Les was comforting his kid. The stockman who'd swung the truck around was as blind as a bat and didn't know the kids were there. The poor feller was that upset. He said, "I thought Gong was going to kill me."

I said, "It was only an accident. We're just lucky the kids weren't hurt. All they got was a mouthful of sand, and they could have got that rollin' down the hills playin'." Lucky it was the front wheel went over them, 'cos the back ones were those dual wheels and the truck was so heavy loaded it could have killed them.

Right after that excitement we heard the Flying Doctor. We got Mary off the plane with the baby. It was late so

we didn't move off till next day. That night the mail truck
came past and on the back were four big cornbags full of
cabbages. None of us had tasted a cabbage for months. So
while Les was talking to the mailman the fellers nicked a
bag of cabbages. We paid dearly for it. Fresh cabbage has
a terrible effect on your stomach when you're not used to
it! One bloke was groanin', "I'll never eat another cabbage
again." I wasn't too sympathetic. "That's what you get for
stealin' cabbages. Why couldn't you climb up and get two
or three. You didn't have to take the bagful." We ended
up feedin' them to the horses. They didn't mind, there wasn't
much green stuff about.

Mary was havin' trouble with the new baby. She was feeding
it on Lactogen, and because she didn't know how to use
it properly the baby had constipation. Les didn't believe
in tinned milk for babies, so he said to his wife, "There's
a cow with a new calf, always seems to have plenty of milk.
We'll turn her into a milker and stick the baby on cow's
milk. It'll be good for the rest of the kids too."

That night they cut the cow out of the mob. She was
wild, and strong as a bull – dust flyin' everywhere, it was
like a bloody rodeo. They drug her over to a tree and tied
her up, and tied the calf to another tree. Cows protect their
babies, they're better mothers than some people. That cow
bellowed all night for the calf, and the calf was singin' out
in his turn for his mother. We were up early next mornin',
wild and all cranky from no sleep.

We had a feed and then started to try to milk that wild
cow. Had to leg-rope her, and she drug us over stumps,
through grass and roly-poly burrs, I had burrs even in me
ears. In the end they threw her and tied her back legs right
back, stretched her out flat on the ground. We got half
a bucket that first day. Mary filled the titty bottle half milk,
half water, and the baby thrived on it. We had no fridge
to keep it fresh, so we put the milk in tins, with little
holes in the lid, in the gauze meat-safe. The meat-safe,

wrapped in a couple of wet bags, hung in the back of the truck where the breeze kept it cool.

As the calf got older, and the cow got quieter, she gave us more milk. I liked it in the morning, warm straight out of the cow. Then we milked in the evening too so rice pudding became a favourite, especially with golden syrup. We were livin' in luxury.

We camped up on the sandhills on Kyabra Station. Kyabra Creek has permanent water so I decided to go down to the lagoon and throw a few lines in. I rode down, put the lines in, then turned back to my horse. Then I got the feeling I was being watched. Now I hadn't got over being chased by that young naked white feller. But it wasn't a feller at all, it was a scrubber bull – an ugly big yellow brute with black marks all over him – standin' in the bushes, almost between me and the horse. I thought, "How'm I gonna get to that horse?" Then "It won't chase me . . . I think . . ." but I was kiddin' myself. I walked slow, but it snorted, pawed the ground and shook its head. I ran for a little windmill the Chinamen on the station had put up for their vegie gardens. I got up about ten foot when that scrubber's rump hit the wooden stand. It rocked and, I tell you, I thought I was going to fall.

I was up there, screamin' and singin' out, and the dogs started chasin' the bull. It lashed out at them and kept comin' back and comin' back, bumpin' the windmill stand. I held on for grim life, I wasn't havin' no grim death! Splinters all on the face and the ribs, and right up the inside of me legs, I was wrapped around it so tight. We were pickin' them out for ages. They heard the racket up at the camp and someone rode down with a whip and tried to flog it away. It ended up knockin' down the horse with the man on it, so the other fellers had to shoot it.

Then we were off again to Quilpie.

On the way we camped on Pinkilla Station, north-west of Quilpie. By rights I should have been on ahead with my horses, but I stayed back with the bullocks to let my horses graze up while I gave a hand to get the mob to the Quilpie yards by sundown. We were just pushin' the mob off from dinner camp down on the flat when a few of 'em broke off onto a stony hill – not knobbly stones, but big slabs lying flattish on the ground, very slippery.

I rode up after them where there was a flat rock almost under a tree with a limb hangin' over. I thought the horse would walk on the soft ground between the rocky patches and avoid the limb but he got onto the slippery rock. I felt him goin' and made a grab for the branch. It broke, the horse slipped and fell on me! My first thought was, "How the hell I'm gonna get out from under this brute?" I managed to wriggle out somehow but I didn't realize my ribs was broke 'til I stood up and started to walk. Then it was just like something grabbed me round the chest and squeezed the life out of me. A couple of the blokes behind me yelled out, "Ev's horse fell," and came racin' over, thinkin' I'd be crushed right underneath it. By this time I was sittin' down again.

"What happened ya?"

"I dunno. My ribs are crook."

One feller felt around me side and said, "Feels like they're broke."

I yelled, "Don't touch 'em again!"

The others came up, took the stirrup leathers off the horse (the poor thing was skinned all down the side), made me hold me arms up high, and strapped me right round with the leathers, both of them, real tight, I couldn't hardly breathe. They said, "At least you won't feel the soreness till we get you to the hospital." So there I was like a mummy in leather. Gong had been down on the flat with the main mob when he heard all the singin' out and he came ridin' up to see what was the matter. He rode a hell of a lot faster when he saw it was me!

We were about seven miles out of Quilpie. The truck

had gone on ahead, so Gong and one of the boys helped me up onto another horse, with me yelpin'. We had to walk the horse those seven miles, tryin' to keep him on the soft parts of the sand wherever we could because every time he put a foot down I'd catch my breath. We had nothing to ease the pain, so I sat on that horse wishin' the hospital was closer. There wasn't much they could do when we did get there, just give me painkillers, strap me up and tell me to stay still. I was lucky because a lady was in the hospital havin' twins so the Flying Doctor was there, otherwise we'd have had to wait for him to come from Broken Hill. He said the boys had done the right thing. It had stopped the ends of the bones from grating together. And he laughed because he said it was the first time he'd ever seen anyone really STRAPPED up.

Les came in that night and said, "You know we'll have to push on first thing, Ev. Don't worry about Maree. Mary will look after her. You can catch up to us as soon as they let you go."

Gong said, "I'm sorry. Looks as if you're on your own again."

"That's all I've been this trip, travellin' on my own. When I get back to Bourke, I'm never goin' away again. I'll stay home with mum and her family."

The plant moved on early the next morning. They left me a saddle horse and a pack-horse. I managed to get myself out of bed and went out onto the verandah lookin' out over the truckin' yards, feelin' so sad seein' them leave. Not until they'd left did I realize they'd taken all the dogs, my two as well in the truck, to give them a rest after the long trip they'd already done. I was there about nine days when the Flying Doctor came back and said I could go, but to be very careful.

"What about all this strapping, your strapping?"

He gave a funny sort of look to the nurse and said, "Well, what about it? You'll lose some skin, girl, when we take it off."

"Why the hell did you put that kind of stickin' plaster on me if you knew it would do that!"

"Get the metho!" he said.

So there I was, topless, and they're pourin' metho, cold metho, on me, and pullin' the stuff off. I reckoned I'd have no skin, no meat, no nothin' left on me bones.

"Now, how's that? Alright, isn't it? "

"Yeah, alright if you're used to dryin' yourself with sandpaper!"

The Sister rubbed some Vaseline over me and bandaged it and said, "You'll be right. You can go when you want to."

Next day I went down to the stable, but I couldn't lift the saddle. So I went back and asked Matron, "Can someone come down and saddle the horse for me?"

"You can't go. If you can't saddle the horse for yourself this morning, you won't be able to unsaddle him tonight after riding all day, and a horse can't sleep with the saddle on."

"These horses can." I was determined to go, but it was no use. I knew that by this time the plant would be almost to Thargomindah.

"Look, just wait. Give it another couple of days. Go down every day and try to lift the saddle up."

So I did, and in the end I got the horse saddled, with the help of one of the rookie nurses, who didn't know what the Matron had said! I went back and saw Matron. She said, "Got your horse saddled yet?"

"Yes."

"Did you put it up yourself?"

". . . buckled it on and everything." By this time the rookie nurse was off duty and couldn't tell on me.

They found out afterwards that she'd helped me, 'cos they dropped a little note to Girdlers telling them how I'd 'escaped'. I didn't try to take the saddle or packbags off the horses, I'd just loosen 'em and pull 'em back towards the rump to let them dry out, and tie the horses up for the night so they wouldn't shake them off. In the morning when I was ready to move, I'd slide the saddle back up and buckle the surcingle tight. That was a cow of a trip. And hot – you wouldn't believe it!

Every night I was terrified of wild blackfellers in country I'd never been in before, and no dogs for company. Every time I'd hear an unusual noise, I'd listen, me heart'd start racing. I could hear it, and feel it banging up against me ribs, and I'd stop breathing altogether. It was a terrifying trip.

Remember that boundary rider's hut between Thargomindah and Quilpie where I saw the big red blanket hangin' on the line? Well, when I came back, a couple of months later, that same blanket was still hangin' there but it was bleached almost white. It was hangin' there for that long you could just see some pink patches on it. What I didn't know then, and found out long after we got back to Bourke, was that the man and woman who lived in that hut had died even before I went past on the way up, and were still there dead in the hut when I passed on the way back. They weren't found till April. Apparently the bracky bore water got too much even for them, and they'd tried to cure it with Epsom Salts and poisoned themselves. They both died because there was no one to go for help. They were a middle-aged white couple with a grown-up family and the kids had moved away.

Boundary riders on big properties often didn't see anyone till their stores were due. This couple had chooks and ducks and turkeys, all dead too because they had no water and food when they'd been shut up for the night. That was probably the last thing that poor lady had done. Even the dogs were dead on their chains. The only things alive were the loose dogs. Lucky for me I'd been anxious to catch up with the plant. I don't know what I'd have been like if I'd found those dead people. That trip for me was bad enough as it was.

I crossed the Bulloo and camped on Ardoch because I was feeling a bit crook. I thought the ribs might have come undone again, so I went to the homestead for a bit of a handout. There was a big gathering there and I could see it was a sad gathering. People were standing round a horse, unbuckling a young feller off the stirrup irons. The horse had bolted with him, he'd fallen off and the horse drug him. He wasn't dead, but he was very bashed up.

They'd called for the Flying Doctor, and I thought, "This is my chance, I'll see him too."

When he arrived, the doctor asked if anyone wanted to see him while he was there, because it must be over 400 miles from Broken Hill to Ardoch.

I went over and it was the same doctor that had treated me when my ribs were broke!

"What're you doing way down here, girl? You should be up in Quilpie."

"I'm on my way back home, tryin' to catch up with the mob."

He found my ribs hadn't mended at all, that they were just fitting back into the cracks, but not joined up, so a slight bump would really bring 'em undone. I wasn't happy about that, but I was more sorry for my poor horses, with the saddle and packbags on all the time for more than a week. The manager said I could camp for a couple of days to give my horses a break.

They were good to me on Ardoch. All the meat was corned beef, but the red kind, not jerky, so even that was a change. The Chinamen there grew more white turnips than anything in their garden so we had boiled turnips and boiled turnips and . . . I thought to myself, "While I'm here I'll get friendly with the cook, 'cos he's the feller I'll really need help from." His wife was good too, and she cooked up some stuff for me when she saw I only had a bit of flour and not much else. She give me a couple of books to read, and that helped a lot when I was camped alone at night. I'd sit near the fire to read them, even though it was so hot.

I caught up to the plant about fifteen miles south of Ardoch. They'd radioed from Toompine for the Flying Doctor to bring them a part for the old truck. The Flying Doctor used to drop things for drovers in the outback, not only things they'd asked for. As they flew over they'd see a mob on the move and know the drovers would have been out of touch for a long time, so they'd drop things on little parachutes – parcels, medicines, fruit, anything. Everybody would watch the plane fly over and if you saw a parachute coming down with a box, there'd be a gallop to see what it was. When it hit the ground, you'd have a few bent bananas, a few squashed apples, a few boiled lollies. You'd cut the squashed part away and eat what was left – we weren't fussy. You'd fold the parachutes and leave them at the next station. Anyway, they'd dropped the part, and a message to say they'd seen me at Ardoch, that my ribs still hadn't mended but that I was alright. Gong decided to ride back to meet me so that last bit was the only good part of my ride.

I was still feeling very sore. I was bruised all down to my stomach, and right round me. My teeth started to play up, so I decided to go to Cunnamulla to see the doctor. Gong and the rest started the bullocks off down to Hungerford. I waited at Thargomindah with Maree to catch the mail truck to go the 125 miles to Cunnamulla. I was down the town talking to a lady I'd got friendly with on the way up, talked too long, and missed the mail truck. When I got back they said, "The truck's gone, your swag and gear's still there. You can catch it on Thursday." About five hours later, a bloke came along on a horse in a real lather. I could hear raised voices so I went to find out what was goin' on. The mail truck had tipped over at a creek crossing near Eulo, five people had been killed, and both the driver's legs were broken. It had been carrying a load of empty 44-gallon petrol drums, and the people had been sitting on top of them. Me and Maree would have been killed, along with two fellers, a girl about sixteen, her mother and a little boy about seven. I didn't bother about waitin' for the mail truck. I just saddled up and rode to Cunnamulla. Took me a week 'cos I was too sore to push ahead. There were some days me and Maree just camped and never moved at all.

When I got there they told me I had pyorrhoea in the bottom jaw. So I had to go into the hospital and the doctor cut the gums on both sides. I remember the camp cook was always saying, "Gee, you're bony, Ev. When're you going to pick up?" but that was what the trouble was.

My Aunty Kate looked after Maree while I was in the hospital. When I came out I was broke, so when I heard that Charlotte Plains Station wanted musterers I headed for there with Maree. I was three days on the way when the police caught up with me. I had to go back to Cunnamulla because Aunty Kate's husband, Alf McCarthy, was missing. He was working on a station near Bollon. He was a drunk, and had been in the horrors and wandered off. Two policemen found him eventually. He'd fallen off his horse, cut his head and lost his memory. We heard they were coming back to Cunnamulla so we all went up to the police station, when they brought him in, laying down in the back of a truck. We just thought he was tired, because he was a thin old man and the grog had taken its toll. The policemen got out and called out, "Come on, Alf. Get out here."

He mumbled, ". . . can't get up."

Aunty Kate walked over to the truck and said, "What's wrong with you?" then she sung out to me, "Ohhh, Evelyn, look what they've done!" They had the biggest chains on him, on both his legs, his two arms and around his waist. There's no way in the world he could have stood up with those chains on him.

I yelled, "What've you got chains on him for? The man's lost his memory, he's in the horrors!"

"We thought he might do some harm."

"To you bi-i-i-i-g coppers!" Big strappin' young fellers they were.

"We can't take chances with mad blackfellers."

"He's not mad. He's SICK."

Aunty Kate called to one of the young fellers standing there to go down and get her boys – they had six sons. Old Alf was still layin' on the truck when her big grown-up sons came beltin' up in the sulky. They had axes to cut the chains. The police pulled out their guns, but the boys didn't care. They kept cutting the chains off that little old thin bony man with a great big gash on his head and dried blood all over him, eyes wandering round, lost eyes as if he was searching for something he could focus on. They were just loose eyes in a sick old man – and they put him in chains like a mad dog!

I wondered how people could be so cruel. How can a human being treat another human being like that? It's an insult to animals to call cruel human beings 'animals'. Animals don't treat each other like that.

I grew up in Yantabulla where you hardly ever seen the police, and you didn't see the bad things some of 'em could do. But when someone said, "P'leeceman there," you'd just run. There in Cunnamulla I saw what they could do to you. Even now, to this day, there's a lot of that in me.

Uncle Alf was a very sick old man, so they sent him to Brisbane and Aunty Kate went with him. I never seen him alive again, and I didn't see Aunty Kate till my father died in Brewarrina, years and years after.

I'd never had much to do with Queensland before that, but if that was the way they treated Aboriginal people there I wanted to get out as quick as I could. I thought if anything happened to me I could be in chains and locked in a jail and they'd take Maree. I saddled up and rode with her back to Bourke, another 160 miles.

It was a bad trip – busted up, left behind. I don't know what I'd have done if Gong wasn't there to look after Maree. But there was still lots of times when that poor little kid only had me to depend on.

On that tough long droving trip, many a time I just wished Mum'd be there to say, "What're you doin', Ev? What're you breakin'?" or that Dad'd say, "Ev, you don't listen!" I'd have given anything to hear them, even if they were rousin' at me, because I never thought I'd make it back – I never thought I'd make it back.

On the way I heard that I'd missed Gong again. They'd already delivered the bullocks and he'd taken another droving job to pick up a mob at Come-by-Chance, between Walgett and Narrabri. So I headed home to Brewarrina. That was the end of long droving trips for me. I missed it at times, but I didn't really regret it. But before Gong's job cut out I took another job. A team of us, four girls and four fellers, were camped out on Naryilco Station, breakin' in horses – a hundred and twenty-three of 'em. That was the hardest job I ever had. When you leg-rope and throw a horse to brand it, it kicks like anything, and I'd be holdin' on to the rope, thinkin' me two arms were goin' to be pulled straight out of me body, and that me head would fall off from the constant jerkin' and jarrin'. I thought I'd never come good after that – reckoned I'd be a milk-shake with scrambled brains all me life!

After that I wasn't back home long, a young mother learnin' about raisin' kids, when Gong was away on another long cattle trip so I went to stay with Aunty Rose Elwood at Number Two boundary rider's hut on Brindingabba Station. It was a full day's drive out from the homestead. Maree was at the big explorin' age, into everything – three or four years old – so it must've been about 1949.

One morning she was playin' on the back of an old wagon with a lot of the other kids and she fell out and hit the side of her head. The feller blamed for pushin' her was Billy Elwood. He was about six, and always in trouble. He was singin' out, "Aunty Dorl's fell out of the cart!" Billy never called her Maree, and I never found out why he called her 'Aunty Dorl'.

Maree was just layin' there – I thought she was dead.
I picked her up, raced over to the bore drain, and chucked
water all over her. She sort of come to, and up came this
great lump on the side of the head. She was cryin' and
cryin', and I was rockin' her and sayin', "Shh-shh, baby,
don't cry, go to sleep."

Aunty Rose was away from the camp, sittin' under a tree
a long way off, away from the noise of the kids playin',
and I didn't know any better, so Maree went to sleep, and
she slept and she slept and slept. Three o'clock in the
afternoon this kid was still asleep. I picked 'er up, and her
arms and legs were hangin' loose. I opened her eyes and
they were just starin', floatin' round loose in her head so
I took her down to where my Aunty was.

"She's real sick, Ev. You'll have to take her in to the
station."

I went back to the camp and Eddie and Bob put the horses
in the buggy and off we went to the homestead. Eddie was
nearly as old as me, eighteen, nineteen or so, and Bob was
about twelve, but a big, solid kid. The station manager's old
mother said, "She's got bad concussion. You shouldn't have
let her go to sleep. Mrs Elwood should have told you that."

"She wasn't there. That's why we've brought 'er in to you."

"You'll have to stay in here for a couple of days till
we see what we can do."

She wrapped her up, and put cold cloths on her head
and was very, very gentle with her – very nice old lady.
Maree was bad all that night, then the vomitin' started. She
was cryin', "Dark, Mum, dark." She couldn't see and I
was terrified. The lady give her boiled water with glucose
and a bit of salt in it. That's all she had for four days.
The boys had to go back to Number Two hut and I just
sat. That lady was so good. I had a nice room 'n all there,
nice furniture, flowers on me dressin' table, pretty mat on
the floor, ricketty old wireless runnin' off a car battery.

Then Maree started to come good, pickin' up things, tryin'

to hold the cup, and her eyes looked as if she could see what she was lookin' at. The old lady said she was getting better and gave me lots of medicines in a good galvanised bucket, and a **big** list of what to do. On the top was 'Keep her out of the hot sun'. Half-way down that list was, 'Keep her out of the hot sun'. Down the bottom, in big words, was 'KEEP HER OUT OF THE HOT SUN'.

On Brindingabba they had telephones rigged from the homestead out to the boundary huts so the old lady rang Number Two and told them to come and get me. But Uncle Ted and the boys had already left to come in because the mustering was on, and Uncle Ted worked on the branding. The whole family came, so me and Maree were in at the station for about six weeks. There were heaps of us, uncles and aunties and cousins.

I never worked so hard in all my life as then – cookin' for heaps of kids, washin' for heaps of kids. There was no wood in the camp so you had to yoke up the horses and go out in the buggy for a load of wood. I didn't git much help, except for Shirley. She's the oldest of Aunty Rose's family and she was real good. She used to get up even earlier than me and cook breakfast for her father and big brothers before they went to work at sunrise. And all this time there was no word from Gong. He was up near Brunette Downs travellin' mobs south.

One day the boss came up to the camp and said "We need someone to do the grooming." The old aboriginal groom, George Weldon, had a heart attack. A station groom had to kill the sheep and butcher them, feed the chooks, water the garden, milk and separate, and do every other odd job around the place – general dogsbody.

Since Gong wasn't back I did that job for another six weeks. And I still had to help look after the kids! When the work cut out, Uncle Ted said, "We're goin' back to Number Two. You comin' with us, Ev?"

"Yes, I'm not stayin' 'ere without you."

I said to the old *wudjiin*, Granny Mumble, at the station, "We're goin' back to Number Two."

"Oh, no! I've just got used to having you here. Did you tell the boss?"

"I'll tell him when I see him."

But she looked sad. All her grandchildren were away at boarding school, so she used to get me to leave Maree with her when I was groomin' around, and she'd make her pretty little dresses with lace and frills on 'em. Every afternoon when I'd come to get her, she'd be waddlin' along, fat as butter, with nice ribbons on her long curly hair. The missus called her 'Sammy'.

"I'll miss Sammy when you take her home."

"We'll come and see you."

When I mentioned it to the boss he said, "What's Mum going to do?"

"What d'ya mean?"

"She'll miss that little girl so much. Could you leave her here with us?"

"No! I couldn't do that. She's mine."

"Would you come and live here at the station then? She's an old lady and at a bit of a loss. You won't have to work. Just be here."

"Nah. I'm needed out at the hut."

So we left.

For ages there was no word from Gong, but I grew up with, 'no news is good news', because people went to any lengths to pass the word along if there was need. Not long after that, we got word that there was more work in at the station, so the big pack-up again. We'd only been in at the station about four days when the mail came in with a letter from Gong. He was at Bourke delivering a mob of bullocks, so I left Elwoods.

I got no pay for all the months I'd been there at Number Two, so I had no money for me and Maree's fare on the mail truck to Bourke. In the end I had to sell my red kelpie dog, Joe, for five pounds. But that wasn't enough to get me all the way from Brindingabba to Bourke, so I managed to hitch a ride on a truck goin' through. But I didn't trust the old white feller who drove the truck, so I pulled me swag out at Yantabulla and we camped in the bushes, just above the pub, beside the same little waterhole where we used to swim when Miss Cook was teachin' us. By gee, we were hungry, but I needed my five pounds for the mail fare.

I knew Brady, the policeman, always had heaps of chooks, so, that night, I snuck into his fowlhouse and filled me hat with eggs. Mrs McGrath at the pub had turkeys roamin' about everywhere, so I sat in the bush real quiet, and when they went past I hit one on the back of the head. He went down, and I plucked and cooked him. Next mornin', she was out lookin' for the turkeys and saw me.

"Hello, girl, where'd you come from?"

"I'm waitin' for the mail truck to Bourke. Just got off a truck." She must've known I was tellin' lies, 'cos everyone knew when anything came through a place that tiny.

The mail truck came that afternoon, and I pulled him up on the road before he got to Yantabulla. The driver had two white ladies in front. He said, "Yes, girl, get up on the top and make a hole among the bags so you and the little girl won't roll off if you go to sleep." That mailman was Tom Lyons, and his son Alan became my first white son-in-law – married Maree! When I told Alan about travellin' with his dad he said, "No wonder Dad was always saying, 'That Evelyn should've been a bloody boy!'"

When I got to Bourke you can imagine the relief. My first thought was, "Gong's 'ere, 'e's got a bit of money, I don't 'ave to worry about gittin' another feed for Maree." I handed the responsibility over to him, off my shoulders that had been gittin' a bit sore. I never had that responsibility all to meself again till over twenty years later.

I stayed a few days in Bourke while Gong finished off his job, then we came back to Bre and we were there when the 1950 big flood came.

# BREWARRINA

*'For the first time I had
something of my own'*

Our second daughter, Lesley, was born on the
10th of July in the 1950 flood, with water lappin'
under the floorboards of the maternity ward.
Gong's brother Tom called her 'little black duck'
as a pet name, and everyone still calls her 'Ducky'.
When I took her home from hospital we had to
move in to the town, with Tom and my sister-
in-law Jean. They were so good to us. They closed
in the end of a verandah with tarpaulins to make
us a livin' space, and we shared the kitchen. Gong
and Tom were moving sheep to wherever they
could find high ground. We wouldn't see 'em for
eight or ten days at a time – didn't know if they
were drowned or not. It rained and it rained! Our
main problem was dryin' nappies for the baby and
clothes for kids.

Water lay everywhere. It rained from that July
till the start of February. All the people from the

Mission land came out onto the higher ground at the Red Hill, just south of the town, like a big island. You could only get to town by boat, and there was only a couple of boats, mostly used for bringing out food.

They rowed the doctor out twice a week and drug another boat behind 'em with medicines in. The water was lyin' for months so they were worried about a big sickness comin'. There were mosquitoes and sandflies, kids with bad bites and upset tummies and sore eyes.

One day I was out there visitin', me and Maree and my brand-new baby. I said, "Who's that comin' in the boat, feller with a great big umbrella up?"

"That's Doctor Phillips. He's comin' today to give everyone hepatitis needles." So I had to line up with everyone else, and Maree was jabbed with all the small kids.

Often the town ran out of food and the only help was when they dropped food, from those big Hercules, onto the racecourse because the airfield was cut off in even a little flood – still is. The only petrol was given to the doctor and medical people. Where your car ran out of petrol, that's where it stood, but in them days no one would've broken into it, or stripped it. Hardly any firewood, and nothin' else for people to cook with.

After the flood went down it was time to set up our own camp and we moved across the river to the bank above the Fisheries. Aboriginal people had always lived there, big mobs of them. Gong's sister Pussy was married to Dummy Smith and they lived in a house there. Gong's leg was still not good so everybody bucked in and helped us set up a camp. We could only afford a small, very thin sort of tent. You could shoot peas through it, as the saying goes. The fly I made of wool-bales stitched together protected us. We had two beds in it, and a cupboard sort of thing where we put our clothes, and the food to keep it dry.

We really lived in the big bough shade outside. That's where Gong made a table – four forky sticks with a sheet of flattened corrugated iron for the top. Pots and pans and pints hanging in the shed, a few tin plates, a fire in the open, a camp oven, a bush broom. We set up house, real happy. That was my first home.

I had the proudest feelin' for that little camp. I was always makin' a new broom, 'cos I swept round all the time. Pussy used to say, "You'll have a deep hole round that tent, and when it rains you'll have to swim home!" Lovely purple flowers grew down by the river and when I went to get water I'd pick some and put 'em in a rusty old peach tin on the table. For the first time I had something of **my own**. It was **mine**, my husband, my little girl, my baby, my kitchen, my tent, my little bit of ground. I wouldn't have called the king me uncle in them days. In that bend in the river I wanted nothing else, needed nothing else. Everything in the world that was of value to me was there. I was very independent then, and didn't think I'd ever have to ask anyone for anything, or depend on anybody outside my family any more. Not that I ever had. It was home, really home. I'd get the needle and cotton and sit out in the sun, and cut up old clothes that was given to me and make dresses for the little girls, and with the little bits left over I'd make rag dolls for them, like Mum had made for us.

In 1951 Maree started school at the same school that I wasn't allowed to go to when I was a kid. The Mission school was still goin', but they'd passed a law in 1949 that Aboriginal children could be enrolled in the local school, but if anyone in the community objected, they couldn't go to school – just had to stay home. Imagine that! When Maree started, her cousins, Dummy's kids, were already at the school but they would pass for white kids anywhere, and I worried that Maree wouldn't be accepted because she was a little black girl. She went across in the boat with them. She was pretty cluey, and in no time at all she was put up into another class. Gong was workin' for John Simmonds, a feller he'd known all his life, puttin' a fence line round his new station on the Bourke road. He'd always bring home tins of Leetona Fig Jam. I said, "Don't they ever 'ave anything else but fig jam at that place?"

"No, that's all Big John likes."

When the place was finished I asked Gong, "Well, what did they call this famous new place?"

"Leetona. What else!"

It wasn't very long after that we found out there was another baby coming along. I thought then that was the end of travelling altogether. So we had to make a bigger camp.

I said, "We'll 'ave to do something soon, boy. This tent'll be gittin' a bit crowded."

"As soon as my leg's a bit better, we'll go over there on the hill and see if we can mark out a bit of ground to build a house."

I was sitting on a little drum near the fire bucket and looked at him side-on. He said, "What's that look for, old woman?" Never called me Evelyn, nothing else but 'old woman', and he was older than me.

I said, "Have you ever built a house in your whole life?"

"No, but I can put up a tent."

"Listen to me. If we're going to have a family, we'll need a house. Our kids'll have a proper place."

"Ye-ah, I s'ppose so."

"And **you're** gonna build it!"

"Yeah, I'll build it."

So I thought to meself, "This is something I've gotta see. This bloke, all his life sat on a horse, and he's gonna build a house!"

But what he didn't tell me was that he had a lot of friends who did know how to build houses, and that they'd already agreed to help him build it. Or that the owner of Walchera Station had built a brand-new woolshed and told Gong that whatever he wanted from the old woolshed he could have.

I didn't know about that until trucks started bringing greasy pine boards, and greasy rails and greasy posts, old rusty-red corrugated iron, – about the only thing that wasn't greasy! – and dumped it all on the hill across from our camp. It was on the Stock Route, surveyed years ago when they'd thought they could cross cattle at the river, but you couldn't cross there – too many rocks. It was land that nobody could do anything with anyway, there's too many gullies as well, so you could get permission from the Pastures Protection Board to put it to use. John Simmonds was a great help in fixing that up.

They seemed to be a long time gatherin' all these things, 'cos Gong would be away on trips. About time it was, too, with three kids already. The tent was dyin' of old age, and I was havin' to sew strips of it together from the inside. When Gong was away Pussy worried about us, and wanted to get Dummy to build us a little house, but I kept sayin', "No, thanks, we're right." I really had meself convinced that we needed nothin' more. She was good and would always mind the kids if I had to take one to the doctor.

One of my big worries when the kids were small and runnin' round was the river, because where I'd grown up there was only little creeks. When I went down to get water they'd all want to come, and their Grandfather Crawford wanted to make little billy-cans for the kids so they could help me carry water. I said, "No. They'll go down there when I'm not with 'em, and fall in." I kept them away from the river – and anything else dangerous – with a little crooked stick! There was always one in our house. It never got to be a big stick, and sometimes that stick would be there on the side of the cupboard from one week to another and never taken down – but it was **there**.

"Well, what you'll 'ave to do, girl," said Grandfather Crawford, "is teach 'em to swim."

"Right!" So I did. We had a couple of dogs that always followed the kids round, so I taught them to swim with

the kids too. I knew they'd 've drug 'em out if anything
went wrong.

Gong and I got work whenever we could, sometimes
separately, sometimes together. We needed the money. The
people who owned the station at Brewarrina where Gong
worked also owned a station near the Bollon. We both went
up to help with the shearing, and camped on the way at
Cunnamulla. Gong said, "You c'n ride up to the butcher's
and git some meat." It was the same butcher us teenagers
used to buy the pig's trotters off. I asked for some pig's
brisket – three flaps. While he was rolling it up, he said,
"I know you. You were here about seven years ago."

"Was it really that long? How much do I owe ya?"

Now the flaps were two bob each, but 'e said, "You
owe me seven quid."

"What? I don't think so!"

"You just think."

I gave him the six bob, and said, "Seven quid? . . . seven . . .
Oh-h-h . . ."

"Yes, and I believe you didn't do any good with the dress
anyway! What did you do with it?"

"Still got it, rolled up in a white flour bag sittin' in me
saddlebag. When I git married, if it'll still fit me, I'll wear
it. But I 'aven't got seven quid to give ya."

"Well, when you get married, send me a picture of you
in the dress."

I got out of there pretty quick.

Soon as I got back to our camp I said, "We'll 'ave a
feed and get goin' to the station." While we were travellin'
I told Gong what had happened. He was ridin' along as
if he never heard me, never said 'Yes . . . no.' That's how
we were then, told things to each other and got no comment
back, but we each knew what was goin' on.

Not long after our third child, Alan, was born in 1952 –
new doctor then, Dr Lopes – I got a short job takin' sheep
up to Come-by-Chance. Gong had already picked up a mob

and was on his way back. It was a funny feeling to think
that I was going one way with stock travellin', and he was
goin' the other way, both obligated to our jobs. There were
seven of us in that plant, the boss and his wife, four stockmen
and me. None of us girls ever took jobs unless the boss
was married and took his family along. We were camped
out on the Cato Plain near the old Mission boundary. Another
plant was camped near the Cato River and we could see
their fires so I rode across to see if anyone had heard where
Gong was. And there he was. He'd had a bust off a horse
and was walkin' on a forky stick.

That's when he said to me, "Well, before we go any
further, what about if we get married and go and live at
Mootawingee?"

"What?"

"We'll get married in the church."

"Yeah ... I heard ya ... I'll be back later on and we'll
talk some more about this gettin' married business."

So I rode back to our camp, thinkin', "It'd be a good
idea, I suppose. At least I'd have another name. Wouldn't
be Evelyn Mallyer all my life."

Next day I rode over to Gong's mob. I said, "OK – we'll
get married."

That afternoon we rode into town, me and Gong, and
went to see the deaconess, Sister Horsborough. She asked
what religion we were. Gong was Presbyterian, I was a
Catholic and she was a Methodist Sister, so we were a great
big fruit salad. It didn't matter to us, and it didn't worry
her either. At the time there was a Methodist Church at
the back of the big school, a little blue building. We made
arrangements to get married there and split off back to our
own camps. We moved the sheep on again the next morning
and I rode with the mob because we didn't have to be at
the church until three o'clock. Then I had to ride back
about eleven miles to get married – in me work clothes,
not the pink dress! We tied our horses up on the fence

and went into the church with our witnesses – Gong's sister-in-law, Jean, and a friend of Gong's, Fred Hilt, a feller they called Booney Hilt. We left straight after, just jumped on the horses, didn't have a cup of tea or nothin', because I had a long way to ride to catch up to the camp. As I rode off Gong called out, "See you in eleven weeks."

So there I was, back in camp, with this new ring on. The cook said, "What're you doin' with that new ring, Ev?"

"I got a husband, you know." And was I proud of it!

We had four or five Christmases in the tent – didn't go to someone else's place. I know Pussy was sad that she was in her house with decorations hangin' all over and we were in the bough shed. By that time we had a proper wooden table Dummy had made, and some coloured paper and a few things out of the lolly stockings hangin', and balloons for the kids. Every Christmas felt like a special Christmas to me in my own private little world. One year was very special – Gong won the only raffle in his life – a Christmas Stocking, eight foot high!

I was pretty independent. One day Dummy was sittin' at my fire, rollin' a smoke, and I was makin' a brownie for the kids. He said, "You know what, Ev. I never seen a woman like you before in my life."

"What d'ya call all the rest of 'em, ham sandwiches?"

"Shut up and listen! Ya know what I'm talkin' about."

"No, I don't. You tell me."

"Ya do everything for yourself. Doesn't seem to worry you if Gong's away weeks at a time. Ya look after the kids, cookin' all the time, washin' all the time."

"That's me job. I'm a mum."

"Yeah, but you're a young person – must be somethin' you want to do or 'ave for yourself."

"I got plenty to do 'ere. The day's not long enough for me. I got all I want with Gong and the kids. That's the way my mum looked after us, Dum."

"Well, Gong's bloody lucky, 'n I 'ope 'e knows it."

Gong did know it. He said to me, "When I'm ridin' along an' I think, 'Wonder how the old woman an' the kids are gittin' on', I'm glad I don't 'ave to worry."

That was the greatest compliment he could've ever paid me, that he could trust me to look after our kids that way he wanted 'em looked after.

I loved doin' things with them. We'd swim across the river to the tip and find all sorts of treasures. I helped Alan make a little cart with wood and a set of wheels we found there. We could drag it to get firewood, and on wash days, when I only had four kids to wash for, we'd use it to pull the buckets of water up to the camp to do the washing. When you washed every day there wasn't a big heap to do, and anyway we didn't have heaps of clothes to let it pile up! It was only later when I had a mob of kids that I had to take the washin' down to the river. At the tip I found a flat iron with a rattly handle and the kids all learned to iron with it – still got it! – chromed over now as a keepsake.

I'd take the kids fishin', boil the billy and have a picnic. We'd go walkin' and I'd show them all the things Uncle Archie had taught us. I never seemed to run out of things to do, but it was always things I **wanted** to do, when I wanted to do 'em, and how I wanted to do 'em . . . in my own time, so life was good and relaxed.

Then Gong had no work for a while, so at last he got started on the HOUSE – went at it in a big white-feller way of building. He got a long fishing line and said, "I have to measure this now."

"Measure what?"

"Measure to see how long we want the house and how wide."

I could have laughed all the time. I thought to myself, "This blackfeller doesn't know a bloody thing about buildin' a house," but I didn't say anything.

Then he called back to me, "Cook up some meat and a couple of dampers. I'm goin' out to the bush with Simmo." So they went out in the truck to the sandhills and cut big pine logs to saw them into blocks.

I was puzzled. "What do you want blocks for, boy?"

"To put a floor in the house. You can't put a floor right on the ground. You've got to raise it up a bit."

I looked, and I laughed, 'cos all my life I'd lived on the ground. I'd never once said to myself, "Gee, I'd like to live in a house with a floor in it," because I knew I'd never get it. Poor old Dad, he did the best that he could for us, and none of us wanted any more than what he provided for us. We never wished for what we couldn't have.

I caught myself thinking, "At last I'll have a house with a real floor in it," then got sad to think that Dad had done his best, and here I was, thinkin' like that. I talked to Gong about it because I didn't feel good. I wanted that house with a floor, and I didn't want to hurt my old Dad. He said, "Your father'll understand. It won't worry him. He'll be pleased to know you've got a house with a floor in it."

They set up a rack to hold the logs and everybody took turns with the crosscut saw to cut blocks all one weekend. They were about four-foot blocks because the house was about two foot off the ground. Gong wanted it high enough for his work dogs to camp under. He really relied on his dogs to help him earn a living, so he looked after them well. Whenever he wasn't away working we sawed more blocks, and a whole mob of helpers landed on us at the weekends – all Aboriginal fellers, and some of them must have been the greatest rum drinkers you ever seen. Some with a little bit of knowledge of building, some with none, but with their bottle of rum they put that house up in no time. By then our fourth baby was crawlin' round, gettin' under everyone's feet, so a couple of years had gone by since we first started. I was so sick when she was on the way, I nearly died when she was born, so Gong named her

'Evelyn', thinkin' he was goin' to lose me. We mostly call her Tiny, I suppose because she isn't!

Just as well we got it built, with nine more babies after Tiny, between 1955 and 1969 – Diane (Bimbo), Rodney (Rocco), Raymond John (Jack), Guy, Val (Chooby), Verina, Cheryl (Dinty), Rebecca (Tilly) and Jess.

In the north-east sky there's a cluster of stars – the Seven Sisters. My six sons can relate to that because they've got seven sisters! When they can get a clear view of each separate star they say, "That's Maree . . . Ducky . . . Tiny . . . Bimbo . . . Verina . . . Rebecca," and the one that twinkles the most, "That's Dinty!" not because she's prettiest or happiest, but because she's so **noisy**!

We had a lot of arguments buildin' that house. Gong'd say, "Hold this tin up, old woman, while I nail it." When he'd finished it'd look crooked so he'd say I didn't hold it straight. I'd git the huffs and throw the tin down and say, "Do it yourself!" There'd be times when I'd be throwin' the orders, and he'd chuck the hammer and nails down. "Do it yourself!" he'd say, and go and sit down somewhere. Couple of hours after, we'd come back and finish it. It surely was a Do-it-yourself house.

Later on there were big decisions where to put the fruit trees. They were precious things. Father Patrick Killeen from Bourke used to come out to Bre. One day he said to me, "Have you got any fruit trees, Evelyn?"

"Nah, we can't afford to buy fruit trees, Father."

Next time he came over from Bourke in his van he had six fruit trees for us, grapefruit, orange, lemon, mandarin – and one little mulberry tree. Now that mulberry tree caused heaps and heaps of hassles. There was times if Father Killeen had've come along, I'd have wrapped him up in it. It caused bellyaches, and stains on good clothes that I couldn't get out. The soles of the kids' feet were purple from runnin' on the ground under the tree, and the stain'd rub off on the sheets. "Just as well he's gone back to Ireland," I'd say, "He's not safe if he comes back 'ere!" Even before he went back I used to go mad at him about it, and all he'd say in his coaxin' Irish voice was, "Oh, but Evelyn, the kids like mulberries. Don't you yourself now?"

"Yes, Father, but if I'd known it was going to be such a hassle I wouldn't have said 'Yes, give it to me'."

He brought some vine sticks too, so we had grapes as well. We had plenty of fruit, plenty of vegetables, plenty of milk, plenty of eggs, plenty of fish, and though there was no money, we had plenty of love. And I think that's what we all survived on.

Like all families, we had some frights with the kids. Alan – oh, he was a terrible boy! – drank kerosene when he was two and nearly died. Kero looked like water in them days and I suppose he thought it was lemonade. I don't know how much he drank. I found him layin' there like he was in a fit, lost 'is breath and went white. I grabbed 'im and filled him up full of goat's milk.

Gong was away on a job, and Alan was gaspin' for breath so Dummy got his old Ford and took us to the hospital. They never had all the equipment in hospitals outback in them days, but Dr Lopes struggled and kept him alive. Alan got pneumonia and was in hospital weeks and it took almost until he grew up to get over it. While he was there they found out he was a bleeder. The doctor explained all about it to me, and that as more babies come along probably more of them would be the same. Just imagine what it was like tryin' to make sure those wild boys didn't cut themselves while they was growin' up!

That was a terrible experience for me. I felt so sorry for Alan and so bad about it from thinkin' it was my fault, that I'd left kero lyin' about. I was still gittin' to know all the things you needed to know and do to be a sensible mum. I had no Mum there with me, and no Grannies. I suppose you have to expect accidents with a heap of kids, but they were always happening. Maybe it just seems that way, and we only remember the unusual things. In raisin' my kids I tried to think of all the things that Mum and Granny Knight and Granny Moysey and Granny Mallyer taught us in the camp when we were kids and then I did that. I think it was thanks to those three Grannies that I still have my thirteen kids alive today.

That kero episode didn't change Alan. He sniffed another bottle when he was about five and it didn't smell like kero so he thought he'd taste it, and – back to hospital. This time it was turps. His father said, "Anything else this boy'd like to taste? We'll get him some sheepdip or paint."

After that Alan was always pale and he was a man before he got really strong again. It doesn't take much to make him sick. If someone's badly hurt or cut, he'll help them, but that will throw him very quick, then he'll be sick himself.

Maudie Barker lived near us and she had sixteen kids, and had learned from her Grannies, so we leaned on each other. But I still kept doing some stupid things. Like the time when Lesley was about five.

A bottle had fallen off the table and broken and I asked her to throw it away. She'd thrown a piece away and picked up another bit, then I heard this terrible scream, **Mu-u-um-m**! I raced out to see what was wrong and the blood was just pouring out of her fingers. I stood there, didn't know what to do, then I started callin'. Dummy ran over – Gong was away – 'n he wrapped her hand and tied it up, and said, "I'll take ya to the hospital." I could hardly hear him over Lesley's screamin', and me own heart beatin'.

At the hospital they said someone would have to sign the paper to give her the chloroform. That was the first time I'd ever had to do anything like that and it really worried me. I didn't know what this 'puttin' under chloroform' was, so I said, "No, no." They told me she'd just go to sleep and not wriggle while they stitched the finger – cut all the way down it was. They could do the job properly and she wouldn't feel any pain. The doctor showed me the pad they'd put over her face and the bottle of stuff, and said they'd use just a couple of drops. But I had pictures of her not wakin' up again! and kept sayin' 'no'.

I went down to the Post Office and rung up the station where Gong was. He said to get Dummy to drive out and pick him up. Dummy dropped me off at home and I stayed there. Gong signed and they stitched her up. When he brought Lesley home he said, "You coulda just put your name on that paper. It said 'father or mother or guardian'.

"I didn't know what they were goin' to do, did I?"

So he took the time to explain why they did these things. There I was, four babies down the track, and I didn't know what chloroform was. I never had needles or chloroform for any of my thirteen babies, and I was pretty bad when Tiny was comin'.

When I took Lesley to enrol her at school I worried again, because she's dark like her father. But she was one of those 'full-of-confidence' kids. "I'll be right, Mumma!" She was standin' there with me while I was talkin' to the teacher, and the teacher looked down at her and said, "Little Lesley Crawford." The kid looked at me as much as to say, "I'm Ducky, not **Lesley!**"

She come home one day and said, "Mumma, I don't like that name, Lesley."

"You'll git used to it, mate."

But she didn't have to. All the other kids knew she was Ducky Crawford, and the teachers soon started using it too.

Diane came along on the 27th of May in 1955 and was mostly called Bimbo. She was a kid always on the go, energy like you've never seen. When she was about four, she was runnin' down the gully chasin' the goats and got a **bad** cut under her foot, nearly cut it in half. We took her to the hospital and they stitched it up and wouldn't let her come home in case she ran round and split the stitches open.

Every day I'd row over and take her something – a rag doll
I made, couple of little old coloured pencils and a picture
to colour in. The first day when I was walkin' behind the
hospital comin' up from the river, I could hear that kid
cryin', "I wanna go 'ome in the boat to my mother." I
went to the front and saw Jan Halbish, the Matron who
was relieving then. Later she came back to Bre, about when
Chooby was born in 1962, and has been there ever since –
a very good support to me when my kids were growin' up.

"Is Bimbo alright?"

"Right as pie," she said, "all the kids are like that. She'll
stop in a minute and be playing again."

"Well, I won't go near her. It'll just make her worse
for you all."

"Good idea," said Jan. "I'll give her the things and tell
her you sent them."

I went every day, and every day I heard that kid cryin'.
She never settled down so on the fifth day they said I could
take her home. When she was nine, she cut that same foot,
crossways in the same place, playing in that same gully, and
as Gong said, probably on the same bit of glass. They didn't
wear their shoes when they were home – kept 'em for school.
Everyone of them, I'd say, has got long cuts under their feet.

Gong would be away on trips, twelve, fifteen weeks at
a time. Once when Rocco was about three, he come inside
and said, "Evelyn – never calls me 'Mum', this boy – Evelyn,
there's a strange blackfeller at your gate."

"Yeah? Who is he?"

"On a 'orse."

I thought to meself, "Wonder who that could be," and
I looked out. "Boy, that's your father!"

Gong had been away so long Rocco didn't know him!
He'd been caught in floods and couldn't get home.

Livin' on the river bank, we had lively times when the floods
came down. One time when the water was high, we were

down at the river washin'. We used to wash all day Sunday so everyone c'd help and there'd be clean clothes for the week. Jack was about six, always tellin' us how well he could swim. What he called swimmin' was his arms goin' and his feet still well on the ground! He 'swam', his friend Johnny Barker with him, from where we were on the bank to a little island the floods had made. They got there, and Johnny sang out, "Hey! Look there!" and it was an old goanna who desperately wanted to git from that island – don't know how long he'd been there without a feed – onto the bank. Jack went back into the water and the goanna must've thought, "I'll tag a ride," and jumped on Jack's back, his head on the back of Jack's head, his front claws on Jack's shoulders and the back ones on his bottom. I was washin', Gong was fryin' meat 'cos we were havin' dinner there, and we heard this commotion.

Gong called out to me, "What's wrong with that boy? He's goin' on like a buckin' horse in the water."

"He's just muckin' up," but of course he was tryin' to shake this big lizard off his back! Soon as he ran up the bank the old *thirridyah* just fell off and cleared!

The Hardys lived near us. Old Grandfather Hardy had a great old saying, when people didn't do what he planned, like having regular claypan dances, "Well, if ya don't wanna 'ave 'em, we'll 'bolish 'em." Always sayin' it about everything, so people got to calling him Bolishem Hardy. That went on for years and years so my kids never knew his name was really Henry Hardy. He was a hard-workin' old feller and liked his drop of rum. In those days Aboriginal people weren't allowed to have grog, so the station owner used to have a few bottles of rum for him, so he didn't have to try to get it in town.

One Thursday we were all down on the river bank gettin' fish for Good Friday, and along comes Bolishem, with a sugar bag of vegetables for us – he grew lots of good vegetables, and he was generous with them – and his bottle of rum, steppin' high and real merry. He sat down and started fishin' with us, talkin' real loud, not too good for the fishin'. After a while he got sick of us tellin' him to be quiet, so he said in a stage whisper to Gong,

"Gonna go 'ome and git a feed, Horse. I've left me shrimp can in the water for more bait." Bolishem called every man 'Horse", like you'd say 'Mate'.

When he come back later he pulled his shrimp can out, and waited till all the water drained out. Then he made this terrible noise, like you see written in comics – ARRRGGHHHH – dropped the can, turned and ran up the bank. He must've tripped 'cos he rolled down into a gully and we never seen him any more!

Gong jumped up, "Gord, what's wrong with that feller? He must've 'ad a heart attack."

We all got to him, and he was layin' there moanin', no hat on, head all scratched, and his nose bleedin'.

"You alright, old feller?"

"Yeah . . . yeah." 'e was pantin' it out. "Yeah, I'm alright, Horse . . . shrimp can . . . shrimp can . . .!"

Gong went and pulled out the can and there's this bloody great dead brown snake in the shrimp can!

Now that morning they'd killed a big brown snake in Dummy Smith's fowl house. Nothin' would suit Alan, about eleven he would have been, but to sneak that snake down to the river, but no one knew that at the time. Course, Alan thought it a good joke to put it in Bolishem's can. His father said, "You get home now. You're not fishin' any more. Take all those fish home, clean 'em and cut 'em up ready for your mother."

Alan was always this stupid joker. But he got his just reward a couple of days after, on the Easter Sunday. We were down fishin' again – we lived on fish – and he was runnin' around in the shallow, muddy water. Now catfish love to swim in muddy water, so what did Alan do? He trod on a little catfish, and the bones stuck in his toe. He cried all the way over to the hospital, and all the way back home, cried and cried, and cried himself to sleep.

The next day his father said to him, "Right, you must've got punished because you frightened that old feller with the snake. God doesn't like cruel jokes."

I said, "Oh, there's catfish everywhere in muddy water. He just happened to tread on one – just bad luck."

So for years he didn't know which one of us to believe, 'cos he was the heathen feller that wouldn't go to Sunday School. Everybody else went but not Alan. But he didn't play that kind of trick again, at least not on Bolishem or any other old feller.

Alan loved to go shooting for kangaroos at night with his friends and in the morning he'd be too tired and sleepy to go to school. But when he was in school he did very well, won a CWA bursary for a sketch he did of the man on the horse spearin' the dragon – St George it was. He went to Melbourne for a year, went to ordinary school and had special art lessons. But in them days boys couldn't grow up fast enough to go to work. At fourteen he went into the shearing sheds, and he's been in the sheds ever since – for years on stations around Brewarrina, then he went to Queensland. He does a lot of sketching now, real quick at it he is, not traditional Aboriginal art, but in the white man's style. While his brother is playin' the guitar, Alan'll make a picture of him that almost talks to you.

Chooby's a feller who worried me almost to death. He was about two, and Guy a couple of years older, and the five or six older ones were at school. With that big mob of kids I'd take the washing down to the river.

One day I had the stones rigged up and the copper boiling on the fire. We had an old stroller that Chooby was really too big for, but he and Guy used it like a play-cart. They'd take turns pushin' each other round. He'd climbed in it and gone to sleep with his feet tucked under that front step, 'cos his legs were a bit too long. I'd gone up to the house to get tea and bread and stuff 'cos we were havin' dinner there. Chooby must've woke up and wriggled and the stroller moved and run down into the fire. The wheels were each side of the fire, the hot boilin' copper was against his two knees. He'd been able to pull the right foot up, but his left foot was jammed, and the fire got to the side of his little toe.

We had a little stumpy-tail dog that loved the kids, the only pet dog we had, the others were all workers. Stumpy ran and met me and was grabbin' hold of my dress, pullin' me. I dropped everything and ran to see what was wrong, and there was Chooby fryin' in the fire. He never made a noise or nothin'. He'd already passed out with the pain. I grabbed that stroller and ran 'im, pram and all, into the river. The cold water brought him around a little bit, and I left him in the the water till he started to cry.

Now it was a Thursday, and every Thursday Doctor Lopes used to come around to the bend where all the Aboriginal camps were, and look at the old pensioners, take their blood pressure, check their medicines, 'cos they had no way of gettin' in to the town. I knew he was due soon. I had no one with me. Guy had wandered off, and I knew no one was at home at Dummy's. So I left Chooby in the pram in the water, with the tiny dog to mind him, and tied him and the pram with a rope onto a tree so they wouldn't git washed away. Then I ran up the bank and along the track to where an old feller lived by himself, one of the people the doctor come out for. I hardly had any breath when I got there. "Tell the doctor t'come straight down to the river when he comes. Me little boy's burnt." I only waited till I was sure he understood and I was off. The doctor came, had a look at him. "I'll take you with him over to the hospital."

"I'll have to find my other little boy first."

"Well, I'll take this one in, and you can come in later on."

"Let me put dry clothes on him . . ."

"No, he'll be right, dearie. I'll get straight off."

The doctor carried him up to the car and gave him a needle. Chooby was a bit whingey, kept sayin', "Mumma, you comin' up? you comin' up?"

"Yeah, I'm comin' up, lovey."

Pussy came home. While I was askin' her to tell the kids where we were when they come home from school Guy turned up from wherever he'd been playin' and I took him with me in to the hospital. We sat there with Chooby for a long time while they done his foot, and he kept cryin', "Wanna go 'ome." The doctor asked if I could look after him if he let him go home, because it was sure he wouldn't settle down if they kept him, and being upset wouldn't give him a good chance to get better. "Yeah, we'll be right," so he put us in his car and drove us home. Gong was away again on a trip. I had a big heaps of bandages and stuff to change the dressing. I wasn't to change it before four days, and it was so smelly from the heaps and heaps of Ung-Vita, that oily, fishy ointment.

His brothers and sisters were very good to him and he never complained. His special place was always the big rock in the river, the one we call Buggy Rock. Every day he'd sit there fishin' with his little line. The hardest for him was not being able to go anywhere near the river, because the foot had to be kept dry.

Chooby ended up with a whole slice off down the side of his foot 'cos the fire had burned to the bone. He told me he really felt it in the Army wearing them heavy army boots. His knees are fire-scarred too, and his hands where he'd kept tryin' to push himself back.

The Buggy Rock stayed a special place for him always. When he was about five, he came back to the house from where he'd been fishin' there callin', in his big deep loud voice, "Mumma, Mumma!"

"What now?" I thought.

"Mumma, there's a white lady lyin' on the Buggy Rock, and **she's got no clothes on!**"

It was one of the young nurses from the hospital who used to sunbathe there every day. I tried to explain to him that she had a bikini on, but he'd never seen one. His biggest worry was that all the crayfish he'd caught would be crawling out of the can!

I saw her in the street the next day and said, "Did you see that little black kid fishin' yesterday?"

"Yes. I tried to talk to him, but he ran away."

"That was my Chooby. He was embarrassed because he thought you had no clothes on!"

Towards the end of 1963, not long after Chooby got burnt, and not very long before Verina was born, Gong got sick. They sent him to Lewisham Hospital in Sydney and took his kidney out. I couldn't go with him, because we had no money and no one to mind the kids. He had to go through that scary time by himself. It was hard for him goin' off, but it was harder coming back. He couldn't handle his case, he was that weak. He said he was so giddy in the head he just sat in the train and hoped for the best. An Aboriginal feller he met on the train, Jack Griffiths, must've had some idea he was sick, talked to him and helped him. Gee, that feller was good – didn't get off at his own town, but stayed on and brought Gong right home. John Simmonds met Gong at Bourke station and when they got back to Bre they had this strange feller with them. He become our life-long friend. So I had Gong sick, Chooby with his bad foot, a heap of kids to look after, and Verina on the way!

Doctor Lopes come around one day and said to Gong, "You're not well enough to work, and won't be for a long time, so you're entitled to the pension. I'll help you apply for it."

Says this old proud blackfeller, "Nah, I'm not applyin' for no pension. I'm right."

"You've got to get it, man. It'll be months before you can work, and your family's got to be fed."

In them days, when we were rearin' our kids, there was no Sickness Benefits, you had to pay for every Aspro, every drop of medicine you got, plus payin' the doctor's fees.

It took a lot of hard talking before we convinced him, and the doctor helped. But Gong was a man with a lot of determination. He picked himself up, even got more weight on his lanky bones.

Not too long after that he got crook again and this time they sent him to Dubbo to do more tests on the other kidney. Pussy said she'd mind the kids for us, and the big ones were great, so I was able to go with him. I seemed to be there a long time, though it was only four days. You know, when you're sittin' in a hospital, everything slows down. I was feelin' pretty sick meself at the time, with the baby I was expecting, so I said, "Reckon I'll 'ave to go home to the kids, Gong." That was me excuse, 'cos I didn't want him to be worryin' about me – he had enough on his plate.

When I got home, everything was right, just like I'd left it. The big ones were wonderful, helpin' out. The kids were at school, nice big fresh damper in the cupboard, the boys had killed a goat and corned some of the meat, and were already in the process of tannin' the hide for a mat. I'd worried about the goats too, 'cos I knew some of the old nannies were due to have their babies. They wander away and hide their kids in logs and under trees, and the silly things would lose 'em and come 'ome with no kids. You'd 'ave to go lookin', and if you don't find 'em the dogs'll git 'em. We had forty-three young chickens and they were still there. In fact a bantam had hatched out four more. It was like as if I'd never been away. The kids had always been like that. When Gong was away droving, and it was time for me to go to the hospital for a new baby to be born, I'd say to the older ones, "Look, I have to go to the hospital now. You look after the kids."

Until the oldest were big enough to take the boat for me, I'd go down to the boat, row meself across, climb up that steep bank on the town side, carry me case to the hospital, have the baby, stay there for four days, then row meself back with the new baby. The house wouldn't be out of place, it would be just like I hadn't been away. The kids were wonderful. They made it possible, and they made it all worthwhile. None of us could have lived without each other. Everyone had his own job and didn't shirk it, 'cos if he did, someone else would have to do two jobs, and we always taught them that wasn't fair. Dummy said, "These kids of yours are better 'ousekeepers than my old woman!"

When Gong got home from Dubbo he was still pretty sick, couldn't work and was battlin' to get well again, and didn't think much of sittin' round at home. Verina was born that January, and when I brought her home from hospital, he had the baby to play with, so she became Dad's girl. It was great for me. I didn't worry then that he had nothin' to do, or that the baby needed a dry nappy or a feed. That was his job. It was 'specially good for me, because I had someone to talk to other than the kids. He took over most of the cooking, and when I came up from the river after doin' a big wash there was a feed ready for us.

Her father called her Verina and I asked him, "Where'd you get that name from? I've never heard it before."

"I was sittin' in the cart shed one day on a station where I was workin', and all these bags was folded and stacked up, and I seen this word, 'VERINA'. I reckoned it'd be a nice name for a little girl. I undone the top bag and it was a fowl food bag from the Ri**verina**! I laughed, but I still think it'd be a pretty name." Her aboriginal name, *Toorah*, means the 'mothering one', and she is just that. Sometimes I think she mothers me!

Verina stayed Dad's girl and she was as much a scallywag as her own kid is now. She loved to stick her finger in the dough when I was mixin' a cake. All the kids knew the rule was: 'one finger each in the basin', and there'd be so much on the fingers I'd wonder if there'd be any cake left to cook! But she'd break the rule – she had to put **two** in.

One day I was makin' an emu egg brownie and went outside for something. When I came back there was no one in the kitchen, but there was a yellow trail of cake mixture along the table and across the floor. She'd taken a fistful. I tracked her out to the shed where she was sittin' with a broody hen, her fist in her mouth, suckin' off what was left.

"You're not gettin' no cake when it's cooked."

"Daddy'll make me a cake."

"Well, I'm not. You and Dad can have your own cake."

After she was pre-school age, she loved playing 'cubby house' with her rag dolls, but if an arm or leg came off, it was catastrophe! You'd have to drop everything and find a needle and cotton, otherwise that kid would cry and cry. That was when Bimbo started to be good at sewing, mending those dolls, and it was a great load off me. As she grew older Verina even become like her dad. She could whistle to his workin' dogs, when they was just layin' on the hill mindin' their own business, 'n send 'em for the goats. Didn't he scream!

"Who's messin' round with my dogs? You got your own dogs to chase the goats. My dogs are sheep dogs! I don't want 'em with them smelly old goats!"

Guy'd say, "Toorah, Dad." But she'd be gone.

None of the kids were used to their father being around all the time so that time after he'd been in Dubbo Hospital was great for all the family. They really got to know him as a person. He used to say to me, "These kids of yours are all friendly, old woman, aren't they, eh?"

"Yeah, when y'git to know 'em, they're real friendly."

222

"What're we gonna do with this bony feller? (that's what he called Guy). He's a bit of a live wire!"

Guy's aboriginal name is '*Ekla*' ... the 'hurry-up, no-patience feller'. I'm always grabbing him by the hair and sayin', "Look, slow down, boy. Don't panic, don't worry."

Val's just the opposite. His Aboriginal name is '*Chooby*'. That's his registered name, but he called himself Val. *Chooby* means 'the slow person', 'the comin'-behind feller', and he's the slowest thing this side of a turtle! Yet he's got all that education. Even at the TAFE College where he teaches they say, "Where's Val? When's he ever going to get here? We're all waiting."

Kids are five or six days old when they're given Aboriginal names, and what amazes me is the meaning of those names is what those kids grew up to be.


When Rocco was about eight, he had a hernia operation. They did it in the morning and I went to see him in the afternoon. Gong was away. That night I was asleep and thought I might've been dreamin'. I heard a far-away voice callin', a kid's voice singin' out, "Jack, bring the boat, Jack, bring the boat!" It was dark outside, and cloudy, so I said to meself, "You're just hearin' things." Then it came again, so I went and said to Jack, who was awake too, "Jack, c'n you hear anyone singin' out?"

"Yeah – over the river – sounds like Rocco."

I looked at the clock and said, "It couldn't be. It's half-past-three in the morning!"

We went down to where we had the boat tied, and could see this little white speck across the river. It was himself in pyjamas – he'd snuck out of the hospital. We went over and got him and brought him home. He couldn't straighten up, with all the stitches across his belly. We put him to bed and I thought, "Well, when they miss him, they'll come lookin' for him."

About seven o'clock old Jimmy Barker came around. He worked at the hospital.

"That little boy of yours, he's not at the hospital."

"No, he's in bed in there, asleep."

"I've come to take him back."

"Yeah, alright," and I went in to wake him up.

It's a wonder they didn't hear him at the hospital ... "I'm not goin'! I'm stoppin' 'ome!"

Jimmy said, "Don't upset him. Go to sleep, boy." He got in his car and away he went.

About eleven o'clock Doctor Lopes came round, and Rocco was sittin' on a rusty tin out the back feeding his little chickens.

"Coming back to the hospital with me, mate?"

"No! I'm stoppin' 'ere!"

So the doctor left him home and came every day. It was about fourteen days before he could straighten up. I worried because I thought he might have got an infection because he mucked around the fowl house with his chickens.

Around that time Lesley – she was about fifteen – won a big bursary for herself. The Rodeo Committee and the CWA gave bursaries for kids who were good scholars and she won it. She'd always fitted into school real well, and went away to a boarding College in Bathurst where the station owners' kids went.

Gong and me had thought ten years of schooling – from five to fifteen – was enough for any kid. The rest of the learning was what would come from life later on. In those days, white man's education didn't mean a real lot to us. You just used it enough to get by, so you wouldn't feel stupid if somebody spoke to you. We didn't want our kids embarrassed. Then as our kids did real well, we were proud of them, but didn't want to flaunt 'em in anybody's eyes, makin' out what great parents we were. It wasn't us that was doin' it. It was the kids themselves who had to work hard to get where they wanted.

Lesley changed then from bein' **our** Ducky to bein' **her**

**own** Lesley. But it didn't make any difference in the family. You know, 'Absence makes the heart grow fonder' and everybody was so glad to see her back. We'd be all lined up on the river bank waitin' for the rowboat to pull in, bringin' her across the river.

In every way the river was always part of our family life – we ate from it, we drank from it, we washed in it, we played in it. Every kid that lived on the bank had to learn to swim as soon as possible. Even kids a few months old, you'd take 'em in with you in the summer time. I hadn't grown up on a big river so I didn't do that for my first kids till Dummy told me.

Bimbo nearly drowned one day when we were all swimmin'. Jess, our youngest, was a baby, so she was about fourteen. She played a lot with the boys and always played to win, played rough. That's why they nicknamed her 'Horse'. I used to say to them, "Don't let her get away with that just because she's a girl. Treat her like she's playing. Play rough with her back." At first they thought I'd go crook if they hurt her, but after a while they took me at me word.

This day the river was high, but not a real fast flood. Gong was with us. All the kids were playin' round and Bimbo could really look after herself, so we never missed her. All of a sudden her father just pulled her up out of the water by the hair! Floatin' by, she was, under the water.

When he got her on the bank and she had her eyes open, he said, "Where'd you come from, Bimbo?"

"Fell off the Guhneet Rock and hit me head."

It's a big rock, like a tiny island, and has a split in it so when the water is runnin' high it makes funny noises. *Guhneet* means 'ghost'.

"Right," says Gong, "That's it. Everyone out." I knew he was goin' to rouse on 'em to stay together in the water and look out for each other all the time.

I was out on the bank with our dog Stumpy, and thirteen-year-old Rocco was up a tree that leaned over the water, with Johnny Barker. Rocco dived, but before he hit the water his arms and legs were going' every way and he was singin' out. Just as he dived, there was a big black snake swimmin' upstream amongst all the kids, and between the limb and the water he saw it. He fell flat on his belly and came up yellin', "Snake! Snake!" All the kids dived under the water then, and all you could see was Gong and this black snake. That was the best thing they could've done, 'cos snakes swim on the top. I was countin' heads as they popped up, then the snake was comin' out right where I was. Stumpy made a grab for him, and I couldn't see where the dog had hold of him, 'cos the snake was wrapped right round the little white terrier. Gong got out of the water, all the kids were screamin' and cryin', and I was singin' out, "Save the dog!" Then the dog keeled over and just lay there. Course, everyone was cryin' for the dog, we all loved 'im. There was no movement at all from the snake. Stumpy heard his name and the little short tail started goin'! We thought he was on his last.

Gong got a stick and tried to unwind the snake. When he did, the little dog wriggled himself out. He 'ad blood all over him. He'd chewed the snake's head nearly off – it just just hangin' by a couple of inches of skin, and he was exhausted. The snake must've been tryin' to squeeze the breath out of him. We washed the blood off and looked for bite marks. He hadn't been bitten and lived for years after that.

The rule was made then that when people were swimmin' there always had to be one on the bank watchin' out, 'specially in flood times when the river risin' would wash snakes out of logs and holes on the bank.

There's a lot more to the Fishtraps in Bre than people realize. They still work. People who know how still use them. When we were rearin' the kids we used them all the time. You've heard of the Bible story – is it 'The Three Little Fishes and the Loaves of Bread'? Right! Well, it's very true, 'cos that's how Gong and me raised our kids. That story's very dear to my old heart. You wouldn't think Guy would be so mad on fishing still today 'cos sometimes that's all we had to feed our kids on. We really needed that food. We had damper, but our meat was mostly fish. I could say to Rocco, "Go down and get a fish."

"Righto. How big d'ya want it?"

"About this big, or that big . . ." or whatever size we wanted.

He could go down to the traps and be gone for about half an hour and come back with just that size fish. They spent that much time on those rocks, them kids, they knew where the big fish were. The boys blocked 'em up and caught 'em with their hands, and stuck a stick in the gills. I suppose they got so good at it from **havin'** to so we could eat. That was before we got the goats, and their meat was a luxury. We had chooks but we couldn't kill a fowl to make chicken soup because we needed the eggs. They were the scraggiest lot of fowls – 'ten-feathered chooks' Gong called 'em. Made no difference, so long as they laid.

One day I was doin' the washing down at the river where the rocks are. We'd put the washing in the pram and wheeled it down, the kids'd lugged the tubs and soap, and we'd lit the fire and put the boiler on.

An old lady who lived a bit further up the river had heaps of white ducks. Me and the kids were gettin' the washin' ready, and these ducks came swimmin' past us – there was no weir then. I kept an eye on them because they were a real pest – always grabbing my little bars of soap. They'd swim off and the slippery wet soap would fall out of their bill and the kids would have to dive and feel for it so I could get on with the washing.

Guy was about six, and he's always said things before he thinks – he's one feller you couldn't trust to keep his tongue quiet.

"What're they like to eat, Mum?" asked Guy.

"They're real good eatin', boy."

Rocco, about nine he was, and the scallywag of the family, was on the bank a bit further down, fishin' for crayfish. A little while after, there was a commotion and the ducks all flew. I thought they went back to the old lady's place. Then round the bend came Rocco, over to me with a duck under his arm and said, " 'ere's one of them ducks."

"What 'appened to him?"

"I dunno. 'e was floatin' past and I just grabbed 'im and got 'im out."

"But they were alright . . . they're not sick, are they?"

"Nah, he's alright . . . but you was sayin' . . ."

Guy was feelin' the duck, liftin' its wing, tryin' to see what's wrong with this dead duck. Guy wouldn't hurt anything.

Jack said, "Why don't we just pluck 'im and chuck 'im in the camp oven?"

There was nothin' else I could do, the duck was dead, so the boys plucked him – away went the white feathers down the stream – cleaned the duck, cut 'im up out on the Buggy Rock, and put him in the oven.

We had vegies growing. The boys used to cart water up the bank to the 44-gallon drums, and it was the girls' job to carry it from there to water the garden. So I sent the kids up to get carrots and parsnips and potatoes, and into the oven it all went with plenty of curry. It was on the fire and goin' good when the dog started barking. It was the old lady who owned the ducks! She said, "Evelyn, you never seen any of them ducks of mine about, eh?"

There was about nine of us there, and we all looked at Guy. He was sort of fidgettin', workin' up to something, as if the words was comin' from the bottom inside him and was gonna fall out. We're all givin' him black looks, and Jack went over and sat on a log and pulled Guy down beside him, and said, "Siddown still, boy."

"I seen 'em early this morning. They come past here, then they flew off. Think they went your way."

"Well, I haven't seen any of 'em anywhere. Dunno where they could be."

Not one kid spoke. She was there talkin' to me for a while, but I can't even remember what the poor old woman was saying. I was too worried about that kid, thinkin' any minute he'd open his mouth and say something about that duck cookin' in the camp oven.

As she was goin' she said, "Ya might git these boys to 'ave a look down the river for me when they've had a feed. I see you're cookin' dinner."

"Yeah, they'll do that."

Off she went, and she wouldn't've been more than fifty yards away when Guy piped up, "Mum, why didn't ya tell 'er we was cookin' one of them ducks?"

"Because she'd've told the policeman and he'd put us all in jail, 'cos that's stealin'."

All Jack's life has revolved around horses. He'd ride anything, and I mean **anything!** . . . could've ridden a buckjumper when he was five, that feller. He could be a scamp with the best – or worst – of them.

Aunty Pussy had a pet pig she reared called Elvis. He turned into a huge long barrel of a pig.

One weekend the kids had coaxed Elvis over to our place. I wondered what they were doin' but I left 'em alone. There was Jack, about ten, Rocco and his cousin Johnny Barker were a bit older. Those two were always together. They were good kids at school, but they sure made up for it when they were home. Of course, Guy was there too. It didn't matter what mischief those big boys got into, he always had his two little grubby hands in it somewhere. Jack was lyin' along that pig's great long back and Rocco and Johnny tied him on, arms round its neck, hands tied with bits of rag, feet tied under its belly. While they were lashin' Jack on, Guy kept runnin' into the kitchen sneakin' pieces of damper to feed the pig so he'd stand still.

I come out to pick some of the long tomatoes I had growin', and I could see the kids so very busy down the back. I was thinkin', "Wonder what they're doin'," when Guy took off over to Pussy's yard and was perched up on a rusty tin, singin' out, "El-l-vis! El-l-vis!" Rocco yelled, "Let 'im go!" Elvis took off, headin' straight for that feller wavin' the piece of damper.

I ran out the gate, but was too late. The pig was goin' flat out, with Jack hangin' on, slippin' down this side, then wrigglin' back on top and slidin' the other way. The kids were yellin' – you know how they do when they're havin' fun – that started our dogs barkin'. I'm singin' out from home – uproar! Down the gully went Elvis and Jack, up the rise, hit the rusty tin Guy was standin' on, Guy shot up in the air, and in the gate went the pig. Aunty Pussy comes out her back door with her broom and she started, "What're you doin' to my poor old pig?" That stirred her dogs up too – you never heard such a row.

Pussy's house had three doors in a line, the back door into the kitchen, the inside kitchen door, and the front door, and they were all open 'cos she was sweepin up. Elvis, and Jack still clingin' on, went straight past her, through that house and out the other side. Jack was on the pig's side then and his back was all skint from the doorway. I'd dumped the tomatoes and raced after them, and all I could think when they came out the front door was, " 'e's headin' for the river, and that kid's tied on!" Then the leg rope broke, and I could see his skinny black legs swingin' up and down, and the big pig canterin' for the river.

Now there were two old fellers comin' across the river, very drunk, in their very old little green boat. One had a big military overcoat on, ten times too big for him. All the bottom of it was stiff with burrs because it was always draggin'. Teddy was only a little man – used to be a jockey years ago. He was half-kneeling, 'cos they only had one oar so he had to use it canoe-way. There were no seats in the boat so the other feller was standin', shiftin' and swayin', carryin' a bottle of Red Mill Rum, and hangin' on to a red cowboy hat full of eggs he'd bought from the Chinamen across the river. Just as the pig got to the bank Jack managed to break the rag tyin' his hands and fell off, and the pig went straight into the river, right when that old boat was comin' to the edge of the water.

Over they went! We were all singin' out! All we could see was the red hat floatin', and a bit of the overcoat. We had to jump in and fish around for them. I pulled at the coat, but it was water-logged so I could hardly move it. I was tryin' to pull him out of the coat. He'd come up every now and then and go "Prr-rr-rr" and sink again. I was callin' out, "Teddy, Teddy!" wantin' him to help me get the coat off. I got him onto the bank and the kids were all divin', lookin' for the other bloke. He surfaced a bit further down river, fetched up against a tree branch, and started singin' out, "Git them aigs, you kids, git them aigs." But the bottle of rum was still in his right hand! He had an old leather coat on, with big pockets, and when he staggered up onto the bank, the water was squirting out of all the little holes in the worn-out leather. He looked like a rusty leakin' tank!

Pussy was cryin', and sayin', "Look at poor little Ted. He must be dead, eh?" I put my foot on him and rocked him a bit and he started groanin'.

"Nah," I said, "he's not dead. Help me get him out of that coat."

He came alive then and said, "Aunty Ev, I had a lot of money. Is it still there?"

We looked and he was lucky, 'cos it was all in silver – sixpences and shillings it was in them days.

When it was all over Aunt Pussy roused on the boys for being cruel to her pig. Jack was skint on the face and on the back where he'd been dragged against the doors, and on the knees when he fell off. Johnny Barker run away, and Guy come in and said, innocent as you please, "Any bread?"

"No. Go and ask Mother Smith for bread. You fed her pig with our bread."

So he went away and come back with an armful of wood and said, "C'n ya cook some pufftaloons, then?"

That was Guy's way of asking. If he was hungry for something special, he'd bring the wood. If I was busy I'd say to one of the bigger girls, "This feller wants this or that – cook him some."

No hassles – all they had to do was mix it up and cook it. He'd climb up on the chair with the long fork, all excited, sayin', "I'll turn it over – let me," splashing them on the arm with the hot fat, splashin' himself on the leg, and he'd be rubbin' his leg but still pokin' in – he was a menace in the kitchen – still is. You've got to push him out of the way to get to the pots when you're cooking.

Those boys, and that Guy! He did the stupidest things – never thought about what he was doin'. Even today when they're both grown men with kids, Rocco says to him, "Smiley, why don't you listen!" – rousin' on him like when he was a little boy.

When he was about nine their father bought 'em a slug gun for Christmas. I didn't say, "No, don't buy it," though I'm terrified of guns, unless it's just one, the one you need to shoot meat, because you gotta eat. Off they went down the river with it, Guy, Rocco and Jack. Like always, they had their knives. They crossed the river just below the house, then crossed it again, and again, 'cos it winds a lot, so they must've been five miles from home, down where there's a little lagoon and plenty of wild ducks. They shot four ducks and were headin' for home, Guy taggin' along, slashin' the tops off the grass with his knife. He sort of missed and it went straight into his leg at the side just above the knee-cap. Lucky it was the bluntest knife in the whole camp. But that feller could hurt himself with a lump of butter!

Rocco swam him piggy-back across one river crossing, and Jack had the ducks and the gun, then they swopped over, 'n kept doin' that till they got home, with Guy on Jack's back. I was outside waterin' some cotton bushes, and the other kids ran round to me yellin' out, "Look at Jack 'n Guy! They're all blood!" When Rocco come up from the gully he was covered in blood too. They'd been in the river three times and the blood had spread pink through their wet clothes. They all looked like galahs.

I thought, "Blood! It's that bloody slug-gun!" and started singin' out to Gong, goin' crook at him. He ran down, and saw that the blood was runnin' out of Guy's knee. Gong grabbed him, then **he** was covered in blood, even his hat, because every time Guy moved, the blood just spurted, even though Jack had torn up his shirt and tied the cut as tight as he could.

The fellers buildin' the new weir below the house took Guy across in their boat, then on to the hospital. That's when we found out that he is a bleeder too. He'd lost so much blood he was just like a piece of old wet rag. As fast as they were puttin' blood into 'im it was seepin' out. The doctor had a terrible time before he could even think about fixin' up the damage inside the knee. Then they had to make that feller keep it still, 'cos any movement would damage it all again. So old Jimmy Barker came along with a piece of deal board and they bandaged it behind his leg. But he'd been a very sick little boy. It took him months and months to restore all that blood and become the happy little feller he'd been.

Cheryl was the worst small kid I ever had for keepin' an eye on. When she was born, her father called her 'Dinty'. That's an Aboriginal word that means, 'you're there, but you're not' – here one minute, then you're somewhere else.

I couldn't keep track of her even in the house. I'd give her something to play with and say, "Just sit there! Don't move!" but turn my back and she was like a snake – just gone. I was everlasting singing out, "Dinty, where are you?"

I had an old black dog that used to follow her about and I got to rely on him. She'd go off, and climb. Climb! She'd be up trees, on top of the fowl house, everywhere. She'd knock herself out, then drop off to sleep wherever she was. When I'd sing out, she'd be dead asleep, but the dog'd give a couple of barks. That Dinty'd be up in the mornin' singin' out, "You fellers gonna cook porridge." You'd look at the time and it'd be ha'past four! Someone'd call out, "Shut up, Dinty. Go back to bed!" Jack would get up for her, 'cos he's the early-bird feller.

All the girls have always been great readers, especially Verina. Whenever their father found books or papers or comics thrown out anywhere, he'd smooth 'em out, pack them in his saddlebag, and bring them home. We mostly didn't have money to spare for candles or paraffin for the lamp, so they were readin' by a fat lamp Rocco made. A fat lamp is a golden syrup tin filled with sand, with a tightly rolled piece of corn-bag standing up through the centre, like a wick. You pour water onto the sand so it sets like kind of clay around the wick, then you pour melted fat down on the wick. Put on the lid with a hole made in the middle, pull some of the wick up through the hole, and it's done. As it burns down, you put a fork under it and prise more wick up.

This night the lamp was burnin' low, running out of fat, the light gettin' duller and duller. Verina was trying to finish the last bit of story, bendin' down close, leanin' over further and further, and her long hair fell over into the lamp and caught fire. Ph-phutt! And what should happen but the flame, just as her hair frizzled, caught the curtain next to her – the only bit of lace curtain in the whole of the house. I was out on the verandah and could hear all the singin' out.

I raced in. Someone was tryin' to put Verina's hair out, Tiny came with a jug of water pourin' it all over her, the other kids got the little ones out of bed and outside, Rocco threw the fat lamp out across the flat so it fell to pieces, and we put the fire out with a bucket of water, the only lot we had.

I said, "Who's gonna go and get more water for the night?" It was summer time and there's always snakes on the banks during the night. Everybody was frightened and we didn't have a torch. We struck matches but the wind blew 'em out. Six of us went down to get the water, makin' a lot of noise to scare the snakes away. Of course, the next morning there was great tears – "I can't go to school like this. They'll all laugh at me." But off she went.

I made the rule, 'No more readin' at night for you lot. Do your readin' in the day." But of course there was no time for readin' in the day. They always had a lot of jobs to do, and I was the Big Boss who made sure they did them. If they didn't do the job I'd have to do it, and I had enough of me own – or so I thought. So I had to let up a bit.

"No readin' at night unless you put the fat lamp in the middle of the table in the kitchen." That way they couldn't get too close.

Our story in Brewarrina seems to be a story of floods. The flood in 1970 was a big one. We didn't move away that time, but our house was just like an island. Gong was home, and him and Rocco and Jack'd row across to bring food. We had seventy goats, all our chooks, heaps of kids – as well as beetles and insects and lizards and snakes that were being washed out of their homes. I don't remember what time of year it was, except it wasn't winter, 'cos our main battle wasn't to get wood to keep warm, but we needed it to cook a feed.

Gong fixed up with the school for lessons for the kids.

One of the teachers would leave the paper work under a rock near where the Museum is now, and when Gong went for bread and meat he'd take their homework and leave it there.

We didn't have much island to move about on at all. What bit of grass there was the goats soon demolished, so the boys had to cut leaves to feed 'em all. They had to row out under the big dead branches of the gum trees and get a boatload of wood for cooking. They were all day and every day tasks for the best part of three months. We got a lot of things done around the house and yard and the vegie garden that Gong and me couldn't have done without the help of the kids. We worked a kind of conspiracy against them then. He'd be doin' something with the boys, showing 'em how, then he'd say, "I'm gonna have a smoke now," and they'd say, "We'll finish it, Boy, we c'n do it!" Big men they thought they were! ... and Gong'd wink at me. I'd do the same thing with the girls. It gave me time to make over clothes for the kids and make rag dolls and patchwork quilts, but we run out of cotton and elastic, and had to wait till we could afford to buy some more. When the floods went down Gong had work all over the place, with the station owners checking up on all their stock.

Jess was only a little feller – he was born in September '69 – and he got sick and real thin. The doctor didn't seem to know what was the matter. He thought one of the crawlies out of the flood might've bitten him. He'd pick up then get sick again.

Life wasn't only kids, but when you end up with fourteen, there's not much time for anything else. There were our thirteen, and Roxanne, our granddaughter. She is Evelyn Junior's eldest, but has always been exactly like my own daughter.

A couple of years before Roxanne was born Evelyn Junior had been working on a station near Charleville and broke her leg. It was bad for months. Then when Roxanne was a month old Tiny's leg got much worse. Dr Lopes thought it was best for her to go back to the doctor who had been treating her. Gong said, "The baby'll be right here with us." Tiny had to go to hospital in Brisbane, and Roxanne was toddlin' about by the time her mother's leg really got better. By then she was callin' us Mum and Dad and stayed with us ever since.

We had a gramaphone that Gong bought for ten pounds. It was as precious to my kids as TV is to my grandchildren today. They used to sharpen the needles on their father's emery stone, if he didn't catch 'em at it! We played the old records on that wind-up gramaphone, and I taught all the kids how to waltz and do the Barn Dance and the Schottische and the Quickstep. The record we wanted was Jimmy Shand, but we could never afford to buy it, and now I've got some tapes of Jimmy Shand, with the same old dance tunes. The kids were all good dancers, boys as well as girls. Alan especially was very light on his feet.

Gong seemed to have two left feet when I danced with him. I told him so too! I thought he'd never dance with me again, because I kept sayin', "Boy, you're treadin' on my toes!" Before we got married he was doin' it, after we got married, the same, amd after the kids came, he was still treadin' on my toes! So I said, "Listen, boy. Either you don't come to the dance with me any more, or I give up and stop home with you." So I'd go to the dances and he'd stop home with the kids. He said to me once, after we had about nine kids, "I never really liked dancin'. I only went because you liked it."

"Course I like dancin', but I don't like people dancin' on my toes."

"I didn't think you'd mind if it was me."

"Of course not. You're only about thirteen or fourteen stone!"

Every October they had the Police and Firemen's Sports.

That time of the year in Bre it's like sittin' in a big bush fire, it gets that hot. But they'd have a street parade and march up to the Showground, and have sports – foot running, three-legged races, bag races. It was a town thing and everybody went, and everybody participated. So that's how I got into the wood-chopping competition.

Gong was working for a station owner, Jimmy Rope, and that feller was a champion wood-chopper, and was teaching Ronnie Burton to be one too. The prize wasn't a big handful of money, it would be a silver dish or something like that. It was the participation and the sharing with other people that was the great thing, and the more people you were up against made it more interesting, and made yourself keener.

There was a Ladies Wood-chopping Championship. Peter Stedman, an Aboriginal person, was one of the organisers, and he said to me, "Come on, Mrs Crawford, why don't you have a go? I always see you choppin' wood."

"Why not," I said, "I know how to use an axe."

Jimmy Rope said, "Would you like to use one of my axes, Mrs Crawford?"

"No, no thanks, I know how sharp your axes are, in those special leather cases."

Then Ronnie said, "Have mine, then. You could handle it."

I don't know why I accepted it, but I did. It went right through that whitewood log – softest timber in the bush – and I won. I was so proud of the little silver teapot, milk jug and sugar basin on a tray. I'd never owned anything like that in me life, and to think I got it just for choppin' a log in half!

When Gong came in from the station at the end of the week, he said, "Ronnie's axe was just as sharp as Jim's, old woman, you know."

"You tell me now! Wait till I see that white feller – I'll sool my dogs onto him!"

"If he hadn't told you that, you wouldn't have competed."

I came second in the Throwing the Broom Competition –
an ordinary straw broom that you swung round and round
over your head and let it rip. Won four new teatowels,
and I'd never bought teatowels in a shop in me life. Teatowels
were what was left of your old sheets, or an old skirt. So
I was havin' a real good day.

Then they called the Driving the Nail Competition, a four
inch nail that you had to drive into a block of wood with
two hits. People were bendin' nails and droppin' 'em, but
I was lucky again, and won a little saucepan with a lid.
Brand-new one it was, so I never used it on the fire. I
used to make jellies in it, cool the custard, set the yeast
to make the bread, because the lid kept it all clean. When
the newspaper came out the next week, there was my name,
Mrs Crawford won... Mrs Crawford... I cut it out and
put it in the photo album.

The next year they gave even the ladies a beefwood log
to chop, after the men had taken the thick hard bark off
it. If the axe slipped on that bark it would've taken your
left leg off. I won a big black enamel pot with a lid that
time, and many a stew and pudding I cooked in it.

Dinty was like her father – could do anything with horses,
never afraid of them. He got her an old white horse, and
everyone in the riverbend knew that horse. What that horse
put up with! It was drought time and all he 'ad to eat was
waterweeds. The kids used to stand him in the river and
dive off his back. They'd swim him across the river, tie
him up, go and do the shopping, then swim him back. Dinty'd
be outside washin' up, and I'd hear everything rattlin', then –
quiet, I wouldn't hear a thing. I'd go out and she'd be gone,
and the horse too. Little while later, the rattlin' would start
again, and she'd be back there, washin' up! In school she
was the same. She used to ride her horse to school. She'd
put her hand up and the teacher would let her go outside.
Next thing, they'd see the white horse canterin' past the

front of the school. "Where the hell's Dinty going now!" A little while later she'd be back in the classroom and finish her lessons.

At that time the school in Bre accepted kids like that. There was a lot of tribal kids and they put no pressure on them. The teachers found that if they let them do what they wanted to do, the kids would come back and do the job they had to do, without the teacher nagging and fighting with them. It was very hard to teach the teachers, "Let 'em go, but make sure the job is done, and done properly, in the end."

A teacher said to me once, "Jess has missed three days school this month, and you are involved in the school. I thought you would have made sure that he came every day."

"Look, mate, Aboriginal people don't put pressure on kids, 'We want you to do this . . . to do that.' That's not our way. We say to the kids, 'You goin' to school this morning? 'No, I'm not goin'.' So we have breakfast and we leave it at that. No one says, 'Why?' If they wanted us to know why they'd tell us. Next day, 'You goin' to school?' 'Yeah, I'm goin',' and off they go. That way there's no hassles in the house, no arguments, and the kid feels he's not pressured, and really he doesn't take that many days off, because if you make a thing of it, you just give him something else to argue and fight you about. I found that out from my own kids, from people like Alan. I learnt a lot of tricks from the older ones that I used on the younger ones. They trained me well, my older kids, fair dinkum they did . . . trained me well! That's why I'm the best-trained Nanna round now.

# MATES

*'One little boy'*

In January 1974 we had the biggest flood people could remember, no rain, just water. The rain was way up in Queensland, and when they had to let the dam go near Narrabri, even the end of the big bridge over the Barwon was under water and we had to move from the river bend.

Gong was sick – he'd never been properly better since the kidney operations – so while I dropped him at the surgery and went to the Shire Office and asked them for two tents, the kids packed up everything we'd need. Tiny and her husband, Teddy, a shearer, were back in Bre with us, because there's no work around the sheds with floods. Most people camped at the Racecourse because of the toilet facilities, but we went out to the Red Hill, on the road not far past the Cemetery. The Shire fellers set up the tents for us and cut us a load of wood.

Gong and I were sittin' at the fire watchin' the water rising. I said, "What're you thinkin' about, boy?"

"I was just thinkin', if I die, you'll have to take me in to the hospital, then bring me back out here to the cemetery to bury me. You know I was born in the 1920 flood."

"Oh, don't be stupid! What's that got to do with anything?!"

Gettin' into February, the water was everywhere and we were cut off from the town except by boat. The kids put in two green forky sticks and strung a wire near the fire, so I could dry things. When we moved back to town we didn't bother about the sticks, and, would you believe it, they took root and they're two fine box trees, still there now!

Jess was goin' on five and always first up in the morning, pokin' round. One morning he wasn't there, and I found him still asleep with Bimbo. He was a funny colour, and when I picked him up he was as stiff as a board. Reminded me of when Dad used to poison foxes and we'd find them in the morning like that. I tell you I was scared. I grabbed him and jumped in the car and drove to the edge of the water where they used to cross in the boat. Gong stayed with the other kids – he was still crook. I tooted the horn like mad and a feller I didn't know came with the boat. He took us across near the football ground, and people in the big house there took us in their car to the hospital. The policeman said he'd go out and tell Gong what was goin' on, and I stayed at the hospital all day. I went back to the camp about sundown, had a meal and changed me clothes – hadn't had time to get dressed properly in the morning, then back to the hospital where I stayed all night.

Next morning Jess just sat up and had a big breakfast. He was talkin', and wanted to see who was in the hospital. Jan Halbish was still the Matron, and he'd known her all his life. So they went off together and after a while Jan came back without him.

"He's talking to kids in the children's ward, Ev," she said, "He's good enough to go home, but you'd better leave him here a bit longer till we see how he goes. You go home now and have a sleep."

"Alright. I'll just tell Jess what we're doin'."

He was happy to stay with the other kids, so off I went and about three o'clock in the afternoon the coppers brought him home. A few days later, first thing in the morning, Jack called out, "Quick, git up! Something's wrong with Jess." And it was on again. He looked different from before, a bluey colour, twice as bad, I reckoned.

The river was much higher. A feller in a motor boat took us, and goin' over a drowned fence he got the wire caught in his outboard motor. He couldn't free it, even when he pulled the motor right off the boat, and then he found he had no paddles! So he lifted Jess out and waded with him back to the track, then helped me till we got back to my car. On then to another crossing place, and the Emergency Service fellers took us to the hospital.

They rang for the Air Ambulance, the policeman went back to the tent to get me some clothes – the kids rolled up what they could in a bag – and away me and Jess went to Sydney, to Prince Henry Hospital. A male nurse looked after him, and I couldn't get over how very, very gentle that great big man was. Good to me too, he was. Showed me where I could sit on a balcony where I could see the sea while they were doin' more and more tests on the 'little feller'. That's what he always called Jess. One of the nurses took me with her to the huge laundry to pick up things she had to get, then to see the gym where there were people in wheelchairs. Some were exercisin', and some were swimmin' in hot water. They were all good to me, probably to get me mind off me worries.

For three or four days Jess never opened his eyes. All the time I sat with him I'd be talkin' to him about his dog . . . and how his favourite little bantam hen was goin' . . .

if she was layin'. Never knew if he could hear me or not, but I kept talkin', like I would've done at home. On the fourth or fifth morning a nurse came and said, "Doctor wants to see you, Mrs Crawford." My heart, I could feel it bangin'. They'd had an American doctor lookin' at Jess, and a Chinese doctor. Then Doctor Duffy, Jess's main doctor, came in and said, "Come on, I want to talk to you, dear."

When we got outside, he took hold of both my hands and said, "Doctor Lopes rang."

"Yeah? What about?"

"Your husband. He's had a heart attack."

"Tell me again. Is he alive?"

"Yes, but Doctor Lopes said, could you go home? Your husband keeps asking for you. Jess will be alright, he might stay like he is for a couple more days. We'll look after him. You could go home and come back if your husband is right."

But I knew how sick Gong must be. He'd already lost so much weight, he was only a shell of a man after being such a big person. The last thing he could stand was a heart attack. I went back and sat with Jess and a nurse brought me a cuppa. Doctor Duffy came back and we were both sittin' there drinkin' tea.

"Doctor, I just wish Jess was awake, so I could tell him that I need to go home to see how his father is, and ask him if he'd be alright if I left him." Then I felt this little cold hand touch my hand. His eyes stayed closed and he said, real quiet, "Go 'ome to Dad, Mum. 'e needs ya. I'm right." Doctor Duffy jumped up – spilled his tea – and everyone was runnin' round, because Jess had come to!

I remembered that in Brewarrina he'd come good so quick, for a couple of days at least, so I thought that would give me time to get to Gong. I felt anxious in me chest that I needed to get home quick, and just then Ray Baker came in. He was Lesley's husband – they lived in Revesby in Sydney.

"Come on, Mum, Lesley's gettin' the kids ready. We'll take you straight home."

I said to Jess, "Will you be right, son?"

"Yeah, I'll be right," still with the eyes closed, talkin' to me.

Baker had come to the hospital with Lesley every night, and he said, "Hey! This feller's awake!"

Jess said, "G'day, Baker," but his eyes still weren't open.

So we got in the car and travelled all night. It was early mornin' time when we hit Bre, and we went straight to the hospital. I shivered cold all over when I saw how sick Gong looked, but he knew us all.

"What're **you** doin' up here, Ducky? On holidays?"

"Just came up to see you. What're you doing, getting sick, frightening everybody?"

"A man's gettin' old and stupid. How's that boy, old woman?"

"He's alright . . . talkin' to me before I left."

"That's good. Now where's Alan?"

"Alan's at Charleville . . . he's on his way down." But he wasn't. Actually I didn't even know where he was, but I didn't want to worry Gong.

"Well, git in touch and tell him to hurry up."

When we left the hospital we rang the policeman at Charleville – a feller we knew – and told him if he could find Alan to send him along as quick as he could. That was on a Tuesday, and I sat with Gong all the time. Every time he'd come to, he'd see me and ask where was Alan. Then he'd wander off, and be whistlin' to his dogs, drovin' sheep, talkin' to old mates that 'ad been dead years . . . back in the drovin' camps all the time, he was.

The policeman in Bre, Brian Schultz, was a very good friend to Gong, and sat with him at night so I could get a rest. He was the first person I ever heard Gong say, "This white feller's my friend." Wednesday dinner time Brian come in and said, "My copper mate at Charleville has just rung.

Alan was there from Cloncurry. When he got word about his Dad, he left straight away, but would be havin' trouble gettin' through the water that's blockin' tracks everywhere." When Alan got to Engonnia, one of the station owner's family was sick and they were bringing him to the hospital at Bre in their plane. When they heard Gong was bad, they went to the Aboriginal camp, found Alan, and put him in the plane too. Then something went wrong with the plane and they had to turn back to Engonnia, because there was too much water to land anywhere nearer!

Wednesday night Rocco's daughter was born in the maternity ward where most of our kids had been born. In the morning we were telling Gong about this new baby, he said, "You c'n call her Jodie." He wanted to have a look at her, so the nurse brought the baby up and showed him, and Anna, the baby's mum, came in and talked to him too.

Brian got word that the plane was ready to take off again and Alan would be in it. All the kids were there by then, except Jess, of course, and Guy, who was away at school in Sydney, at Sylvania Heights High School. He lived in the Hostel there with about sixty other Aboriginal students.

On Thursday morning, about half-past-nine, Alan walked in the door of the ward, just off the plane, whiskers, wool all over him, still in his shearer's clothes. Gong looked at him and said, "So you got here, boy. Bloody long time you were about it! How far away were you?"

"Cloncurry, Boy, and ya know there's floods."

My fellers always called their father 'Boy'. The old chap brightened up a bit then, yarnin' away to Alan, and Jan said to me, "Do you want a cup of tea, Ev? I'm having one now." I went out with her, and we were sittin' talkin' with a couple of others. Alan came out a bit later, with a puzzled look on his face.

"That old feller, Mum, he's not good, eh?"

"No, he's not good."

"He's talkin' to his old friend Bruce . . . thinks they're

out bush puttin' up a break ... he's tellin' him to hammer in a peg here, not there!''

That afternoon the Sydney hospital rang and let Jess talk to me on the phone. He told me he'd been to school – the hospital school – and he'd been drawin' and colourin'. He sounded real bright.

He asked about his dad, and I said, "Not good, mate, not real good."

"Tell him I've got some paintin' for him – I'll show him when I take it home."

"That'll be great – he'll like that. I've gotta go now."

Then, before I hung up, he said, "Ya don't have t'worry about Dad, ya know. They'll look after him."

"Yes, they're all lookin' after him here."

Then he said, "Don't mean them fellers there, Mum," and with that he put the phone down.

I was sittin' in the chair beside Gong's bed. I looked up, and Alan was standin' there and he had Rocco with him, and Jack and Val. Brian had gone out in the boat and fetched them. Maree was in Bourke and held up by the floods, and the other six girls were out in the tent on the Red Hill.

Gong said, "Guy's not 'ere."

"No, still at that Sydney school."

Then he said, "You look after your mother, Jack. I won't be goin' home."

"Don't talk silly, Boy ... you'll be comin' home."

"No, you see you look after her. And Rocco, you look after everybody else. That's your job from now on. And by gee, if you don't do a good job, mate, you'll be answerin' to me."

Then his mind sort of wandered off, but he come good again so I went outside for a couple of minutes, and Alan was talkin' to him. I must've dozed off in the chair. It seemed just a minute when Alan was standin' in front of me sayin', "He's gone, Mum." It was within an hour of when Alan arrived. It seemed like Gong was just waiting till he came.

It was the 19th of February, 1974.

Two persons never became better mates than we were, you know. We yarned as husband and wife, we yarned as mum and dad, but the most yarns, and the best times, was when we sat down and talked as mates. We had the best sharing times, just the two of us at the fire. One of us would say, "Will we go to bed, or chuck another log on the fire?"

"I'll put the billy on, make another pot of tea."

So we'd sit there, and talk about the things we liked, the places we'd been, the people we knew . . .

"Wonder where old so-and-so is now?"

"Last time I heard of him he was . . ."

It was important to us to keep track of our friends, or we'd be cut off from a part of our lives that we didn't want to lose.

After Gong died, year by year his mates died too. My world, that was so solid, like a big rock, just started to fall away in little bits, chip by chip knocked off it. With each little chip, part of me went too, because those people were part of Gong and of the world we both lived in.

My kids say, "Mum, you goin' to that funeral?"

"No, you go for me."

"But, Mum, you've known that person all your life!" But if I went, it would be like watchin' Gong being buried all over again, we'd all been so close. Rocco mostly goes for me, so he's my link with that old friend, because he saw them last. I don't know if it's fair to him, but I've got to build on somebody.

When Gong died, no way could any of my people get to us with the floods everywhere. That afternoon Brian came out to the Red Hill and told us that Jess was doing well, but they were keeping him longer. We'd buried his father before he got back, and the floods stopped Guy getting back too.

The day we were burying Gong was totally clear, not a cloud. I was walking to the grave between Maree and her husband Alan Lyons, who knew Gong very well, and our boys were carrying the coffin. I looked at Alan and said, "I know I shouldn't say this, mate, but I can almost hear that old bloke sayin', 'It's a wonder you fellers are strong enough to carry a bloody man!'" He'd been such a big powerful man most of his life. We still talk about it sometimes and I say to Alan, "You don't think I was a silly old woman for sayin' that, do you?"

"No, Mum, it sounded just like him."

While the preacher was prayin', this **black** cloud came over, out of nowhere, and a wind whipped up really powerful. It seemed to have the people pinned against the fence. Then the rain. I couldn't see Rocco, just see his white shirt, and Jack's and Alan's – the rain was blindin' me. They were hurryin' to try to get the grave filled in. I don't know how I got out of that cemetery, but I found myself out on the road, walkin' back out to the Red Hill camp. It was twice as worse out there. The kids were cryin', one tent was almost inside out, tables knocked over, plates and pints and food everywhere. By the time the boys got back, it was all over, no rain, no wind, just a dull cloudy day. We read about that storm in the paper. It was a very narrow, thin storm, and we were in the path of it. It went for miles, and the damage it did!

The next day the smaller kids and I went back to Sydney with the Bakers. Right away I rang the hospital and found they'd just sent Jess back home on the plane, with a little tag pinned on his clothes, 'Jesse James Crawford, Red Hill, Brewarrina'. When the plane landed at Bre, someone said, "His mother's not here. She went to Sydney with her daughter." They put him straight back on the plane, took him back to Sydney. Doctor Duffy met him at Mascot and brought him out to Revesby. He was a good friend to us.

Jess is the youngest in the family, so when his father

died, he became the head of our family. I'm nothing. I've done my job. That's the tradition of his father's people. He's the youngest so he's got the longest to live.

I thought the older ones would say to him, "You're only a snotty-nosed kid. You don't know what you're talkin' about." But it's not that way. With people reared traditional, the respect for tribal custom is much, much stronger than that. He talks to his brothers and sisters about things, then whatever he decides they all go along with it.

I was sort of at a loose end. We had the home we'd built on the river bank, but to me it seemed like an empty house, and for the kids who were his mates, his good mates, it wasn't a home any more. The kids didn't say they wanted to go back home, and they didn't say they didn't want to, but there was a funny feeling, vibes I was gettin' from them that they didn't want to go there. I didn't want to say how empty it was for me, because we'd all built it together.

Some of the traditional feeling in me of not goin' back to where someone died – sort of 'burnin' the camp' idea – I could've been unconsciously communicating to the kids. They knew about that, because when Dummy died, Aunty Pussy moved back to Charleville. At the time if they'd said, "Mumma, we want to go home," I'd 've gone with 'em. My married daughters said, "Mum, come and live with me . . . come to us." They were all good to me, but I didn't want that.

There was a little house near the school the Shire said we could live in. It was in pretty bad shape, so we didn't have to pay rent. It had a kitchen, and toilet out the back, so we moved there. It was just before Bimbo and Red Kelly got married and Red soon fixed it all up for us. When the floods dried up, my dad came over from Wanaaring and stayed with us for a while. I was glad to see him, and my younger kids got to know him a bit better.

I had all my kids – many still at home or at least in Bre –

grandchildren, my Dad, plenty of cousins and uncles and aunties, but I was alone. I was that used to being with that man for nearly thirty years. Gong made all the decisions. We talked about the way we were goin', to make the road straight for our kids. If one of us pulled one way, and one the other, what would the kids be like? So in the end I'd go along with his decision. I'd never made decisions alone in all my married life. Where the hell was I gonna start now? And if I wanted to discuss something important, who of my own age was I gonna talk to? I was beginnin' to withdraw myself even from the kids.

The only person that drew my attention to that was Rocco. He lived away at the time and when he came home he must've noticed the distance I was puttin' between me and the kids. He said to me, "You alright, Mum?" and he never called me 'Mum' except when he was really serious.

"Yeah..."

"These kids say you're not alright. Ya won't talk to 'em half the time."

"I talk to them."

"They said you don't."

So then I thought to meself, "What'm I doing to me kids?"

I was just sort of worryin' about the mate that **I'd** lost, the mate I'd had for years and years, and I was feelin' sorry for **myself**, and forgettin' that the kids had lost someone very precious to them too. When I thought about them, I could see that they were the saddest-lookin' little kids I'd ever been near in my life. There was times I didn't want to be near them, they were that sad. They'd lost their Dad, and I think they were afraid they were losing me, too. It took me a long time to realize my kids worried about me, like I worried about them. I found out later that they became closer and closer and leaned on each other. Because they thought I was wrapped up in my own thoughts, they talked to each other. Even today I don't think there's a single thing that happens that they don't discuss between the lot of them. I'm very lucky, and grateful to have a family like that.

Havin' that little house so close to the school was good, too, because Jess was school age and after he'd had such a good time in the hospital school, he was dying to start in Kinder. That's the first year real school in New South Wales, not Pre-school. He was still pretty short-winded so I'd carry him across to school and upstairs to his classroom. Then I'd wait, 'cos I'd finished my work early in the morning, to take him down to the toilet at recess time.

I'd be sittin' on the verandah near the windows of the Kinder room, and I'd hear that first-year-out young lady teacher strugglin' to get through to little kids who used a lot of Aboriginal words in them days. Even though it was less than twenty years ago, lots of them were minded, or reared, by their Grannies, who spoke traditional languages. Today not many kids would have more than a few words.

While I was there waitin', I'd talk to other kids that didn't have a sad look on their faces. I'd talk more to them than I talked to Jess and Rebecca and Dinty and the bigger ones. I leaned on those happy kids, because I'd have to go home to my sad lot. But then I found those kids that seemed happy had their own problems too, especially learnin' in the classroom, and I tried to help them. I needed to get away from that deep depression at that particular time.

Sitting outside the classroom, I'd pick up, every now and then, the teacher's voice raised. I'd wonder how many mothers back in the camps knew a white person was shoutin' at their kids. So I'd listen, to see why the voice was raised. Or I'd hear an anxious kid, who wanted to go to the toilet, but couldn't make the teacher understand what he wanted.

I told Rocco about this, and he said, "Why don't ya just tell the teacher what the kids are sayin'? That way, then, there won't be so many wet pants goin' home."

"You got a point there too, boy."

Up till then I'd thought, "Teachers know everything. They've got it all!"

So I said to that Kinder teacher, Debbie, "Look, I know how to get through to those kids that you can't understand."

"Do you, Mrs Crawford? If you could just tell me the word they use for going to the toilet it'd be a great help."

We practised that afternoon when the kids went home, together on the verandah in the sun. I worked out the different languages in her class and we wrote down each kid's name and how he'd express it in his language. It took her about a week of school days to catch on. She told me that one day in the staff room she said to the other teachers, "Aunty Ev's teaching me some Aboriginal language."

"Huh! what for?" That was the feller who had the First Class.

"So I can understand my little kids."

One day that young white feller said, "What about helping me?"

It wasn't till about Third Class that some kids would want to speak English outright. If the teachers picked up some of the kids' language it made for a better understanding. Kids'd come home and say, "Gee, Mum, my teacher can say Aboriginal words. She said this today ... he said that," just like we'd said about Miss Cook. They'd be so proud the parents would think, "If that teacher's taken the trouble to say an Aboriginal word, to make my kid feel good, that's a white person we gotta meet." And the flow between teachers and parents would begin. Parents would come, just to sit in the classroom where their kids had to be five days a week.

Next thing Debbie said, "Aunty Ev, this little feller wants to read and the other kids are interrupting him. Would you mind listening to him for me?" The teacher might've thought I was a clever old mum, that I could read really well. But that wasn't it. I had a good memory, and when I'd heard the story once I could act as if I could read it all easily. Of course I said, "Not at all."

**One little boy** really started it all for me, on a Tuesday morning, about half-past-eleven, just when they went back inside after recess. By the next Tuesday, I had **five** little boys! We all had the same story, and one would read till he come to a word he didn't know, and another one would go on. We did it till each one could read the whole story all by himself. It was a big morning for us that day. One feller read it all and went inside to tell the teacher how good he was, then another feller, and another feller – talk about copy cats, but they were so proud of themselves.

Their teacher was proud of them too, so I said, "If there's anything else I c'n help you with ... I'm just sittin' here." By this time Jess was able to come down the stairs – it took him a while – but he still couldn't go up by himself.

So I spent all the last term of 1974 as a Reading Mum. I listened not only to the Kindergarten kids, and helped them write their name, but First, Second and Third Class in that Infant section. The next year I was at the school most of every day, still as a volunteer.

It's funny how life works out if you let it. If Jess hadn't been sick, and if the classroom had been downstairs, I wouldn't 've been there at all. Verina would've taken him to school. In Year 5 she would have been, and it's an all-age school – littlies to Year 12. At that particular time I didn't want to hang around **anybody** at all, much less round white fellers. The school was good for me, gettin' me away from the house, and from sad feelings. I felt we were all startin' off a new life, only this time without Gong. We couldn't fill the gap he'd left, but we were all hopin' that for a long time there'd be no more gaps.

My kids seemed relieved that Mum was comin' good. I could talk to them again, about their schoolin' as well now. I got to know them better than I'd ever known them before. Up till then I'd been too busy, rearing babies, keepin' them all fed and looked after properly, that I never took the time to see what made these little fellers of mine tick, or wonder what sort of people they were. I suppose I was like someone that looks at a tree, just sees a tree with bark and leaves, without realizing every tree is different. We'd all go over to school together, come home for lunch together, back again, then home. One morning I woke up, and they were in the kitchen, laughin' and talkin'! I thought to meself, "This sounds just like the kids were in our home over the river." I knew our family was back. And when Bimbo married Red Kelly and moved into the old house she'd grown up in, everything settled down.

I couldn't be mum **and** dad to the kids, so I settled to be their mate. Most of them were grown-up, so if they fell I couldn't pick 'em up, they'd be too heavy. The only support I could give was to be behind 'em, back there with some of the family. My kids became my very good friends, and advisers too. If I had a problem about a student, a kid of mine about that age would say, "Mum, don't forget the age gap!"

"Well, how'm I gonna treat it?" and they'd give me a bit of an idea, and I'd work on from there, at home as well as at the school.

I'd had enough of livin' in the town, so we moved back across the river to a small house on the river bank at Barwon Four. Dinty would have been about ten. Some kids who lived near us were stirrin' up her horse, chuckin' rocks at it, so Dinty went over and threatened to punch 'em up and they ran away and told their mum. Of course she came over to my place, and I said, "Now look. That's between the kids. There's nothing there for me and you to argue about."

"Alright, old girl. We'll leave it at that." And off she went.

The next Saturday there was a merry-go-round over in town. Dinty went on her horse, and I took the other kids in my old car. Who should be there too but those squabblin' kids and their mum. Dinty left to ride home before we did, and what did we see near the big bridge on our way home but Dinty on the white horse chasin' that woman and some of her kids round and round a tree, the woman yellin', "I'll break 'er leg!" One of those same kids had thrown a rock at her this time and she'd started to chase him, and his grown-up sisters – and mum – joined in.

I pulled up and raced over and yelled at Dinty, "Git out of 'ere right now and go home!" I was thinkin', "Gee, now there'll be nothing but trouble from that family." I was right. About four days later I was driving the kids home from school. We were almost at the bridge when Verina said, "Look, Mum, there's Dinty's horse tied up to the fence."

"Where's Dinty, then?"

"Dunno, Mum, but there's a lot of kids there."

I pulled up and said to Verina, "Go over and see what Dinty's doin'."

Over went Verina, singin' out, "Come here, Dinty, Mum wants you."

There was bony skinny Dinty, no shirt on, just her singlet, knucklin' up to this young feller who'd sworn at her in the shop. She caught him on the way home and got into him. When his mates jumped in, she couldn't beat 'em all, so she grabbed a big stick and laid into the lot of them.

I hunted her home, and was thinkin', "Next thing there'll be people here, sayin', 'We've got a complaint against your daughter,' and no Gong to back me up, and straighten her out." Dinty always carried her own little load, fought her own battles.

At the end of that year as a Reading Mum, 1975 it was, the Senior Infant Mistress said, "What're you going to do next year, Ev?"

"I'll be back . . . I like it."

I spent all the next year in the classroom all day, every day, but as an unpaid person. There was always something happening in that school, little things and big things. We had a class of kids, about eight-year-olds, havin' a Nature Study lesson one day down at the creek near where the animal park is now. There were three kids to a team – one had a little net to scoop up tadpoles, one had a jar or tin, and one had a board with paper, doin' all the writing. Big project it was. Believe me, I never looked at tadpoles when I was a kid at Yantabulla. They weren't tucker – or danger – so they were just there. It was a new thing for me as well as for the kids. Here I was, nearly fifty years old, lookin' at tadpoles for the first time! I was standing a bit back up higher on the bank where I could see 'em all. When you take kids to the river, you're countin' 'em all the time. You don't take your eyes off 'em. We had a first-year-out teacher, and she was sittin' down on her haunches, kids all round her, so all she could see was the little bellies of this ring of kids pushin' closer.

Next thing, a kid yells out, "Miss, Jamie's gone!"

Every class always has a little know-all kid, thinks he knows things better, can do things better, even than the teachers. In this class it was a little white kid, the bank manager's son, only come from Sydney a few weeks before. You tell a know-all kid not to put his foot on a rock – he puts his foot on that rock! That's what happened. The rock wasn't secure, it rolled, and away he went.

The river was risin' at the time, full of muddy water runnin' fast – there was no weir then to slow the water – and he was bein' dragged along under it. I happened to see one foot, just come up for that second. Lucky we was in a bit of a backwater so I ran down further, went in till the water was up to my waist and I could just keep me footing, and waited. I was hoping he was still in the stream of water where I'd seen the foot, and not been carried to a faster stream further out. If he had, I'd've had to swim in, and let the teacher call for help, but I don't know how I could've found him when I couldn't see him. I never saw another bit of him, didn't know which way the eddies was takin' him, till he hit my legs. I got him out, very cut and bruised he was, pushed against branches and rocks. The first thing I seen was the gash in his forehead, blood pouring out, and with the water, the blood looked like it was runnin' out of him everywhere. When I knew he was alive, I sure wanted to slap his bottom! The other kids were screamin' and cryin'. They all run over to me when I put him on the bank. The only one that didn't come was that teacher! She couldn't move, she just stood there, a scoop in one hand and a piece of paper in the other.

There was an old feller who lived on the little hill near there, and a couple of kids ran and got him. He picked up the kid, cryin' by this time, and said, "I reckon he's alright, but we'd better take him to the hospital."

I said to the kids, "Gather up all your things, we're going back to school." All of a sudden I remembered, "We've got a teacher here somewhere."

She was still standin' there, and I went back to her. "Are you alright?" and I shook her. She started to cry, the tears just rollin' down. "It's my fault... I should've watched him... I should've..."

"He's **alright!** C'n you carry these things and take the kids back to school."

"I'd like to go to the hospital with him."

"Alright, I'll take the kids back." I was thinkin', "There's young white women there at the hospital, they'll be able to talk with her and help her."

I was walkin' the kids along the street and someone said, "Where's their teacher?"

"Oh, she's busy at the moment."

I was a stickler for the rule that the kids were the teacher's responsibility, not an aide's, Aboriginal or otherwise, but there was no rules in this situation. We got back to school and went in the gate, the kids not dawdlin' and sayin' nothing. A teacher saw us and asked me, "What's wrong?"

"Nothing. Where's the Principal?"

"Over in the other building."

"Could you tell him to come to the Third Class room, please, straightaway, now."

The kids sat down all subdued and put all their gear on their desks, mud and weed and everything, and the Principal came in, and I told him what happened.

"Is he alright?"

"I think he is," so he sent another teacher to the front office to ring the hospital and stayed himself to talk to the class. They were only little kids and pretty upset. He told them Jamie was alright, but he warned them about water too, that you can get just as drowned in a little creek as in a big river, and you'd be just as dead. Then he went to ring the parents.

That night the dad came round to where I was living across the river. We were sitting outside round the fire when he walked over and said, "I wanted to see you and thank you for what you did today."

"That's alright. I'm glad I was there and able to help."

"I'm more than glad that you were there. Jamie wants to see you. His mother is at the hospital with him, and she'd like to thank you too."

"Right, I'll come with you."

When I walked in Jamie sat up in bed, all cut and bruised and sore. "Hello, Mrs Crawford. Gee, am I glad you can swim! If you wasn't there to catch me . . . I tried to get my foot on the ground . . . I tried to grab the rocks, and look, my hand's all cut with broken glass. I thought I bumped into the bank and it was your legs!"

It was a terrible shock for the young teacher. The Principal said to me, "What can we do for her, Ev? You should know, you're working with her."

"**Workin'** with her! The poor kid can't do anything. Why don't you ask her if she'd like to go home for a week or a couple of weeks, and be with her family? That's what she needs. She's a good teacher. It would be a shame to let someone like that go down because we didn't see she needed help."

"Good, I'll suggest it to her."

She jumped at the chance, and said to me, "Somewhere along the line, I think I've got you to thank for this two weeks off," and gave me a big hug.

"It doesn't matter who you've got to thank for it. You go and have a break, and the tadpoles'll be frogs by the time you get back."

I knew how important it is for all parents to know what their kids are doing, but I also knew that most of the Aboriginal parents were scared about the school – it was a white man's place and they didn't feel comfortable about goin' there. So whenever a kid did something good, I'd go to his place – in the town, down the river bank, or out at Dodge – and show his parents. That sort of gave me a bit of a right to go when I knew something was going wrong – first the good news, then the bad! Aboriginal people had been sayin' for years, ever since our kids were allowed to go to the public schools, "Our kids'ud get on better if they had Aboriginal teachers."

I was just a Reading Mum when Olive Mitchell and I first got talking about white teachers and Aboriginal children in the schools. Olive was an Aboriginal lady, born in Brewarrina and there all her life. She said, "These schools need black people in 'em, mate . . . teachers in the classrooms." But nobody was prepared to make that **big** move on.

At that time, Bill Rose, a white man, was one of the 'heavies' in the Education Department. Later on he become Chairman of the Far West Children's Scheme, based at Manly. He used to come out to Bre, where we had close on six hundred kids in the school, most of them Aboriginal. He introduced himself to me at the school.

"There's a lot of Aboriginal children in this school, Ev."

"Yes, Mr Rose."

"Wouldn't it be good if you had Aboriginal teachers for them?"

"Yes, that'd be great."

But I just said it to answer him, because I knew nothing would come of it. No one'd be bothered training Aboriginal people to be teachers. They certainly wouldn't give them a classroom, make them responsible for a heap of kids, white as well as black. I thought that was a **long** way ahead, too far to see.

He came in another time, a very quick visit on his way back from Weilmoringle and that's when he met Olive. He said, "Would you like a cup of tea? Come over and we'll sit down and have a yarn."

So we talked. He said, "We might be able to get a group together. There's an Aboriginal person teaching in a school in Sydney, Yvonne Bolton, who'd be interested."

We said, "Alright," but after Bill Rose had left, Olive looked at me and said, "What was that white feller talking about?"

"I dunno!"

It was only about four days later he was back again, all the way back from Sydney, with Yvonne Bolton. I think he felt he never got through to me and Olive, so he brought back an Aboriginal person to talk to us. But what he didn't realize that this was a **Sydney** person! So the poor feller didn't make much progress there. He was doubly confused! and so was she! But we got through it. We went down to the river, where the weir is now, and sat down under a tree, on the roots, and we talked till dark. We knew what he was talking about then. If we could form a group of people, we could go to the Education Department, and say, "Would we be able to get Aboriginal people trained to be teachers out in the outback Aboriginal areas?"

Bill Rose was saying how good it would be, and I was sayin' to meself, "Yeah, but it'll never happen." It seemed a long way down the track to us. But at that particular time we didn't know how far we'd be goin' down that track ourselves. We **weren't** successful with that request! So our next step was to ask to have Aboriginal people trained as Teacher's Assistants to help our kids make some headway in out-back schools. The Education Department agreed to that and set up the Course at Sydney University in 1976.

At the end of the year the school gave me a cheque, and the Principal said, "How would you like to work here officially, and we could pay you properly, every two weeks?"

"That would be great."

Then they sprung it on me that they wanted me to go away to Sydney University to do the training as an Aboriginal Teacher's Assistant, the course we'd got them to start the year before. They showed me a picture of the University, and the lecture rooms, auditoriums with students and someone up high in front talkin' to them. I said, "Cripes, I'd get lost in a creepy big place like that!"

The Principal said, "Would you like to go?"

"No, I wouldn't!"

The teacher I was working with was Joan Hart, and she said, "Why don't you want to go, Ev?"

I wasn't afraid of talkin' out in front of that lot any more, so I said, "To be in one of them places you'd have to be able to read and write good, and that's one thing I can't do."

"But, Ev, they'll teach you to read and write properly. And over the time you've been here, you've picked up so much ... your work's improved ... you'd be great."

"M-m-m-m, if you think so. But what'm I gonna to do about the kids?"

"You work out something, Ev. I reckon it'll be real good for you to do it."

Well, the older kids came home for Christmas, and I was tellin' them about this plan. "If I did it, then I'll be paid for doin' the job."

They said, "If you want to do it, Mum, you go. We'll mind the kids. You can't sit around doin' nothing ... and you're good at it. It'll only be for the year."

"That's true. They said it's three weeks at a time – three weeks in Sydney, and then three back home in the school, with work to do, all the year."

I had a lot to think about. And the thinkin' excited me, and scared me too.

The day school started, I told the Principal I'd do the Course. When Gong died I'd felt like an old tree way out in the middle of the desert, just space all round me, not another tree beside me. After I was in the school I never felt I was in the desert any more. I was in among other trees, and lots of little bushes, and I liked it. So I went to Sydney.

# OPENING GATES

*'We just went ahead,*

*very, very, slowly!'*

At six o'clock in the morning, I got off at Central where I'd been a scared little black kid years ago, and there I was, just as scared again. Bill Rose, and Alan Duncan who was in charge of the Course, met me and took me to International House at the University where we were going to live. We went down to breakfast and I met the other people who'd come from different places. I knew only one of the group, Pat Doolan from Bourke, but apart from that, we were all strangers to each other. They came from Taree, Moree, Forbes, Peak Hill, Hilston, from everywhere. There were young men, too, twenty-one of us altogether, and only one lady older than me! We were the second batch, all ages and shapes and colours.

Living conditions were good, nice rooms – two people to a room. I shared with Hazel Rhodes from Lismore. They put people from far-apart areas together deliberately, like me from the dry sandhills outback with a coastal person. Gave us plenty to talk about too. We'd ask each other questions about our lives and places. It's marvellous what you learn when things just come up in conversation. The first week was a 'gettin' to know each other' time, really interesting. Here I was, learning about people I'd never seen before, finding out that so much of their lives was the same as mine.

The only thing I didn't like about International House was the food sometimes. Because the students came from different countries, they'd have different food week about – all Chinese food for a week, such-and-such food for another week. I really enjoyed it when it was Australian Week, and we'd have feeds of chops.

We had a full week for Orientation, findin' out what Universities were all about. Interesting week that was. I'd assumed that universities were for white people, and young white people at that. When I saw people my age and older I thought they were the teachers, the professors, then I found out they were students too. That surprised me, because I thought that when you were old you knew everything, you didn't need to be taught anything any more. Seeing those older people helped me to settle down, to dig in. They took us all through the University – into the Great Hall which is a beautiful place, a beautiful place. I was walkin' round, and lookin' up and lookin' up, to think people had done all that.

We listened to lectures, listened to all sorts of things that went over our heads. In one room they said there was a Professor Someone lecturing on Child Psychology, and I said to meself, "What's Child Psychology?" Didn't mean a thing to me, that word, it was too big, too far off for me. We were listenin' to that professor talkin' about Child Psychology. Faith was sittin' beside me. She bumped me and whispered, "Look over there near the wall," and jerked her head at these statues, all white, with bits of sheet on 'em, half-naked. I could feel her shakin' beside me, tryin' not to laugh out real loud. Then Jean bumped me from the other side, and her eyes were rollin'. She muttered, "Look at the statues!"

Under me breath I said, "What's wrong with 'em?"

"You watch 'em."

So we clean forgot about the man talkin', and in the corner of my eye I thought I saw a statue move. I said to myself, "I've never been in this kind of a place before, but you can't tell me statues are movin'! Statues are stone."

That's what we thought, but these were live ones. Yep! Talk about bein' took in! They were young people with white paint all over them, and a bit of cloth across them. They were movin' that slow you wouldn't see it if you looked at them, you'd have to catch it in the corner of your eye. So for the rest of the lecture that took up all our attention. The next morning, when they asked us "What did you learn?" we said, "We learned there was live statues in there!" We just thought they were a queer lot of white people. But we found out it was the 'muck around' week at the start of their year, so we saw some pretty strange things.

After that it was 'Get out your books and pencils' time. I was thinking, "This is it. Now I'm gonna be embarrassed. I won't know what they're talkin' about." I got depressed about it. I worried about me grammar, I worried that much I made a mess of it. Alan Duncan is a marvellous man and he must've seen this, and he said, "Ev, what's the matter? You're not worrying about the work, are you?"

"I'm worryin' about the bloody lot, Alan. 'ow do I know I'm not down here wastin' my time and wastin' other people's time tryin' to teach me?"

He sat me down and said, "Now, you're not a brand-new person in the world. You've been around a long time. Think of all that's happened to you, all the things you've learnt. You put a value on them and you think, 'I'm not as uneducated as I think I am. I know a lot. I'm educated in a different way.'" I'd never thought about it like that, and Alan made me feel a little bit better. He must've said it to the lecturers too, because they talked to me about things that were part of my life. So I settled down after that.

One of the courses was Communications. We wondered why we had to do this course, because we didn't think we had any problems communicating with each other. The teacher showed us how we could use the skill we had, and how it could be beneficial in our work, that it wasn't about just havin' a conversation with Tom, Dick or Harry.

I'd been working in our school over a year, and thought I knew the short cuts to a lot of things, but to become a reliable person in the classroom, to be able to help the teachers with the kids, I had to learn the 'proper' way.

At the end of three weeks, they gave us our travel tickets and back we went to work in our home schools for three weeks. Then I worried that the teacher would think I was tryin' to take over her class because I was talkin' to the kids in the Aboriginal language while she just stood there with the chalk in her hand. I worried about how I could have her included as part of it, even though I was usin' our language. So I had to spend time with her so she wouldn't feel left out.

They gave us assignments to do while we were home. We had to pick a child in a class we worked in, and do a Child Study. I picked a kid I thought was a quiet little feller and wrote about him. I still got a carbon copy of the things I wrote about him nearly twenty years ago. One time, when the teacher was reading them a story, he was sittin' on the floor real quiet right close against her, tying his shoe laces to her laces. And me writin' it all down!

Not long ago that feller showed me his new baby, and I said, "Keith, when he gets to Kindergarten, is he going to do the same things you did?"

"I hope not, Mrs Crawford."

When we'd got so many pages done we had to send it back to Sydney. They'd read it before we got back and were ready to have talkin' time with us. They worked hard, and they worked us hard too. The ones who worked us hardest were Aboriginal themselves, Margaret Valladian and Natasha McNamara. They were both very clever women and good teachers. I called 'em the 'bullock drivers' – behind their backs, of course. But they did so much for us. And it was them sendin' Chris to talk to me years later that started this book.

I was still wonderin', "What the hell am I doin' here? It's not my kettle of fish, bein' at Uni." Then when we started gettin' results back I was gettin' nice comments, heaps and heaps of comments. I got more confident.

We all heard the others' reports, and it was a fascination to me that a person from Moree could have the same things as a person from Peak Hill or Brewarrina, and almost in the same words. We wasn't copyin', so it showed me that kids are much the same everywhere. The lecturers got us older ones to work with the young men and women who had no children of their own. That sort of drew us all closer together.

Before I'd leave Sydney each time to go home, Bill Rose and Olive and Yvonne would meet me, and we'd go to a meeting all day about Aboriginal educational things, have a bit of a meal, then I'd be on the train goin' back to Brewarrina. About this time, white education people were agreeing with what we'd been talkin' about on that tree root on the river bank at Bre – that it would be good if there was someone who could advise them about Aboriginal people. It was us four that started what became the Aboriginal Education Consultative Group (AECG).

We had no idea what our little group, three Aboriginal women and one white man, would become in later years. We were just thinking – at least I was – from one week to another. It wasn't anything pre-planned. We never said, "If we get this done, we can surely get that done." We just went ahead very, very slowly. That white man, Bill Rose, played a very important role in my life. Talks that I had with him changed the attitude I had towards white people, made me take on the challenge to get to know school teachers, whether they were black or white. To me he seemed to have the inside knowledge of them, what teachers are made of, or what they should be made of anyway. I listened, and I learned from Bill.

Yvonne was a teacher herself, and I thought, "If all teachers (I didn't think specifically Aboriginal teachers) were like Yvonne Bolton, we're heading for a rosy future, us Aboriginal people." She is a person who can work with both peoples, she can talk and hold her own in an argument with both peoples. And Olive – Olive was like me. We were both sort of hungry for knowledge because it was from Bill Rose that we both got a taste of how important education is. We knew that if we wanted to be in that education system, and get other people to come forward and do the same thing after us, we'd have to work bloody hard to git in, and to be accepted, because we started from scratch. The challenge was there for me, an old woman almost fifty, and I never, ever walked away from a challenge in my life. And I'm sure Olive and Yvonne never did either. So we hung in there.

Sometimes later on we felt a bit on the edge, being outback so far from Sydney. I stumbled a few times, but there was always a hand put out to stop me from fallin', and I appreciated that. When a person put that hand out for me, there was more than just a friendly 'I'll-help-you-up-mate' feeling in that hand. It was a good feeling, it was wonderful.

I'd never seen the real ocean, just Botany Bay and the Harbour over thirty years before with the Bloxhams, until Olive Mitchell and some of the others in the AECG and me went over on the ferry to the Far West Children's Home at Manly. That was an experience! I never moved, just sat there, inside, of course. I was a bit braver comin' back, and stood at the door, but I wasn't brave enough to walk round the outside.

We went for a walk along the ocean beach, and that

was the first time I seen anyone riding the waves on the surf boards. It was really the first time I seen waves, that you'd call **waves**, great big things. I wondered what was making them when there wasn't much wind at all. You could see big white marks of 'em way out. I didn't ask anybody because I didn't want people to think I was a bush bunny. Some of them might've been doing the same thing as me – not lettin' on that they were scared! Bill Rose was with us and he would have explained without any embarrassment to me. But I didn't ask. The sea just fascinated me, but it scared me a bit too.

Back in the classrooms in Brewarrina, I was tryin' very hard to get to understand these people I was workin' with five days a week. Me, after promising myself when I was a kid to kill every white person I could when I grew up, not because I hated them, but they were like a burr when you wanted to walk with no shoes. You just want to git rid of it. I wasn't going to change my opinion of them till I found out what made them tick. Of course I found they were all different people too. The first time I heard a teacher runnin' some other teacher down I laughed to meself and thought, "Gord, these white people are just like black people! – only they've got white skins, flasher cars, prettier dresses."

When I was a kid, I didn't know if we were allowed to teach Miss Cook about our Aboriginal culture, but there was nobody now stoppin' me teaching these Kindergarten teachers so they'd git to know us, perhaps understand us, and make for a better feeling between everybody – so we could talk more freely to each other.

I never went near the Primary section of the school, neither did the other Infant teachers, and the Primary section never went near the Secondary, unless they wanted to borrow equipment. They were like three different schools, only the Principal did his rounds a couple of times a week. If anything went wrong, especially early in the year, the Secondary teachers would blame the Primary for not teachin' properly, the Primary would blame the Infant school. I used to think just to meself, "If you were more friendly towards each other, and worked together, you'd all be able to understand the kids."

Up to that time, the white teachers had assumed that the Teacher's Aides were there to wash the cups and tea-towels, and if the teacher or kids made a mess it was the Aboriginal person's job to clean it up. After about nine weeks in Sydney, I found myself in the staffroom telling them that wasn't our job at all.

They said, "Well, what are you supposed to do?"

I got out my work and showed the Principal what we were doin' in Sydney. He could hardly believe it. "Evelyn! That's the same sort of work the teachers do at College!" And he said it to them all at the staff meeting. "Thse people are not being trained to be 'wood and water joeys', as Ev calls them. They're being trained to be to aides to **teachers**." He passed round all my work.

Just before I went back to Sydney for the last three-week stretch before we graduated my Dad came to visit us. Some of my bigger girls had got jobs, so he said he'd mind the kids for me. He got himself a little caravan and camped in that at our place at Barwon Four. One night we talked till late at the fire then went to bed. Early in the morning one of the kids sung out to me, "Quick, Mum! The caravan's on fire!" Everybody around came runnin', the dog was inside yelpin' and the back of the caravan was burnt right out. I reached in and grabbed something – it was the dog, and some-one pulled Dad out through the back. They got the ambulance but Dad died before they put the trolley in the ambulance.

Seems like all his family were to die in fire.

When I finally came back to Brewarrina, a fully qualified ATA, Joan Hart said, "You're becoming a teacher in your own right,

Ev," and she let me work **with** her. She'd say, "About our teaching programme for next week, Ev, what do you think we should put in it?" We'd sit down and discuss. I think that was the first time ever that Aboriginal Aides had any involvement in the teaching programmes in any school.

If there was a kid who could not, or would not, learn to read and write, he'd be handed over to us and in no time at all we'd have that kid out of his shell, startin' to read and write, talkin' up, mixin' at sports with the rest of the kids. When other teachers seen what we were doin' on a one-to-one or small group basis – there were two more aides then – they'd send us more kids and we'd send 'em back to the classroom confident kids.

People underestimate kids.

Kids have got brains in their heads and they like to be able to use them. Parents, and grandparents, don't give the kids freedom to do the thinkin' for themselves, they're all the time tellin' them what to do, when they should be askin', "What d'you think about this... about doin' that?" I know there's a certain amount you have to tell kids when they're small, but there comes a time when the kid likes to use his own initiative.

I was with a kid once and it had been rainin' for a long time. There was a bloody great puddle on the road. I said to myself, "Walk right round it and you won't get muddy feet." But the kid just took two or three back steps and he jumped over the water. His way worked just as well as mine, and it was fitter for his age. That's only a little thing, but it tells us a lot.

There are parents who take the responsibility of rearing their children very seriously, and there are ones who don't give a damn whether their kids learn anything or not, or who they earn it from. And these are the kids who learn it from the wrong people.

Aboriginal kids didn't go to Pre-school in them days. I watched in the Kinder and First classroom, and could see that the best teacher in the room was the kid who'd been to pre-school. I said to Joan, "Don't you get the feeling that this McKenzie kid is teachin' us all in this classroom?" He'd show us grown-ups how to get the little kid who'd never been to Pre-school started. When I realized this, I went out to the Aboriginal families at Dodge and told 'em about the Pre-school the Save the Children Fund was building and we lined up about nine kids from there. I even went and picked them up in my own car, before they had a Pre-school bus. I pulled up and the teacher said, "Oh-h-h! We've got that many kids I don't know where we're going to put them all! What're we going to feed them all on?" (They give the kids a mid-morning snack and lunch.) Until they got it sorted out, the three-year-olds went in the morning, and the older ones afternoons.

I was still spending nearly all my time with the Infants, but as the year went on, if I saw any older kids that needed help, I got game to ask the Primary teachers, "D'ya need any help over there with so-and-so?"

"Yes, but I was afraid to ask you."

"Why didn't you want to?"

"Because I thought you might say, 'You're just picking on 'em because they're black!'"

The two other aides, younger than me, were nervous about doin' things with the Primary teachers. Blanche Gordon had done the Course in its first year, and as the years went on, even though she didn't do full Teacher Training, she was better than most teachers! Kevin hadn't been on the Sydney Course and he said, "Look, Aunty, you start with them and open the gate for us." So people called us 'gate openers'. Some teachers welcomed it, and some flatly refused to work with us, but you've got to expect that in any part of life. Then we got a new Principal, Frank Shaw.

There was a morning tea the first morning to welcome him, and the only ones who turned up in the Home Science Room were High School teachers. He wanted to know, "Where's everybody else?"

"Primary and Infants have their own little kitchens."

"Not any more, they don't. This is the one school, and we'll all use the one staffroom."

The teachers in the room just sat there, and away he went. Then we could hear voices and the others all came in. When he started talkin', there was a few grunts, and shufflin' feet, and movin' chairs, but he went on with his quiet voice and nice little smile.

That Principal made us three ATAs part of staff meetings and saw to it that we got to put more and more into the teaching programme so that the kids didn't find it frustrating that they were doing nearly all white-feller things.

The school had a big staff turn-over. One year we got eleven first-year-out teachers. Imagine that in any school, and in an isolated school like ours!

When kids were going from the Infant school after Grade Three, we sat down and worked out who would be the best teacher for each strugglin' kid to go to – kids we'd worked with from Kinder. Some were comin' out of the fog, some were right out of it, but didn't need much to go wrong to drop 'em back into it again. If they knew some kid was havin' trouble Blanche and Kevin would say, "Go on, Aunty Ev, you go and tackle the boss."

"No, let's give the new teachers a few weeks to settle in and see how they go."

Then I went to Frank Shaw and said, "Fourth Class needs an Aboriginal person in it. That new young chap's havin' trouble."

"Right, you work out which one of you is to go in there." He gave me a lot of responsibility, but backed me up too. Off I went myself to this new teacher, hat in hand, and the kids were playin' up in the classroom. I could hear the callin' out and the bangin' as I went across the yard. Now and then I could hear him shout, "SIT DOWN!"

I went to the door and he came over and said, "What can I do for you?"

"No, what can **I** do for **you?** Do you want a hand in there?"

He stood as straight as any man could stand, hands down his side like a tin soldier – in fact I called him that later – and said, "Certainly not!"

"By the sound of that class in there, mate, someone needs something!" and I went off.

On his way home from school he called in at the Principal's office and said, "That Aboriginal woman had the audacity to come and ask me if I needed help. I told her that I did **not** need any help."

Frank asked, "What did Evelyn say to that?"

"She said, 'Someone needs something in there,' and walked away."

The Principal had time-tabled two mornings every week for the three of us to meet with him, and it didn't matter who came along, that time was ours. Monday we'd talk about what happened last week, what went wrong, what was good, what kids did, what the teacher did. We'd write down incidents as they happened so we'd have a record, and leave them with him, so he could think about it. On Thursday we'd tell him our plans for the following week.

The day after that incident was our 'talking time', as we called it. He asked Blanche, then Kevin, then me, how things were, and I told him about that teacher.

"Right. At the staff meeting, you can talk about teachers needing any assistance."

When we got through the business set for the staff meeting, he said, "Evelyn's got something to say."

I'd started about if any teacher needed help – not sayin' who it was – and he jumped up, hands down the side again, and said, "And I told you I don't need any help!"

I just leaned on the kitchen sink – we used the Home Science Room as a meeting room, it was the biggest place – and said, "Now look here, mate. 'Course you don't need help. You just come out of Teachers College, didn't you?"

"I did."

"But those kids you're teachin', **they're** the ones that need the help. We worked very hard to get them where they are, and the way you're going, they're going to drop right back again. They'll be the laughin' stock of the kids in the playground and you'll have fights everywhere."

He sat down then and said, "I never thought about it like that."

"Well, while you're thinkin' about it, perhaps some of you other teachers might think along the same lines. I know you come here, so proud you've done your teacher training, you know how to read, write and count, and how to teach it, but how many of you know anything about the kids that live out in the bush?"

"Aboriginal kids?" asked someone.

"White kids too. You've been here months, even you new ones. Can you tell me anything about any of the kids in this school . . . their kind of life? "

Nobody said anything.

"Seems that College don't teach you anything about people, just academic things. You don't know the **kids**, and we're here to help you to get to know them, so you can become the good teachers you want to be. If a kid talks to you, especially in the street, he's offering you the only valuable thing he's got . . . his friendship. If you don't answer him, and you knock it, then you're no friend of his in the classroom. You're pretty lucky being teachers, because a teacher gets to meet all kinds of people, future people, from the littlies up to Year Twelve. Other people don't get to meet so many individual people as teachers do. So a teacher should be a person with an open mind. You're spendin' a whole year with these different people, so there should be a lot you learn. Do some comparin' along the way, comparin' with your friends, or your little brothers and sisters, the teenagers next door."

But that little talk didn't seem to make much difference with a few of them.

Later it got back to the Head of the Infant section that one of them had said, "I didn't expect I'd be in a place where I'd have an Aboriginal telling me what to do."

At the next meeting didn't she jump up and down! She said, "If I sent seven of you people away now, Kevin, Blanche and Evelyn could teach all those classes, and do a good job! Don't underestimate them! They're here to help you. They're **not** telling you what to do."

We tried our level best to become friends with all the teachers on a professional basis, as colleagues. One of the white teachers said, "Where do you get all the confidence from, anyway?"

Blanche said, "Well, me and Aunty Ev got ours from Sydney University. We trained there."

One of the Senior School fellers said, "What? You didn't come in from the cowdung pats?" He really said that.

"No, mate, but I've burnt a few in me time for the mosquito smoke!"

Lots of teachers just assumed that we were picked up out of the gutter, dusted off and put in the classroom. They had no idea that we were trained people, and they never asked.

In classrooms where the teachers worked with us, the kids done marvellously well, but if the teacher resented us, we could feel it, and so could the kids. But because we were Aboriginals, and the kids were Aboriginals, who was the bird on the biscuit tin – the feller on the outside – like on the Arnott's Biscuits? The teacher! And it would take 'em a full month – some of 'em a full year – to realize that they **were** the bird on the biscuit tin. We had to be very careful that we kept coaxin' him in from the outside, so he could eat a real biscuit, be part of it all. But one teacher said, "If you're going to put those people in the classroom with me, I'll walk out."

There was a big to-do about it. The Inspector was there, the Principal, the teacher and the three of us. The Inspector said, "If that's what you want to do, it's all up to you. I can't make you go, and I can't make you stay, but I'd rather see you stay. At least give these people a chance."

I said, "No favours, now! No beggin' for us! We can stand up on our own two feet... on our own six legs, the three of us."

In some ways I'd feel sorry for these young teachers coming outback. They didn't have the nice flats the Education Department has for them now. They had to make do with old broken-down houses, walls cracked, power goin' off all the time, no hot water. I'd see some of them cryin' and upset, away from home for the first time, needin' someone to talk to, a shoulder to lean on. I lent many a shoulder – thought I'd have permanent rheumatism with it bein' wet!

The things I listened to weren't all sad. Some were interesting and funny. One young man teacher in his first year at Bre went on and on about his brother's wedding. I had a picture in me head of the dresses and the party and the cake as if I was there. By the time his third year was comin' to an end, he came over to me in the staffroom and said, "Guess what, Aunty Ev, I'm an uncle! And they've named the baby after me!"

Because the job for the kids needed to be done, I tried to let the teachers who resented us know we were no threat to them. I wasn't goin' to come in with a spear and a boomerang, and hit 'em on the head with a waddy. There we were, and there we stayed.

Sometimes you'd get a stupid remark, or a sarcastic tone of voice, that ordinarily, if I was Blanche or Kevin's age, would have hurt me deeply. But as you git older, your skin gets a bit thicker and harder, and half of the things bounce off you. But I never forgot 'em! There'd come a time, if I waited long enough, when there'd be an opportunity for me to come back at them with that same word, and remind 'em what they'd said. They hurt quicker than I did. I never felt good about hurtin' people's feelings, but for the sake of all the Aboriginal Teacher's Aides, I let 'em know that I wasn't the stupid old woman they thought I was.

Gong had been a quiet man. He used to say, "When you're wild with anybody, and you're feeling cranky and arguing, you can say a lot of mean things. You can never take 'em back, and all your life you'll be sorry and wish you cut your tongue out. Get right away from them before you do."

That helped me to cope with a lot of hassles I've had at work too. I did that. I've walked out of the Principal's office and come back two days later.

When I was drovin', all you've got to think about is people, and dogs and horses, and you know how to work 'em out, but the school world was a different lot of people, so I had to learn about them.

Yes, there was a lot of learning in that world. Not only for the kids but for the teachers. And for me too – I learnt a real lot.

I didn't let myself really **like** any of the people I worked with. I respected them. They were my colleagues. But I never let it get to the 'they're my friend' stage. What would we have in common? I felt I didn't know them young white teachers well enough to let that barrier down. My mother used to call it a 'little cold stream of water' that kept people apart. It's hard enough for young people and old people of the same background to git close. I kept them off as much as they kept me off. Perhaps I was too late startin' in this education business – I was set in me own ways then. Ten years before I might have thought differently.

With older people it was different. I felt closer to them in a friendly way, but a real **friend** can share and understand every part of your life. Towards the end, before I retired from TAFE, I did let a couple of people in, special people, my age.

# BROKEN HILL

*'Everything was right,*

*everything was good for me'*

Eight years I did in the Brewarrina school. Two
of those years I was seconded to the Aboriginal
Education Council as Home-School Co-ordinator.

Many Aboriginal kids go into High School with
a big chip on their shoulder, and they meet teachers
there with bigger chips on their shoulders, and
in some schools the Principal's carrying a log, or
a whole tree! Because many of our kids were
dropping out of High School at fifteen, the AECG
felt we needed somebody to pick up those kids
to do courses better suited to them in TAFE. The
Deputy Principal at Bre, Denis Bishop, said to
me one day, "Look at this, Ev. You could do
this job with your eyes closed."

"So, what is it?"

I looked at the paper, and saw the advertisement
for a TAFE Aboriginal Regional Co-ordinator for
the Far-West Region of New South Wales. That's

everywhere west of Dubbo, from the Victorian to the Queensland border.

"Yeah, would be alright, eh?"

A few days later, he gave me an application form and said, "Come on, I'll help you fill it in."

"You tryin' to get rid of me out of this school?"

"No, certainly not! Not while I'm here, anyway. But you'd be really good in that job. You know a lot of kids in this Western Region, you get on well with them and their families, and someone needs to coax them into College. You've got nothing to lose if you don't get it."

So we sent the form off, and next thing, I was summoned to Sydney for an interview. There were two Aboriginal school teachers on the interview panel – John Lester and Linda Burney – as well as a person from Special Programmes and from the Regional Directorate of TAFE.

Only seven days later I got a letter to say that I was accepted, then another to tell me I was to go to Griffith for three months to work with Bill Powell, the Aboriginal Co-ordinator there, to learn the ropes. Then I would work out of Broken Hill. I was pleased about that because of growin' up in the far west. I really put in for the job in Broken Hill because I thought, "A better school for Rebecca and Jess and Roxanne. It'll give them a better start in life than here in Brewarrina. And a change in a new place won't do me any harm either."

When I went to Griffith the kids stayed back in Bre with Bimbo, just until I settled in and got a flat, I thought. At first I stayed with Bill, but when I did get a flat, only Roxanne came. Rebecca and Jess were well into their school work and sport, so they stayed in Bre to finish the year.

We had Christmas in Bre, and when I had to go back to Griffith Rebecca, just like all teenagers, had her own friends and didn't want to move.

I said, "Alright," but inside I was brokenhearted, because my whole purpose in moving to another place was to make a better life for the kids. But, of course, it didn't matter in the end, Becca still did well, still came out on top, with her University degree and working with the Aboriginal Legal Service and visiting the International Court of Justice in Geneva and all. But I missed her growing-up years. She was one who didn't match her nickname. When she was little, Rebecca loved to do things with my brother Lionel. When she messed something up, she'd say, "Gee, Uncle Lou, I'm tilly." Couldn't say 'silly' properly so of course the boys soon called her Tilly.

Jess came to Griffith with me and Roxanne. It was a good school for him. There were all sorts of nationalities there and he was the only Aboriginal! Maybe all those Italian kids knew what it was like to be an outsider and that could've made 'em more ready to be someone's friend. We were in Griffith for longer than they'd said because the person normally based there was sick, so I had to work from there to places as far away as Wagga Wagga, Tumut, Young – all over.

In the winter of 1983 I moved to Broken Hill. When I got the letter to say I was to go to there, I thought, "Here I go, packin' up and movin' again! It's as bad as when I was a teenager!" Jack had been doing a welding course in Griffith so he was there to help us move.

It was really dark and very late when we got to Broken Hill, and just near the Mine we nearly ran into a mob of bikies – almost literally **ran into** them, because in a gully where there's a lot of brunda bushes growing, Jack yelled, "Pull left, Mum!" I pulled over and slowed down. "What was that? I thought it was a horse."

"Bikies, Mum."

I looked back in the mirror and I could see our tail-lights shining on all the chrome on the bikes.

"This is no place for us to be, boy ... in a strange town where we don't know anybody."

The two bikies that were closest to the road, no lights

on, parked just behind a big rock, I nearly hit 'em because I couldn't see them. I found out who they were, about a month later. They were bank johnnies from the Westpac Bank, and, boy, didn't I tear strips off them.

We stayed a few days with my cousin, Eileen Hunt and her husband Roy, then we got a house in Argent Street, so close to the College I could even walk home for lunch. Jess didn't want to go to the High School at Broken Hill, so he decided to go back home to Brewarrina, and I didn't see much of him again till he was way beyond school age. Nobody ever gets beyond learning age. So there was just me and Roxanne. Val was in the Army, and he came and spent some time with us whenever he got leave. Then after he finished in the Army, he got the job in Broken Hill TAFE teaching Carpentry and Joinery.

I have good conversations with him. He's an initiated Aboriginal, so we talk about trackin', medicines and traditional Aboriginal things. And he brings all that back into his teaching – in his everyday teaching of white students! I say, "Why do you talk so much to those kids about Aboriginal things?"

"Look, Mum, they don't really know me. They just see I'm an Aboriginal feller and I'm a teacher. They must have their own curious mind sayin', 'What's he like? What makes him tick? What sort of person is he?' The outside part of me is the TAFE teacher, but the inside part is the Aboriginal man. So I tell 'em about my life, the things I like and the things I do, and what's part of me, and that way they get to know me, as a person, right through."

I was walking down the street with him one day in Broken Hill and two of those white students said, "Good morning, Mr Crawford."

I looked at my young feller and I said, "**Mr** Crawford!"

Val said, "Yes, all the students call me Mr Crawford."

"But in the street!" and I felt so proud. I felt as if I was taller than him, you know, and he's six foot four, but I didn't tell him, but I knew it was good for him.

Then Verina, who'd been working for the Police Department in Sydney, got a transfer, and she was entitled to a Government house in one of the posh areas of Broken Hill, in Willyama Street. She always took her school work very serious, and went on to Year 12. She'd gone to Sydney and lived with Lesley while she went to Bankstown College and then got a job. I sort of lost touch with her for a while.

I never had the idea that any of my kids would want to pitch their camp with me, so I suppose that's why I made myself so busy with TAFE so I wouldn't have time to miss them all. I was so happy later on when she got the transfer to Broken Hill and was with me again.

Roxanne made a lot of friends in Griffith and was ready for High School. When we moved on to Broken Hill she asked me if she could repeat Year Six. I couldn't understand, because her marks had always been very, very good, but she was adamant, so I let her. Later on I realized that she was scared of starting High School not knowing anyone. She knew that it would be easier in the primary school set-up, and then she'd take her friends with her to Willyama High. She's got a shrewd head, that one! Her Aboriginal name – *Gookandi* – means 'smart little black girl'. Uncle Mick Knight named her that, and rubbed her legs with his hands and said, "She'll be a smart one when she grows up."

Not long ago I said to her mother, "My word, when you named her *Gookandi* we never knew that she'd be off to America in 1988 with an Australian Softball team."

Her name became something special, very bright and loud in Broken Hill. She showed me all the things she could do, that surprised her as much as me. She was in the running teams, in softball and basketball, everything – very good at her school work too. It was a very happy year for her. She's one little girl that smiles all the time. The better she did things, the more she always had the thought that she had to prove herself twice over.

I asked her, "What do you mean, 'twice'?"

"Well, I'm an Aboriginal, and I've got to prove that I'm a good Aboriginal, that I'm a good citizen, that I'm not nasty, or selfish or mean. Then I've got to prove myself academically, that I can read and write and learn as good as the next person."

So, with Verina livin' with me, Val teaching in TAFE, Jess with a job at the Water Board, Jack not far away on Naryilco Station – right then, almost for the first time since Gong died, everything was right, everything was good for me, and it went on like that for four or five years.

When I first went to work in Broken Hill I used to sit around with the Senior Citizens a lot. We used to talk and laugh and do a lot of Aboriginal things, and we'd go with Pro Hart up the hills painting pictures on Sundays. That went on for two years. Aboriginal Week came round. Of course Aboriginal people were bringing things in to the Senior Citizens Club to display. The old white men and ladies were interested so I said, "I'll bring some of my Aboriginal paintings in."

"You can do Aboriginal painting too, Ev?"

"Course I can." And I was telling them the story of the painting one of the fellers had brought in.

"How do you know all that, Ev?"

"How? Because it's about our people, I'm an Aboriginal."

"Wha-a-t! But I've known you for years!" Chorus from everyone!

"Yes, but I'm still an Aboriginal. Three of my grandparents and my father and mother were full-bloods. My grandfather Knight was a white man. My husband's father was an Irishman, Bon Crawford, blue eyes and red hair – but he told everyone he was called Bill. His mother was Aboriginal, Isabel Murphy, and she was about as dark as my Jess."

"Well, what do you know about that! We thought your tan was like ours. We got that out in the open."

"No. If you lift up my shirt in the front you'll see my belly is the same colour as my arms."

There they were, all saying to each other, "Ev's Aboriginal, Ev's an Aboriginal," like it was big news!

I was at the football in Broken Hill one Saturday afternoon and my cousin, Badger Bates, saw me sittin' down by the fence and was singing out to me from up on the hill. He is Granny Moysey's grandson and she'd never allowed Badger to speak English, so it was only when she died that he started to speak it most of the time. We knew Granny Moysey could speak English when she wanted to, when she was talking to white people, but she always talked to us in the *Baarkanji* language, and we had to speak back in the language. "That's our lingo, so we'll use it."

Badger is in the Parks and Wildlife Service, and lots of people in the district know him well. We had quite a long conversation before the game started, talking in *Baarkanji*, without thinking. There were some young coppers and their girl friends near me. On the Monday, I had to take Verina's car keys over to her at the Police Station, and one of the young coppers said, "Mrs Crawford, I never ever heard people speak Aboriginal language before. A few words on TV, but to be near people really talking it!"

"Where did you hear it?"

"You, at the match, and Badger, having a good old go. What were you talking about? It must have been something funny, 'cos he was sittin up on the hill, laughing away."

As Aboriginal Co-ordinator I had a lot to do with the schools in Broken Hill. The principal of Willyama High asked, "Will you do a painting for us, Aunty Ev, so that we can raffle it to raise money?"

"What are you raising money for?"

"Well, you know kids go on excursions, and when they get there the Aboriginal children don't have any spending money. The money we make with the things we raffle, that could be their spending money."

"Hold on a minute. I don't like what I'm hearin'! That's gettin' things for nothing. You don't pick up a fortnightly pay packet for nothing, do you? You work for it, don't you?"

"Yes, and pretty hard too."

"Right. Then you work out something that these kids can do to make some money and then I'll do a painting for you so you can raise some more money. I don't give nobody nothing for nothing, not anyone's kids, not even my own kids."

So at Assembly he talked to them all, and told them that I would do a painting. Then he said, "You tell them about it, Aunty Ev."

"Yes, I've agreed to do it, but I don't want you just sittin' back and waitin' for me to paint, and for me to get the raffle tickets and for me to raise the money and all you do is spend it. I don't think that would be fair, would it?"

"No-o-o, Aunty Ev." You know how they all chorus it.

"Well, is there anything that you could do . . . work that you could help me do, and we could all make some money together."

Then they all started givin' ideas,

"I c'n help you paint . . . I c'd do frames in Woodwork . . . I'll cut your lawn for you . . ." I smiled at that one, and thought to myself, "Cuttin' buffalo grass, mate, you'll sure know you're cuttin' a lawn."

Each time I'd go to the school they'd ask, "Started your painting yet, Aunty Ev?"

"No, not yet."

"Gee, look what we've been doing," and they brought out all their work.

"Right, mates," and I got going.

We ended up getting $800 altogether between all of us. They were that proud of it. "We made a lot of money, didn't we, Aunty Ev?"

"Yes, **we** did, mates."

It's always best to show people how they can do things for themselves. Kids need a lot of encouragement, but so do parents. Most people lack confidence, so we all need somebody to build us up.

The Principal of the TAFE College was Ian Fraser, one of the nicest white men I've ever met in my life. He really helped me settle in. The staff at the College had just taken me as Ev, a new person, not an oddity. In that staffroom, anybody sat wherever there was an empty chair. Whatever was on the plate on the table, anybody ate – it didn't matter if it was a brown hand reachin' for it or a white hand. Whenever I came to the office with paper work, always someone would say, "Do you need any help with that, Ev?" That really broke down any barriers. Because my job hadn't existed before, there was no job description. My understanding of it was going out into the community and talkin' to the people, but nobody from Head Office had told the Principal that – probably left it all to me. He had his ideas what a Co-ordinator (Liason Officer it was called then) should do. He could only think of it like for the other teachers, be there at nine and still there at five, and never leave, only at lunch time.

For a while I thought, "I'll let him run along for a while, till he comes to the barbed wire fence . . . he'll go back and start again on a better track." But the poor feller pressed on the barbed wire fence that much I'm sure it stuck in him somewhere.

He'd say, "Look, you'd better tell me what you're doing. I saw you talking to a group of Aboriginal people down in front of the baker's."

"Yes, you did, too."

"And one of the secretaries saw you talking to another group in a cafe."

"Yeah, that's part of my job."

"I beg your pardon?"

"That's what I'm paid to do."

"To stand in the street and talk?"

"How'm I gonna liaise with people in the community if I don't pull up and talk to them? They don't know where my office is, and there's no notice at the front of your College to say ABORIGINAL OFFICER IN HERE. As for **college**, my people've always assumed that was a white man's place . . . no place in there for blackfellers."

"Yes, yes," and he put his hands in his two pockets and went off.

Whenever he put those hands in his pockets, that meant that he was gittin' out of that argument. One time I joked with him, "I'm gonna sew up those two pockets! Then you'll have nowhere to put your hands, and you'll have to pull up and talk!" We soon became good mates. One day he said, "Ev, tomorrow, we'll have the day together."

"Oh, we goin' somewhere nice?"

"You know the Menindie Lakes? We'll pack a lunch, and we'll spend all day in the grassy place near the camping ground."

Early the next morning, away we went. He had folding chairs so we sat under the trees and looked out over the lake, and we **talked**.

He said, "First thing I must tell you, Ev, is I know nothing about Aboriginal people, I've never been near them, you're the first I've spoken to. You've got some idea what white people are about . . . in here (pattin' his chest). I don't have anything like that on Aboriginal people. I want you to tell me."

"Right. But before I tell you, I'm gonna tell you that I'm **me**, Evelyn Crawford, and all those Aboriginal people out there – they're all different. You get to know me as well as you want to know me, but then when you meet another Aboriginal, remember, he's a different person altogether."

"I realize that, I realize that."

He said it as if he was very sure. But he didn't realize it, because when he met another Aboriginal who wasn't me, the two hands went straight in the pockets!

"So . . . tell me about your people at Wilcannia."

We had all day, and I told him about my *Baarkanji* people, about totems, about the languages . . . him writing all the time in a big writing pad. After that, there was no hassles between us. I could go into his office at any time, and mention anything I was doin' or wanted, and he understood what I was talking about. Things he thought I didn't know, or wouldn't ask, he'd volunteer.

I'd say, "You know, I wondered about that for a long time."

"I know, but you wouldn't get around to asking me, would you?"

"Didn't want to be a nuisance to you, Ian," but it wasn't that at all. I didn't want people to think that I was a dumb Aboriginal. Ian was an old-fashioned man, and would be very careful to phrase things so they wouldn't come out in a way that might be hurtful to me. Work became heavy and fast, and I leaned on him a lot. He had to sign every proposal that I put up. He'd talk it over with me, whether we could put more in, or would have to take something out, and always told me why it could be changed. But he never said, "I'll change it this way . . . I'll do that." It was always, "What about if you did this?" So it was always **my** work.

His secretary, Estelle Finch, was wonderful to me. She said, "Anything you want to know, Ev, just ask." and I knew she meant it. I got the feeling that the other people in the office were like that too. One day I went to the office and leaned on the counter and said, "Anyone here help an old Koorie woman?" They all looked up and laughed. Later on, Jim Gleason, the Registrar, said, "Ev, the other day when you said 'old Koorie woman', that new teacher who was there said after you'd gone, 'I'm glad she was the one said that, and not anybody else.' I told him, "Ev's an exception. You can joke with her."

"Yeah. I know when friends are jokin' friendly."

Sometimes they'd ring me at morning tea time and say, "Ev, would you come up, please. There's something on the table for you." So I'd turn up with me pint of tea and say, "Any cake left for one old Koorie?" They got that way they could say, "Every time I turn around, here's this old Koorie woman standing behind me with a piece of paper and a job of work!" I felt I was part of them, and they never said anything about my Aboriginality that would hurt my feelings. We were comfortable enough to tease each other.

Ess became a good friend, a real friend. She helped me with a lot of things, not just College work. She had sons and daughters, and her husband had died, and we'd talk about our kids. Then she got grandkids, and the stories and yarns we'd share would be about grandkids. I'd be talkin' away while she'd be knittin' for the babies. She said I could talk under water with a mouth full of marbles, and we both laughed, because she was right!

My job made me the person who went into Aboriginal communities to introduce TAFE to them. I'd explain how, if anyone wanted courses like Literacy, Numeracy, Secretarial Studies, Sewing, Typing, Carpentry and Joinery, Microwave Cooking, Aboriginal Arts and Crafts – any course, if enough people were interested, TAFE could do it. They even had a mobile thing they could drag out to where students were and set up a Welding Course.

I'd find out how many students would like to do which courses. I'd take the names and addresses back to the College, and discuss the programmes with the Principal. If there was enough students for a Course, I'd go back and ask what they wanted in the course, because they didn't always want what the white feller's got in the book. Otherwise we wouldn't've got any students at all. I'm not sure if we were supposed to do it, but we did it, regardless! And it worked. They'd all get ready for the little Maths and English test they had to do. I'd say to the College teachers who'd go out to give these academic tests, "Now, many of these people only went to sixth class, they're not good readers. They can count money, and that's about all their Maths."

Back at College we looked at the tests and sorted them out accordingly. We found generally we had to split the classes, two classes in one Course, until they got used to doing the lessons. In a little while we'd put them all together, 'cos the ones who'd learnt a little bit could help the ones who were still strugglin' behind. The strugglers could lean on the others.

The white teachers said, "You can't do that, Ev."

"Look, these people are all learning together and they **need** to help each other. You can't keep one lot behind, else they'll be behind for ever and ever, Amen."

"Alright. But there's some with good academic ability, some with less. How'm I ever going to teach them together?"

"You're so crazy for this 'top class' and 'low class'. We don't have any of that in our race. It's up to you. If you're as good a teacher as you think you are, you can do it. And somewhere along the way you'll find you've brought those stragglers along to catch up with the front ones. They'll ask each other questions when they won't ask you. You'll find one of those front ones game enough to ask the questions that maybe five other people want answers for."

So they did work like that, and they **did** bring the tail up to the head.

When courses first started out in the smaller communities, Ian had it in his bonnet that, if I was there, the Aboriginal students would come in, and I suppose he was right. They might have felt a bit more comfortable, especially in classes where the white teachers didn't talk much to them, except for givin' instructions. Especially in sewing courses the women valued me being there. You know how sewing time is chatting time for all women. Things weren't always easy – sometimes the road was pretty rough and rocky. But by the middle of the year, everybody was pullin' up a chair sittin' near anybody, black or white didn't matter.

In the general office they said to me one day, after I'd been there about four years, "We don't see you much these days, Ev. Who's typing your letters?"

"Didn't you lot know? I've got a secretary now, with a brand-new 'lectric typewriter, in my brand-new office."

"Where?"

"Right! Stop everything now. Leave someone on the switchboard. I'll take you on a guided tour."

Down we went to the classroom they'd made into an office for me, flowers on the desk, pictures on the walls, new furniture. When I got a new phone, it took me forever to learn it! But for all that, I never went into a colleague's office unless I was invited, and never sat down in anyone's office unless I was offered a chair. Ian would say, "What're you standing up for, Ev? Sit down."

"Thanks. This is your office. I can't just sit down without being asked."

He used to show me the same courtesy in my office, and I appreciated it. It spread to the other staff too, and it made me feel good that I was part of the College, that they respected me like that.

Ian was the only white person I've been able to tempt to try *gweeyuhmuddah*. The doctor had told him that he had 'junctivitis. He had dark glasses on in the office, so I said, "Try it, just try it." So I cut a branch when I was at Wilcannia, took it home, boiled it, and gave a bottle of the liquid to his wife.

"Now warm it a bit and put it on cotton wool over his eyes. He can open his eyes if he wants to."

In three days he was as good as new.

I went to a meeting in Sydney for Principals and Heads of Sections of TAFE Colleges, organised by American education people. Two of us were sent from Broken Hill. The other person was one of these up-date ladies, no place in the world for Aboriginal people, and having them in College! they shouldn't be there – even as students, and as for being on the staff!

We got out to the airport and she said, "Where're you going to, Ev?"

"I'm going to Sydney, same place as you."

When we got to Sydney, we were both to be picked up and taken to a motel somewhere in the middle of the city. When the car pulled up she thought it was just for her and said, "Where're you going now?"

"I'm going in this car, if that's alright with you."

When the car stopped at the great big brand-new building, would you believe it, she said again, "Where're you going now?"

"I'm going with this bloke."

"Will you be staying here?"

"If it's alright with you."

That was the end of her talking to me, all the time we were there. It turned out that my room was next to hers. She was sharing with somebody from Adelaide, and I was with somebody from Gosford. Lucky they'd decided to mix us all up – I don't know what she'd have done if we'd been put together.

That meeting went for six days and there were forty-one people, and the one was me, the one Aboriginal with forty white people. They were there to talk about Equal Opportunities in Education, and the person who was running it couldn't quieten the people down. There were too many teachers, talking all the time in the back. And a few seats from me, this lady from Broken Hill was saying quite loud, "I don't know what Ev Crawford's doing here at this meeting."

While we were having a cuppa, one of the older Education fellers I'd known for ages, Evan Sutton, said to the organizer, "Can't you quieten them down?"

"No, I can't. I just can't get that lot at the back. They're very ill-mannered. They wouldn't let their students act like that."

Evan said, "Can't you turn the programme round and come on to the Aboriginal part and TAFE, and put Aunty Ev up on the panel for questions?"

I pricked up my ears. "What's this, Evan? I'm getting this second-hand, and don't know if I like it or not."

"Come on, Ev, anything's worth a try."

We were only halfway through the first day and it looked already as if the whole thing was falling apart. So I got up on this panel and they shot questions at us. One of the ones at the back asked what was my attitude towards teachers in the Colleges.

I stood up for that one, and in the biggest voice I could muster I said, "I don't **have** an attitude towards white teachers or white students. You lot, you've got an attitude towards black people in Colleges, not me, mate." And from then on, they fired all the questions at me.

I said, "I feel so sorry for Aboriginal students in your bloody classes with the attitude you've got. Then you'll say, 'Aboriginal students won't stay. They just get out and they won't come back.' And not once would you ever say to yourself, 'Is it because of me?' Nah, you wouldn't say that. You'd blame the Aboriginal students. Don't forget, you're not all perfect, you could be to blame too."

I could have said, but I didn't, "Some of you would've made bloody good Mission Managers!"

Frank said to me after, "I should have put you up there before. You chopped their legs from under them. You certainly quietened them."

"Someone had to do something. It's no good comin' all this way and sayin' nothing. It wouldn't be fair to all the Aboriginal people."

"We'll put you up there again tomorrow, because after all, the emphasis of the Conference is for people who have Aboriginal students in their courses. Tell them what your Aboriginal education programmes are."

"Listen, I only came down as a sidekick, and an unwanted sidekick at that!"

But I did it, and I ended up by saying to them that never in my life could I have dreamed that there would be people like me working for Education Departments. That we could go into a classroom and if we saw that the teacher wasn't suitable for our Aboriginal students we could say, "Right! We don't need him. He might be a good teacher in an all-white school, but he's out of his depth here. We need someone else." And we had the authority to do that.

The next day, that lady from Broken Hill shot all kinds of questions at me. When we got home I wasn't her most popular person. At the next staff meeting, someone asked her, "What was the Conference like?"

"M-m-m-m, I suppose it was alright."

The secretary, my friend Ess, must have heard somehow what had happened in Sydney, and she sent a little note down the table. I could see this note travelling and thought, "Wonder who she's writing to." People were looking at this little piece of folded paper as they passed it along. When I saw it was marked 'Ev', I opened it up. It had 'DID THAT CANARY TASTE GOOD?' When she looked at me I just nodded.

Later when I told Val all about it, he said, "No wonder Ess was asking about the canary. You ate a whole bloody chook!"

About that time I was saying to Ian, "There's nowhere to set up good courses at Wilcannia. We need a proper TAFE College Campus out there." They'd had a bit of a place but it got burnt down and we were teaching in sheds.

The Education Department was building a new school, and the old school had a lot of demountables – pre-fab classrooms. Rodney Cavalier was Minister for Education then and he was out at Wilcannia. I met him in the dining room at the Golf Club, and said to him, "What about giving us a couple of those demountables to set up a College Campus here?"

"They're earmarked to go to a Migrant School." You'd think they were a mob of cattle!

"Hold on a bit! Who was in this country first?"

He looked straight at me with a mouthful of prawns – he had the biggest dish of prawns in front of him – and finished chewin'. When he could speak, he said, "What do you want them for?"

I told him and he said, "Do a bit of ground work, and let me know what's going on."

Back in Broken Hill, I told Ian about the new school, and he said, "Did you meet Mr Cavalier there?"

"Yeah, and I asked him for a couple of demountables."

"**You what!**"

"Asked him for a couple of demountables when the school's completed."

"What do you want them for?"

"To set up classrooms for a proper campus out there."

"I should have thought of that. It's a good opportunity."

"It doesn't matter who thinks of it, so long as it gets thought. Let's keep our fingers crossed and hope we do get them."

"But what if we don't?"

"The world won't come to an end if we don't get them. We can pay rent for someone's garage."

"Now, what do you want me to do?"

"Well, you could write a letter as Principal and say how valuable they would be to us. I'll whip back to Wilcannia tomorrow and get the local AECG to write. While I'm there I'll line up a community meeting for tomorrow evening late and get signatures from the community."

He wrote his letter, I got the letter from the AECG in

conjunction with the school. The Wilcannia Sergeant of Police rang me and said, "I'd like to put my name on that letter."

"What about if you wrote one for yourself, you and your Department?"

"Right, I will."

The Matron of the Hospital and some of the visiting Flying Doctors thought it would be good if the older teenagers were occupied, then there wouldn't be so many with busted heads and sick from drink.

While I was in Wilcannia I went to see the Shire President. He looked up from his desk and said, "What can I do for you?" I told him about our idea. A young lady brought us a cup of tea, and we talked.

"Is this TAFE campus for black people?"

"No, it's for every people. If a Chinaman comes along and wants to do a course in Chinese Cooking he can do that too . . . might have to teach himself. Why would I want to set up courses in this small community for just one part of the community? Everyone can use it."

"Well, what do you want me to do?"

"I want some land to put it on."

We finished our tea, and he said, "Come on. Get in the car and we'll go round and see what vacant land there is."

When we drove along I asked, "What's the Shire going to do with the vacant allotment over there on the corner? Mt Murchison Hotel used to be there, with big stables at the back. Then it was a petrol station."

"I don't know. We haven't talked about it."

We drove all round, and found about ten other vacant blocks but none big enough. We wanted room for two demountables – I still assumed I was getting them! – a workshop for Welding and Motor Maintenance and all that sort of thing and a garden where we could put a flagpole and seats.

"You tell me what you're really looking for."

"That corner block."

He rubbed his chin and said "M-m-m-m."

"Have the Shire members planned to use it for something?"

"No, no. Nobody's discussed that block of land, not since I've been here. But we will. When do you want it?"

"Three weeks ago!"

"That soon! We had a Shire Meeting a few days ago, and because of the rain, most of those men are still in town. What about if I call them together . . . mind you, I can't promise you anything . . . I'm not the only one on the Council."

"Right, I hear all this and I understand." Then I headed back to Broken Hill.

Next morning I showed Ian all the letters and he gave me his. Real formal, it was. "Gee, there's a lot of big words in this, boy!"

"I think it's appropriate, Ev."

I thought to myself, "If it gits us what we want, let him use all the jaw-breakers in the whole dictionary."

Estelle sent off all the letters to Rodney Cavalier. In my heart I wasn't too hopeful, because too often we'd written about things and never even got an answer. I thought this would be another one of those times too. I kept copies of letters that I could look at when I was old and could say to myself, "At least I tried to get something done."

Writing submissions and getting the Government to help made me prick me ears about this politics business and get on the voting roll again.

After about three months, there was some function on at the College, and Cavalier, still Minister for Education, came out. I'd been out around the traps for about nine days and didn't know about it. I came to work as usual and was just near the door and saw all these cars pull up. The Mayor was there, all in his regalia.

Rodney Cavalier got out – very tall man he is, a man

that never combs his hair. He said, "Here's somebody I know. You'll be at our meeting, won't you? "

"If there's a cup of tea and a piece of cake I'll be there."

He looked a bit surprised and said, "Yes, there's a luncheon."

Estelle pulled me aside and said, "We couldn't let you know, Ev, because you've been away, out of touch. If you'd seen the Flying Doctors they'd have given you the message. We asked them to tell you."

"Tell me what?"

"That there's a luncheon today to welcome the new members on the College Council, and you're one. That's why the Minister's here."

I remembered then that Ian had asked me to sign some application form for the Council ages ago. I'd joked, "You'd better tell me what I'm signin' for. You white fellers might be goin' to hang me!" Then I mostly forgot about it. I wasn't anxiously thinkin', "Will they put me on the Council?" But sometimes the Koorie came out in me and I'd be thinkin' "They wouldn't want a black person on such an important committee."

"Do I go along today, then?"

"You'd better! I'll be there, taking notes."

"Right, I'll come with you." Ess was always a great support. So we went to the luncheon – pretty good too it was.

Rodney Cavalier stood up and welcomed all the new members. Everyone was clappin', I was clappin' up for everybody, then he said my name, and people were clappin' for me as representative of the Aboriginal community. Estelle and I were at a small table and Rodney Cavalier came over, got himself a chair and sat down. I introduced him to Ess and she said, "I'd better go and see if Ian needs me."

He said, "Don't go unless you really have to."

I said, "Sit down, Ess. I don't like talkin' to white fellers on me own!"

She looked over her glasses at me, because she wouldn't

say anything silly in front of important people. I'd got to the stage when 'Minister for Education' was just a title. But a man wasn't born with that title. He was born a little boy, Rodney, and I found myself relating to Rodney Cavalier, the man. There was no way I'd know how to talk to a **Minister**, but I could talk to a **person** who was part of the education system, concerned for the same things as I was.

He laughed and said, "I got all those letters you sent."

"What did you think of them?"

"Pretty good arguments were put up in them. I've taken them with me when I was travelling . . . pulled your letter out again and thought about it."

"And now you're going to tell me we can get the demountables? You're going to give us the go-ahead?"

"Yes, I am. But I'd like you to come to Wilcannia with me, and show me the land."

It was just after lunch, so I said, "Gee, I don't know about today, mate . . . go over there and back? It'll be the middle of the night by the time I get home."

"There's an aeroplane out at the airport. We'll fly over and look at it."

Rodney looked over to Ian and said, "I'm taking Aunty Ev over to Wilcannia to see the land."

Ian sort of er-er'd, and the hands were reachin' for the pockets. I nudged Ess, thinkin', "Soon as the hands get in the pockets, we'll know I can go."

Off to the airport, into the private plane, and ch-oo-ff, we're in Wilcannia. The school people met us at the air field and Shire members who lived in town went round the properties with us.

Rodney Cavalier said, "Yes, I do like your choice." Then he turned to the Shire President and said, "Ev's got the land, hasn't she?"

"Yes, she's got it. We passed it at the last Shire Council meeting that it would go to TAFE."

"Great!" I said, "and as soon as you can get your lot crackin', I'd like them to take out those old underground petrol tanks. And see those peppercorn trees down the side, I don't want them touched, and them in the middle, not them either, I want the demountables in their shade. And leave that one in the front. The rest you can take." Throwin' orders I was, right away!

As soon as we left, the President rang Ian Fraser in Broken Hill. "Evelyn Crawford showed me what trees she wanted cut down and those she didn't. What'll I do about it?"

Ian said, "You'll do what you were told to do with them, you won't cut any more or any less than what she told you."

"But you're the Principal."

"Of this College, yes, certainly, but that Unit is her territory and if she wants it that way, I would appreciate it if you did just that."

"Has she got the go-ahead to do all that?"

"Yes, with the backing of the College, and, if necessary, of the Minister for Education."

I knew then I had all the guns, and I was firing them the way I wanted to. I said to myself, "I'll never git a chance like this again, to do things for my people in this little town. I haven't jumped on anybody's head to git this, or browbeat anybody. I've just talked and let 'em see how important and helpful it would be for this little community."

The next week when I went over it was like a **beehive** on that corner, diggin' out the tanks and huge rocks, old posts, wagon wheels – it had been a stopping place for Cobb and Co. on the road to Tibooburra and White Cliffs. The town people didn't know what it was going to be used for, then when they knew it was TAFE the white people just assumed it was something for only black people. So we put all about it in the local newspaper, the *Paddlewheel*. We also let them know that we hoped to get part-time teachers for the Courses from Wilcannia, because there were married women, ex-teachers, in the town, but we didn't get any. Teachers had to travel over from Broken Hill three times a week for different subjects – a couple of hours each way. Welding, Carpentry and Joinery – my Val taught that – and one of the Secretarial Studies groups were night classes, so the teacher had to stay overnight, and in the morning he'd pass the others on the road comin' from Broken Hill. Later on, some of the station owners and their wives came in and taught courses.

Ian had said, "You'll have to make a list of all the things you'll need for your college over there."

"**My** college???"

I made the list, and the only thing I forgot to put on that long, long, long list was a wheelbarrow! I thought of everything else – tables, chairs, office equipment, heaters, air conditioners, spades and hose and garden tools, and I clean forgot about the wheelbarrow! We bought it out of Petty Cash from Broken Hill College, and paid them back when we had some money. I got an Aboriginal girl who'd just finished Year Twelve to be part-time secretary, mainly to answer the phone and take messages. When we'd come across we'd pick up the messages and deal with them.

# STANDING TALL

*'Ready to take on*

*the world'*

I got an invitation from the Premier of New South
Wales, Nick Greiner, and his wife, to a luncheon
with Her Majesty Queen Elizabeth and Prince
Philip at the Opening of Darling Harbour.

I felt very special, but I couldn't believe my
eyes. I got this beautiful big envelope and opened
it up and saw the gold writing. I was so proud
of it and showed it to my friend Estelle.

"Ess, **you** read this and tell me if I'm seeing
things or not."

She read it and shot round her desk into the
main office. Each person there had to get it and
hold it and read it for himself. One little Greek
girl said, "I'm glad. It couldn't have happened
to a nicer person. You deserved something like
that." I felt good when she said that, and just
imagine how I'd have felt if it had been an Aboriginal person telling me that.

My kids were very proud. We put copies in the mail to all the family, up to Cunnamulla, to Newcastle, to Sydney. Got some beautiful letters back, I've kept them all.

Ess said, "Could I have a longer look at that? I'll give it back to you lunchtime." So I let her have it.

Three days later the Broken Hill newspaper was printed and what was on the front cover, right in the middle of the page? A copy of my invitation! I was interviewed by the paper people, by the radio, and the TV rang up. When the TV people came I was up to my sleeves in paint, painting a picture for the Willyama High and said I'd get around to talkin' to them, but I never did.

I put that invitation in a frame, I valued it so much.

*Her Majesty The Queen*
*and His Royal Highness The Duke of Edinburgh*
will be present

*The Hon. Nick Greiner, M.P., Premier of New South Wales*
*and Mrs Greiner request the pleasure of the company of*
*Mrs Evelyn Crawford Snr & Guest.*
*at the Official Opening of the Darling Harbour Project*
*by Her Majesty The Queen*

on Wednesday, 4th May, 1988, commencing at 11.00 a.m.
to be followed by a
*State Luncheon*
at the Darling Harbour Convention Centre at 12.15 p.m.

A reply on the accompanying                    Dress: Lounge Suit
form would be appreciated.                          Day Dress
Entree cards will be forwarded on receipt of an acceptance.

I took Verina with me to Sydney. I went to the Big Girls Shop and bought a very, very expensive dress. I could have eaten for six months on the money I paid for it. Shoes to go with it. They had little studs on the heels, the kind of shoes I'd never worn before. A bag to go with them, some jewellery too. Verina had her hair done, but I'd had mine cut in Broken Hill a couple of weeks before, so it was good enough. Then the big day came. We could see the *Britannia* sailing in as we came around to Darling Harbour in the car.

We were all out in the open near the Japanese Gardens when the Queen came to speak from the little stand they'd built for her there. After she finished doing all her talking and we were all going to the room for lunch, we met some very interesting people walking along. There were all these famous people whose faces I'd seen in newspapers, and read about. One of them was Bart Cummings, the racehorse trainer. Then Verina said to me, "Look there, Mum. That's Tommy Smith over there."

I said, "Yes, and this is Bart Cummings." I'd started to talk to him.

Verina knew how great I thought Bart was so she said, "Would you mind if I took your picture with my mother?"

"Not at all, dear. Come over here, Tommy, and have your picture taken with us." I stood in the middle and Verina took the photo. When we showed that around at home, because everybody is racehorse mad, they were saying, "Well, you should get the inside running on all the winners now you've had your photo taken with the best trainers."

We walked to where the lunch was to be, and it seemed a real long walk, there were so many people and they walked real slow. You got to be really sedate. It was a new experience for me, but I could handle it by then, being around white people for sixteen years. I could even use some of the great big words that I'd learned over those years, words I'd never found it necessary to use anywhere else. I didn't want to show off, but I didn't want anyone to think I was a bush bunny because I'm an Aboriginal and couldn't speak their language. If they were using big jawbreakers I used jawbreakers too. Every now and then Verina would poke me in the back, when something or someone tickled her fancy. Verina is a jolly person with a great sense of humour, laughs all the time.

There was a big turn we had to take, and all my life, if there was ever a short cut anywhere, I'd take it. I said, "We don't have to walk all the way round. Besides, these steel studs on my heels are gettin' at me. I'm afraid I'll fall over, this road feels like it's been polished. It's like walkin' on glass. One slip and I'll hit the ground."

We went on a bit, then I asked Verina, "What's that there for?"

"It's the red carpet, Mum. The Queen always walks on a red carpet."

There were crowds of people all standing along the sides, but I saw some going inside where there were tables and chairs.

"I'd like to go in there and sit down too," says I.

"Come on then."

I couldn't walk in a hurry, 'cos I was frightened of slipping – and there was this red carpet. I thought, "I've spent so much money to come and see her, surely I can walk on her carpet," so I stepped on it. Verina was walking on the road at the side, click-click-click. There were two old ladies on the side near her, holding each other and shivering, thinkin' they'd slip over too.

A feller came over to me, all dressed up in some kind of uniform and said, so-o-o politely, "Excuse me, ma'am, the Queen hasn't walked on that yet. It's for the Queen to walk on."

"I'm sure the Queen wouldn't want one of her visitors to be sitting in the dining room with a broken leg because she slipped and fell over, so will you please just move away and let me pass so I can go in and sit down. Besides, I'm tired, I came all the way from Broken Hill."

"Oh-h yes, ma'am," in such a sympathetic voice as if I'd **walked** all the way from Broken Hill.

I said to Verina, "Quick, grab them two old ducks and bring 'em along."

She hissed at me, "Mumma, you can't walk on that carpet!"

"I'm on it, aren't I?"

"Well, I'm not walking on it."

So she put the two old ladies on the red carpet behind me and away we walked into the dining area.

Inside people showed us where we had to sit. We were at a big round table for eight. The others were Presidents of Shires and their wives, one was from Glen Innes. At the next table, back to back with me, was Barry Unsworth. I'd met him several times when he was Premier. He poked me in the back and said, "What're you doing here?" but he said it in a nice way.

"I'm just lookin' and listenin'." At the moment that's all I could think to say. I should have said, "Same as you. I'm a guest of the Queen."

"How long have you been down here, Ev?

"We came down a couple of days ago. I got an invitation to this, you know."

"I didn't doubt that at all, Ev."

"Here, not too much of that 'Ev'. We're in the presence of Royalty, you gotta call me 'Mrs Crawford'."

Then everyone had to stand when the Queen and Prince Philip came in, and stay standing while she talked again. Then she sat down, and we all sat down. Home Science students from the TAFE Colleges were waiting on us. I knew some of them from the Sydney Tech, some were Aboriginals too. I leaned over to one of them and asked, "What's the tucker like?" They were bringing lovely jugs of orange juice to start with.

She whispered, "Oh, Aunty Ev, I don't think you'll like it."

They brought out this meal, three-course, five-course, I dunno. I lost track, because I didn't enjoy it. I bumped Verina and muttered "What's this?"

She said, "Have a good look at it."

I didn't like what I saw. It looked as if it was somebody's black eyelashes around a little yellow thing, but Verina told me afterwards that it was caviare that was dressed up! I tasted it with the little silver fork and managed not to pull a face. The main course was Tasmanian Cod, and it looked to me like the smoked fish we used to buy in Brewarrina on Good Friday, with that yellow stuff on it where it's smoked. It looked like it hadn't been cooked. They brought vegetables on a silver thing, and they all looked raw. Chinese people must have catered for it, and they have everything half-raw, and Aboriginal people don't eat anything half-raw. So I didn't eat them, just had another drink of orange juice.

Verina muttered, "Eat something, Mum. The people who catered for it, they're watching you."

She was goin' crook at me. We were both goin' on under our breath. "What's the good of eatin' something I don't like?"

"You haven't even tasted it. Taste it . . . I'm not coming anywhere with you any more . . . you can't even behave yourself when we come to see the Queen . . ."

When I'd been looking forward to going to the Queen's luncheon, I was thinkin' about beautiful food – corned beef and cabbage with boiled potatoes, or roast beef, roast turkey with baked vegetables, and my appetite sort of worked up to a feed like that, but when it turned out like it did, my appetite was worse. It took me all my time to sit there, without saying, "I'm gonna go and buy a pie."

At last they took the main course away and brought the sweets, pecan nut tarts that you couldn't stick the spoon in, they were so hard. The others at the table could see I was uncomfortable, but I bet they weren't used to eating that kind of food either. And of course, they talked louder and louder. I notice that when white people want to cover up for something, they talk louder and louder but really say nothing. So I started talking about Mootawingee. I know the white feller calls it 'Mootwingee', but he's wrong. It's an Aboriginal place, and the proper Aboriginal name is 'Moot-**a**-wingee'. A feller at the table, when he heard that I came from Broken Hill, asked me about it, so I started to tell him, not in a loud voice, but I suppose others could see he was interested, and they got curious and listened too.

When I noticed people at tables around ours half-turned round listening to us I wished that I could have got **under** the carpet!

Anyway, the meal was over at last, and She done some more talkin', then She stood up, and we stood up, and away She went. She had to go and look at the railway thing then, the Monorail. When we went in, it was parked up above us, and when we came out it was still there. I heard some person say, "Have they got two of those trains?"

"N-o-o-o-o. It broke down. It's been there all the time we've been inside."

It was a pretty warm day, so I don't know what the poor people were like who were sittin' in it, with kids.

Verina said, "Well, Mum, we'll go home." We were staying with Tiny.

But then they mustered us into a line to meet the queen. She's only a **little** woman! She had an apricot shantung suit on. It was the wrong colour for her to wear that particular day, because it was so hot, and she was looking sort of pink. She was kept walking, smiling and nodding to people as she passed them so I got a shock when she stopped in front of me and said, "Evelyn Crawford . . . Junior or Senior?"

I said, "Senior."

"Ah, you're the one who works so hard for her people."

I thought, "This woman lives way across the river. How does she know about these things?" and I said, "I'm just doing what I can, what anybody would do."

Then she said, "One thing you always have to remember, that you're a very special person."

But I said, "We all are, because there's only one of us."

"I do hope your people appreciate all the things that you've done for them, and tell you so."

Then she had to move on.

Verina said to me, "I thought the two of you were never going to stop talking."

The Minister for Education was with the Queen so he

would have told her, but she was a gracious lady to talk to me. That made me forget the terrible food I couldn't eat. I went home feeling ten foot tall. It wasn't only because I'd met the Queen. That was part of it, but mostly because someone from way over on the other side of the river, you know, pulled up and had the time to talk to me about things that mattered to me, about the things I'd been doing, or trying to do, for my people, for the kids. Yeah, I felt pretty good about that.

When I got back to Broken Hill I had to sit up and relate everything that had happened. One of the first things they asked me was "What was the food like?" Verina happened to walk into the office at the very minute and she said, "Don't talk about it! Don't ask her."

"Why?"

So Verina related the whole thing. All I could hear them saying was, "Oh-h-h, Ev, you didn't! . . . Oh-h-h, Ev, you shouldn't!" I was being reprimanded, in fun of course, all over the office. But I really enjoyed that experience. I thought that was it. I said to Verina, "There's nowhere to go after that, is there?"

"I don't know, Mum. You always seem to find a gap somewhere, with a little road in it. And if there's not a road, you'll **make** one!"

But at that particular time I felt, "Well, what else is there?" That was a big reward for me, for all the times I put up with the bad stinkin' meat, and the toothaches on the drovin' trip, and the horses throwin' me and runnin' away from me, the sleepin' on the hard ground in the rain, and the ups and downs we had rearin' the kids, and the ups and downs we'd had with white people in the schools, I thought, "Well, people **do** get rewards, and this is mine."

I felt ready to take on the world, all fresh again at sixty years of age. It gave me a new lease on life, not just on one life but on forty lives, getting that invitation and having that chat with the Queen.

# SITTING BACK

*'It sure makes for
real good thinking'*

But I was gettin' tired – not in the head, but me
old body sort of run down. I've got to remember,
since about eleven years old, I've been workin'
hard. It was beginnin' to tell on me. Not that
I'm griping about it. Rearin' my family was my
life. I looked after 'em to the best of my ability,
and nobody ever had better kids. I was very proud
of them. I still am, I still am. Must tell 'em that
some day. They might know – they might have
a bit of an idea – but I must tell 'em, just the
same.

I hear a lot of remarks about Aboriginal people
that make my hair stand on end, but I think, "They
don't know about us, so why should I worry, and
waste me time tryin' to explain to 'em. They don't
want to understand. They can say what they want
to say, it's not hurtin' me." When you get old
your skin gets a bit tough, but I have young fellers

who jump off the mark pretty quick. I can understand that when people say and do things that hurt your feelings, rather than show that hurt, you get aggressive. I have to explain to them what Sister Clare explained to me all those years ago. You can't go punchin' and knocking the glasses off everyone who says those things to you.

These days I see Aboriginal girls and boys that are just like the young white teachers back when I started in the schools. They seem to stand very tall, and solid, because they have to. For them, now, things've got tough, and I think, "Yes, we were the gate openers, and I'm proud of the ones that come through that gate." I want it to stay wide open. But it's not all plain sailin' for our young people either.

You'll see a kid, he'll go away to study, will work his guts out in a College, and become highly educated, well-dressed, his speech beautiful. He comes back to a small place, usually the place where he grew up, and often, within a month, you wouldn't know him from the kids who never went away, never got out of the ashes, because he's become one of them again. He's had to do that to belong. Peer pressure is heavy on him. If he doesn't want to be just like the rest, back to being what they are, then he's shunned, not only by his friends but by his family too, he becomes an outsider again – this time with his own people.

Yet all he thought about when he left home and went away to do his training was to come back and help his people to understand, to make a better life for themselves. That's what helped him struggle through the homesickness and loneliness and hard study.

He comes home after four or five years and he's different, and he knows he's different too. The kids he left behind are four or five years older too, more outspoken and more outgoing.

He might have a dad or mum who'd been drinking before he went away, and now they're further down the drain.

Maybe they'll only want to see him when they run out of grog money or they're sick. If he hasn't got the money they want, or even says, "I'll have to go to the bank for it," they'll fight with him, and **he's** the bad one.

That young person's got to cope with the personal problems first, because that's his family. So he gets back to the question again, "What do they want me to do?" and feels pretty hopeless.

He's got to work out how he's going to fit back into that family again. He doesn't want to live the way they're living because he's used to living some other way. It's not his style of living any more, not his way of dressing. So what does he do? Gets himself a little flat up town, and works in whatever Department he's been trained to work in, and comes to be seen as the enemy of his people that he went away to work for. It's not good for those young people who've really tried so hard, and made big sacrifices, most of all puttin' up with all the loneliness and misunderstandings, sacrifices that their people back home in little places don't understand. There's got to be understanding from the parents to explain to the home-staying brothers and sisters why the boy or girl who went away did it, and why they've come back – to explain that they need support as much as anyone.

I know people might say, "It's alright for Evelyn Crawford to talk, because she just lives and breathes and sleeps 'education', and looking towards better things." But I've lived like them too. I grew up living in a tent, and it wasn't all carpeted floors and frilly curtains at windows, but now that I have got those things I'm really enjoying them. But it would be unfair for me to say that other mums and dads should be doing this or that for their kids. We are all individual people, our ideas, some of our values, may be different.

Me and Gong always said we didn't want our kids to grow up in the situations we grew up in, and we both worked very hard towards that. Not long before he died, he said to me, "Look, old woman, you push these kids as hard as you can. We don't want 'em to go through the life we went through, to have to work their guts out for the few simple things we had to work for."

There's always a lot to be done with family. Kids come into the world, brand spankin' new, they have to be taught. And sometime along the way some of your own kids might get a bit off the track, and you have to sort of hint at them about gettin' back on . . . like, "You know, mate, that's the wrong way to go . . . that's not leadin' any place you want to be."

But you can't pick 'em up and **put** 'em on that straight track. I never planned on pickin' any of my kids up once they fell in the dust, and dustin' 'em off. I left that to them, but I'd be in the background if they needed help. If they'd looked back, I'd be back there, but they didn't seem to look back much. They became self-reliant, or their brothers and sisters were there beside them, so perhaps they didn't know I was always there for them.

I would've loved to have carried on working, for a lot of reasons. But I guess it was time for me to sit back and do my own thing.

They gave me a retirement party. I sat at the table at dinner that night before the party began, and I looked at them all – three big tables full, and one small one. I thought to meself, "When'm I ever going to see any of you lot again?" and I felt real sad.

I miss Broken Hill and the people there more than I realized I would.

I miss Wilcannia – my work there, all my family ties and very good friends there too.

I miss goin' away to meetings, and seein' again the people I'd worked with for so long. They were very happy times.

I thought I had a duty to perform, as a granny and as an elder, so I come home to the little town where I lived for about forty years. But it's not the same town. I've got my kids and grandkids, but I'm too much on my own. I paint a lot, but I think a lot too. I work in an advisory capacity at the school and at the Museum, but it doesn't fill all my time. The day to me is like a big empty cup, never gets filled to the top.

When Tilly cuts my hair we get into **very** close conversation. I said to her, "Look, I always thought when you get old, you're like an old boot just put to one side, out in the sun thrown away. Dust accumulates on you, then it gets that way there's so much dust nobody sees you any more."

"No, Mum! You can be an old boot covered in dust only if you **want** to be an old boot covered in dust. No one else can put you there. If you put yourself there, well you'll stay there, 'cos people will think that's what you really want to be."

But I guess life's like that. You can't always have what you really want, not if you plan on helpin' people out. I could be a hermit, I suppose, but who wants to be a lonely old woman, anyway? It's just that I have little lapses in loneliness. I think all old people do.

While I've been workin' with Chris on this book, it's been drainin', yes, **very drainin'**. Sometimes after we'd been talkin' for weeks, it took me **months** to come back to livin' in the present.

But it's been good too. I felt the white people I met while we were doin' it didn't look **at** me as an Aboriginal person, but **into** me, to see what sort of a person I am, to see me for what I really am, under my glorious colour of tan! That made me feel good, because all Aboriginal people are conscious, when they go to meet new people, of what those people will think of them.

One of the good things about being retired is I can read and listen and think. I read a lot of poetry – Banjo Patterson,

Henry Lawson, Will Ogilvie. The ones I like I read onto tape, and then when I'm painting, I turn it on and listen to the stories, 'cos they're all stories to me. There's one bit,

*"I've seen the plains lying cracked and dry,*
*And bleaching bones 'neath the pitiless sky."*

I've seen that all right, and all the other things they tell about in their poems.

Thirty, forty years ago, that's when the world was good. You felt so safe in it. Everybody waved and said 'G'day'. Always someone would pull up for a yarn. Yeah, the bush was my life, and I made the most of it when I was young. I filled up every day with a lot of things. There was so much to talk about, so much to do, so much to see.

I can't complain. I stumbled a few times along the way, but there was always a hand put out to stop me from fallin'. When that person put a hand out for me, there was more than just a friendly 'I'll-help-you-up-mate' feeling in that hand. It was a good feeling, it was wonderful. I don't think I would have survived that long in education at all if I hadn't had so many people lookin' after me, respectin' me, and, yeah, I guess, lovin' me too.

During 1992 I'd been pretty sick off and on for a long time and was feeling like an old T-Model Ford under a beefwood tree in a paddock just rustin' away. Then a letter came from Canberra offerin' me an Australian Award. It knocked me bandy to think I would become part of something that important. I was so pleased I wanted to stand on the highest building in Newcastle, 'cos I was down there with Maree, and YELL IT OUT. But they'd told me I had to be very discreet.

It was a great honour but for me to know that there were friends out there who still think about me, and would go to all the trouble to nominate me and write references for me – well, that filled my old heart. Now that they know my family are all pretty proud.

I'm pretty lucky – haven't got much money, but I'd be one of the richest old women around, with the friends I've got, with all the respect and love I've had shown to me. Yeah, I'm pretty rich – I'm pretty rich.

And the thinking – there's all the time there is for that now. There's so much good to look back on, the happenings and especially the people, and they're all part of the **ME** who's here now.

The past is not for livin' in, you know, but it sure makes for real good thinkin'.

### Put Your Whole Self In  Meme McDonald

Meme McDonald took her camera to the City Baths and her photographer's eye focused on the colour and movement of a circle of older women, splashing and laughing in the pool. This was her first meeting with the Northcote Self-help Hydrotherapy & Massage Group.

The stories of these women, in and away from the pool, are told with tenderness and simplicity. Provocative opinions on youth, marriage and motherhood, women at work and at home, love and the loss of it, life and death, are shared with earthy humour, courage and dignity.

Lovingly photographed and, above all, listened to, these women have something important to say. They challenge all of us to question the way we perceive our lives.

This is a journey of women, re-empowered, reaching out and learning together to 'put their whole selves in'. You will laugh and cry with them, and in the end, you will love them.

**Heroines: A Contemporary Anthology of Australian Women Writers**
Edited by Dale Spender

Who are the heroines women look to? Twenty-two Australian writers of fiction, drama, poetry, journalism, TV scripts and non-fiction reflect on their heroines: from a rewriting of 'The Drover's Wife' to an unforgettable story of a mother in another land in the midst of a revolution.

There are ordinary women and extraordinary women; mothers, detectives, old women, teenagers, sisters, lesbians, rural women and urban; women who kill and women who resist violence; women who masquerade as men; women from the past and women from the present; there is comedy and music, satire and calls for action; a story that takes us back to the roots of human history and another that explores the impact of modern technology and the media on human consciousness.

## PENGUIN – THE BEST AUSTRALIAN READING

### The Harp in the South   Ruth Park

Since it was first published in 1948, Ruth Park's compassionate novel *The Harp in the South* has become a favourite with generations of Australian readers.

It is a nostalgic and moving portrait of the eventful family life of the Darcys, of Number Twelve-and-a-Half Plymouth Street, in Sydney's Surry Hills. There grow the bitter-sweet first and last loves of Roie Darcy, who becomes a woman too quickly amid the brothels and the razor gangs, the tenements and the fish and chip shops.

### Poor Man's Orange   Ruth Park

She knew the poor man's orange was hers, with its bitter rind, its paler flesh, and its stinging, exultant unforgettable tang. So she would have it that way, and wish it no other way. She knew that she was strong enough to bear whatever might come in her life as long as she had love.

Only Ruth Park understands so well what it is like to grow to womanhood in the inner-city slums of Sydney during the years immediately after World War II. She likes the people she writes about and has a rare skill in evoking them. In *Poor Man's Orange*, the poignant third part in *The Harp in the South* trilogy, she tells of the Darcy family, and their vitality and humour in the midst of acute poverty.

**Missus**  Ruth Park

*Missus* takes us behind the lives of Hughie and Mumma, out of the gritty realism of inner city slum life and into the past of the stations, the bush and the country towns. We meet them as they were in the early 1920s, drifter Hugh Darcy, the unwilling hero who sweeps the dreamily innnocent Margaret Kilker off her feet. Ruth Park richly creates the turmoil of those early days of their courtship – in the dusty outback.

**Swords and Crowns and Rings**  Ruth Park

Growing up in an Australian country town before World War I, Jackie Hanna and Cushie Moy are carefree and innocent in their love for each other. But Jackie is a dwarf and his devotion to the beautiful Cushie is condemned by her parents. This is the story of their life-long odyssey and the triumph of a special kind of courage.